Religious Ea
the Challenge of Pluralism

RELIGIOUS EDUCATION AND THE CHALLENGE OF PLURALISM

Edited by

ADAM B. SELIGMAN

OXFORD
UNIVERSITY PRESS

OXFORD
UNIVERSITY PRESS

Oxford University Press is a department of the University of Oxford.
It furthers the University's objective of excellence in research, scholarship,
and education by publishing worldwide.

Oxford   New York
Auckland   Cape Town   Dar es Salaam   Hong Kong   Karachi
Kuala Lumpur   Madrid   Melbourne   Mexico City   Nairobi
New Delhi   Shanghai   Taipei   Toronto

With offices in
Argentina   Austria   Brazil   Chile   Czech Republic   France   Greece
Guatemala   Hungary   Italy   Japan   Poland   Portugal   Singapore
South Korea   Switzerland   Thailand   Turkey   Ukraine   Vietnam

Oxford is a registered trademark of Oxford University Press
in the UK and certain other countries.

Published in the United States of America by
Oxford University Press
198 Madison Avenue, New York, NY 10016

© Oxford University Press 2014

All rights reserved. No part of this publication may be reproduced, stored in a
retrieval system, or transmitted, in any form or by any means, without the prior
permission in writing of Oxford University Press, or as expressly permitted by law,
by license, or under terms agreed with the appropriate reproduction rights organization.
Inquiries concerning reproduction outside the scope of the above should be sent to the
Rights Department, Oxford University Press, at the address above.

You must not circulate this work in any other form
and you must impose this same condition on any acquirer.

Cataloging in Publication data is on file with the Library of Congress

ISBN 978–0–19–935947–9 (hbk); 978–0–19–935948–6 (pbk)

1 3 5 7 9 8 6 4 2
Printed in the United States of America
on acid-free paper

Contents

Preface	vii
List of Contributors	xi
Introduction: Living Together Differently, Education, and the Challenge of Deep Pluralism—ADAM SELIGMAN	1
1. Teaching Religion in the European Union: A Legal Overview—SILVIO FERRARI	25
2. Religion and Ethical Education in Divided Societies: The Case of Cyprus—DILEK LATIF	45
3. Teaching Religion in Bulgarian Schools: Historical Experience and Post-Atheist Developments—MARIA SCHNITTER AND DANIELA KALKANDJIEVA	70
4. The Vanishing State: Religious Education and Intolerance in French Jewish Schools—KIMBERLY A. ARKIN	96
5. The Crises of Liberal Citizenship: Religion and Education in Israel—SHLOMO FISCHER	119
6. Secularism(s), Islam, and Education in Turkey: Is *E Pluribus Unum* Possible?—AHMET T. KURU	150
7. Walking the Tightrope: Prospects for Civil Education and Multiculturalism in "*Ketuanon Melayu*" Malaysia—JOSEPH CHINYONG LIOW	168

8. Educating Citizens in America: The Paradoxes of Difference and Democracy—ASHLEY ROGERS BERNER AND JAMES DAVISON HUNTER 193

Afterword—ADAM SELIGMAN 216

Index 223

Preface

THE CHAPTERS IN this volume emerged from a series of workshops and conversations run by the *Institute for Culture and World Affairs* (CURA) at Boston University and by *CEDAR—Communities Engaging with Difference and Religion*. The workshops organized by CURA in Boston were devoted to exploring the theme of Religious Pluralism and Civic Peace, and the role of religion in the enculturation of citizens. These workshops were held over the 2010–2012 academic years, with the generous support of the Henry Luce Foundation. The workshops focused on the role of religion in developing an ethics of civic virtue and a commitment in religiously divided, as well as in post-conflict, societies. The conversations—held internationally with volume contributors and others—were all focused around how to "live together differently," and what that entails in the organization of learning, pedagogy, and cultural production.

Much has been written on religious education in the Western European context, especially about such educational initiatives in the United Kingdom, Austria, Germany, and elsewhere in Europe, as well as some initiatives in the United States. While not ignoring these cases, this volume sets out to bring a very different data set to the attention of its readers. We are less interested in covering the ground that scholars, the likes of Robert Jackson, have covered so well, in the British context, especially. Rather, we are interested in exploring and bringing to the readers' attention the results of the work occurring in lesser known contexts. We have thus integrated the studies of more-researched cases (like those of France and the United States) with those devoted to the lesser known cases of Turkey, Cyprus, Israel, Bulgaria, and Malaysia. This volume also contains a broad legal review by Silvio Ferrari on the state of religious education throughout the European Union.

Our avowed aim has been to encourage a dialogue across these different cases, to juxtapose their commonalities and differences, and to bring into the more accepted conversations around pluralism and religious education cases that are often less heard. Such an exercise also highlights unimagined similarities between such disparate cases, such as those in Malaysia and Israel, for example. Thus, simply bringing material from Cyprus, Israel, Malaysia, Turkey, and Bulgaria into the broader context of such discussions is, we feel, an important starting point for the type of comprehensive approach (so sorely needed) to the problems of religious education. Post-Communist societies (especially those that were traditionally associated with Eastern Orthodoxy) present very different scenarios than those of North Atlantic Protestant ones. Countries riven by ethno-religious hostilities—as Israel and Cyprus are—again, present markedly different experiences from those of secular Western European societies. Asian societies, let alone Muslim Asian societies, present yet another dimension that must be considered, as must the phenomenon of private religious instruction in France and the United States.

Most of the cases analyzed in this volume have not been studied at all in the English-speaking world—and in some cases, only marginally in their own countries (Bulgaria, Israel, Cyprus, Malaysia). The empirical data presented here (whether of a statistical or ethnographic nature), is brand new and has not been published in any language. It is a pleasure to be able to make it available in this format. With the exception of the United States and more-general studies of religious education in the EU countries, there is in fact little work on religious education and citizenship, despite the growing importance of this subject, in more and more countries the world over.

Citizenship is the key element in all the studies selected for this volume. More specifically, we have chosen studies that focus on the challenge of articulating the terms of citizenship in a manner that includes religious and ethnic minorities, and not solely those majorities identified with the national project. This is the challenge in Cyprus, Israel, Bulgaria, Turkey, and Malaysia. All are cases, we should note, where the nation-building project differed greatly from that of post-Reformation Christian Europe—given the different developmental trajectories of Eastern Orthodoxy (Cyprus, Bulgaria), Islam (Turkey, Malaysia, TRC), and Judaism (Israel). In the case of Jewish schools in France (studied by Kimberly Arkin), the very terms of shared citizenship are questioned by a state policy of non-engagement with parochial schooling, a development usefully compared with the types of civic education promulgated in the United States. The marked contrast between the role of parochial schools in civic enculturation in both countries is, in fact, striking.

It is thus by widening the conversation and bringing hitherto unstudied cases into the purview of those concerned with the more general problems of citizenship and living with difference, that we hope this volume will find its interested readers.

List of Contributors

Kimberly A. Arkin, Assistant Professor, Department of Anthropology, Boston University

Ashley Rogers Berner, Deputy Director of the CUNY Institute for Education Policy and Senior Fellow at the Center for the Study of Law and Religion at Emory Law School

Silvio Ferrari, Professor of Law and Religion, Università degli Studi di Milano

Shlomo Fischer, Lecturer, School of Education, Hebrew University of Jerusalem, Founding Director, Yesodot: Center for Torah and Democracy

James Davison Hunter, Labrosse-Levinson Distinguished Professor of Religion, Culture and Social Theory Director, Institute for Advanced Studies in Culture, University of Virginia

Daniela Kalkandjieva, Project leader at the Scientific Research Department, University St. Kliment Ohridski of Sofia

Ahmet T. Kuru, Associate Professor of Political Science, San Diego State University

Dilek Latif, Senior Lecturer, Department of International Relations, Near Eastern University, Turkish Republic of Cyprus

Joseph Chinyong Liow, Professor of Comparative and International Politics at the S. Rajaratnam School of International Studies, Nanyang Technological University, Singapore

Maria Schnitter, Associate Professor and Chair, Departments of Ethnology and Theology, Paissiy Hilendarksi University of Plovdiv Bulgaria

Adam Seligman, Professor, Department of Religion, Senior Researcher, Institute for Culture, Religion and World Affairs, Boston University. Director, CEDAR—Communities Engaging with Difference and Religion

Religious Education and the Challenge of Pluralism

Introduction

LIVING TOGETHER DIFFERENTLY, EDUCATION, AND THE CHALLENGE OF DEEP PLURALISM

Adam Seligman

ALL SOCIETIES AT all times face three fundamental challenges. These include the need to (1) organize their division of labor; (2) to expand trust beyond the primordial unit of family (however conceived), that is to generalize the terms of trust beyond the narrowest of circles; and (3) to provide some sense of meaning to both individual lives and collective endeavors (Eisenstadt 1995). All social institutions can be understood ultimately in terms of their reference to one or more of these three sets of challenges. As such, they will always carry with them particularistic, local, and specific characteristics. They will be in some sense different in each and every locale, and so their content will not be fully generalizable. While the division of labor may well be developing on a global scale, it is clear that the generalization of trust and the terms of meaning in different societies are different and likely to remain that way for the foreseeable future. Indeed, many papers in this collection stress precisely the particularistic, local character of those challenges tied to the provision of meaning and the establishment of the basis for social trust in different parts of the world. Many papers go a long way in showing just how circumscribed and ethnically defined communities (of trust and meaning) present a continual challenge to the generalization of the formal aspects of democratic membership as well as a sense of belonging within the nation-state. Local cultures count, and they count most in the formation of citizens who are, after all, the carriers of those ideological programs of trust and meaning around which societies are formed.

The chapters that make up this volume address these issues through the very particular lens of religious education. Religion and religious education have, as Silvio Ferrari points out below, traditionally been seen as the arena par excellence for the inculcation of meaning, a problem exacerbated by the "collapse of the great secular ideologies" of the 19th and early 20th centuries (Ferrari 2008, p. 109). In traditional societies, but increasingly in secular European societies as well, the problems of meaning; of understanding our place in creation, the meaning of good and evil, and the definition of the good life; of virtue and of moral action, are addressed primarily in the religious idiom. Despite the promise of the Enlightenment and of the 19th-century ideology of progress, it seems impossible to come to grips with these issues without recourse to religious language, traditions, and frames of reference. It is therefore not at all surprising that different countries approach religious education differently, in accords with their different understandings of their own religious tradition (or traditions) and the relative saliency of different ethno-religious groups within the polity.

The problem is that in most cases, it is impossible to provide a framework of meaning, let alone religious meaning without, at the same time, invoking a language of community, of belonging (and so also, one of borders, of definitions that consider "who is like me" and "who is not like me," or like "us" and unlike "us"), of who we can trust and who we cannot, and in addition, where the boundary of membership in "our" community runs. Thus, and to take only a few European examples, the Italian Concordat of 1984 emphasizes that "the principles of Catholicism are part of the historical patrimony of the Italian people [and] continues to ensure within the school system the instruction in the Catholic religion in non-university public schools at all levels and types." In Greece (with strong implications for Cyprus) the Constitution, "framed in the name of the Holy Trinity, consubstantial and indivisible," defines the mission of the state, among others as being responsible for the "national and religious consciousness" of the Hellenes peoples. In Baden-Wuttemberg, Germany, education is to take place "in responsibility before God and Christian love" (Willaime 2007, p. 58). The following chapters will present further examples of this connection between peoplehood and religious belonging in the context of a reflection on the very problematic nature of this connection.

Indeed, the specific cases that make up this volume were chosen in no small measure to highlight precisely this issue. The interweaving of ethno-national identities with specific religious meanings, commitments, and identities in places like Cyprus, Israel, Bulgaria, Turkey, and Malaysia all provide immense challenges to the enculturation of a religiously diverse citizenry. Moreover, and as we shall see, in the case of France, simply leaving religious minorities to develop their own religiously defined curricula does not seem to be a solution either. Paradoxically, we will find that in the United States, civic enculturation seems to be furthered most by parochial schools that invest students with a sense of communal responsibility and belonging, rather than in the state-supported and secular public schools.

If, as in the case of many of the countries studied here, religious belonging is tied to ethnic and national belonging (and so also to very particular terms of trust and collective membership), and if religion is also seen as the realm par excellence of meaning and the inculcation of virtue, and if societies are made up of different communities of meaning and belonging—then the problem of "living together differently" takes on a significant new dimension. In such circumstances, moreover, religious education becomes the critical arena for the making of citizens whose bonds of trust and communal identity are not limited to their own ethnic (or—in some cases such as Israel, Malaysia, and Cyprus—national) collective. Religious education becomes one of the primary realms where an expansive definition of citizenship is either proffered, or revoked. This is the challenge of religious education in deeply plural societies, and this is the challenge studied in the following chapters across a very wide array of cases.

The cases analyzed in this volume range well beyond the often-studied Western European ones, where linguistic and cultural integration developed prior to post-Reformation processes of state formation (Rokkan 1975). Bringing such cases of "late modernizers" into the same framework as countries such as France and the United States (or for that matter, the wider EU survey as supplied by Silvio Ferrari) is one of the very reasons for this volume. The focus on Christian Orthodoxy, Muslim majority, and Jewish cases are meant to highlight the broad ranges of challenges facing different religiously inflected nation-building projects in the contemporary, postcolonial, and post-Communism world, and how they stand in relation to more long-standing democratic nation-states in Europe and North America.

From Cyprus to Malaysia, from Israel to Bulgaria, the terms of meaning are deeply rooted within very particular, often primordially defined communities. In Cyprus, religion—most especially Greek Orthodoxy—is clearly identified with the Greek national community. As Dilek Latif explains, it was the British who, essentially, turned Orthodox Cypriots into Greeks, and Muslim Cypriots into Turks (though, to be sure, Islam was not traditionally associated with the Turkish Republic of North Cyprus [TRNC], although as she notes, that may be changing). Needless to add, the island is split in two along the lines of these two religio-national entities. In Malaysia, Islam is identified with the Malaysian majority in a manner that provides unending tensions with Tamil and Chinese minorities. Israel is, as is well known, a "Jewish state," and the current Prime Minister even demands that the Palestinians recognize it as such. With Jews accounting for only around 75 percent of the population—and the majority of those, non-religious—serious problems exist along the axis of communal belonging and trust, and who is privy to the dominant terms of meaning and membership in society. In Bulgaria too, the terms of community and trust overlap with those of religious affiliation, and since the first Balkan War at the beginning of the 20th century, the issue of minorities has been a major challenge to the Bulgarian polity (such minorities include Greeks, Jews, Pomaks [ethnic Bulgarian converts to Islam], non-ethnically Bulgarian Muslims, and Roma). Interestingly, three of the four cases listed here—Cyprus, Israel, and Bulgaria—are all successor states to the Ottoman Empire. There is a fourth case studied below by Ahmet (Kuru), of contemporary Turkey—that is, also a successor state to the Ottoman Empire. With the exception of the Kurds (who are Sunni Muslims, like other Turks) and the Alevis (who are not), Turkey does not face the same challenge of ethnic or national pluralism due to the transfer of populations at the time of nation formation and the second great exodus of minorities in the 1950s. Non-Muslims constitute only 100,000 of Turkey's population of 72 million (Kuru 2009, p. 179). Even so, and as Ahmet Kuru's analysis of contemporary Turkey highlights, the difficulties faced by the Turkish state in its attempts to create a "homogenized society" and so deny its ethnic diversity has always been fraught with problems. While the Ottoman Empire certainly had its own very workable system of dealing with the deep pluralism that defines empires—it was not "exportable" to the post-Empire nation-states that emerged in its wake. Its heritage was one of deeply pluralistic societies with no clear mechanisms of accommodation (we will return to this theme in the following section). Modern Turkey, especially, was built on the denial of all ethnic differences and in the marked rejection of the religious heritage and commitments of the preceding Ottoman regime (Kuru 2009, pp. 161–236).

Somewhat overlapping this category (of chapters dealing on the one hand with religious education in successor states to the Ottoman Empire, and on the other with societies where religion is tied to the ethnic or national identity of only one among many social groups) are those chapters that deal with EU countries; Silvio Ferrari's survey of the legal aspects of religious education in the European Union as a whole, Kimberly Arkin's study of Jewish education in France, Dilek Latif's aforementioned study of Cyprus, and Maria Schnitter and Daniela Kalkandjieva's paper on Bulgaria. Cyprus and Bulgaria are both EU member states. There are, in addition two "outlier" cases: that of Malaysia and the United States. Tied neither to the European Union nor, in their pasts, to the Ottoman Empire (though at different times, both were in fact tied to the British Empire)—both are deeply pluralistic, but there the similarity ends. Malaysia reached statehood in the 20th century, the United States in the 18th century. Malaysia has an ethnically and religiously segmented education system, while the United States maintains the myth (if not always the reality) of a "melting pot." Malaysia is a predominantly Muslim country, while the United States is a predominantly Protestant Christian one. Both deal with their pluralistic civil society in very different manners.

Problematizing the Religion/Secular Divide

Fundamental to the ability of these countries to engage with different communities of belonging, to maintain different interests, beliefs, and desiderata among the members of society without the societies tearing themselves apart is thus the provision of a shared sense of meaning that will somehow bridge the different communities of religious, ethnic, and national identities existing within the nation-states. Education provides one of the most important venues for such engagement, and religious education has come to be seen as one critical component of this process in Europe and beyond (Jackson et al. 2007). In essence then, the problem is one of managing different communities of belonging, rather than—as is so often the default of liberal-individualist societies—of "privatizing" these differences and keeping them out of the public space. In fact, in most of the cases presented here, such privatization is not possible, as the very terms of collective belonging are tied up with one particular ethnic or religious group among many. In some cases, such as in Liow's presentation of the educational system in

Malaysia, the rifts of society are reinforced, if not reified in the national educational system. In other cases, such as Bulgaria, there seems to be much more negotiation, and the process is more open and even hopeful. As religious and ethnic differences are thus central to these problems, it is these categories that we should first address before going on to discuss the problematic aspect of most liberal solutions for the cases studied here.

When thinking of civic enculturation, most citizens of Western European and North Atlantic democracies have in mind a markedly secular process, that is to say, a process spearheaded by secular agencies and elites. Many may indeed bear the French model in mind—where the consolidation of the Third Republic was achieved, to a great extent, through the establishment of a nation-wide secular educational system that successfully competed with that of the Catholic Church in the provision of education to generations of school children. Others may think of the type of separation of Church and State, religious and secular spheres that has characterized American national development. Interesting in terms of our cases here, is the seeming divergence between the United States and France—in terms of the role played by parochial and religious schools—in fostering a sense of civic belonging and connection to the broader collective. In the United States, such schools seem to play a very positive role, while in France, the earlier hostility of the Catholic Church and its schools, to the Third Republic and a republican sense of belonging seems to be almost replayed in the attitudes of today's students in Parisian Jewish day schools.

Given the deep bias among many in the West, against even conceptualizing the role of religion and religious elites in the enculturation of a state's citizens, it may be useful to begin by problematizing the very separation we are wont to make between religious and secular ways of life, thought, and indeed, social action. We tend, after all, to use the concepts of religion and secularity or secular culture as if these were objective, universal, and value-free concepts that can be used to characterize aspects of shared social life that are not religious. However, whether approached from the perspective of state education and the use of religion by the state as a form of civic enculturation (Fischer, Liow, Schnitter and Kalkandjieva, Latif, Kuru) or from the perspective of civil society (Berner and Hunter, Arkin) and the more bottom-up engagement of religion in civic affairs—all of the papers in this volume challenge such clearly defined boundaries between secular and religious worlds of action and meaning.

It may then be useful to recall that both religion and secularism are concepts that developed in a very particular and Western Christian context and can be used, helpfully, to describe aspects and periods in the unfolding of that particular Christian civilization, but do not actually serve us well when we come to discuss, analyze, and understand other traditional civilizations or other civilizations within which tradition is changing and being renegotiated. What, for example, is a secular Jew? What of a Jew who observes no commandments, goes to synagogue only on Yom Kippur, and does not otherwise maintain any traditional practices? Is he secular, or partially religious—or neither? How do we characterize China and its 1.3 billion inhabitants? China has been called the most secular country in the world. But when we observe the proliferation of spirit cults and other forms of worship there, we realize that this is not secular in any usual sense of the term. What of the case of Islam? What of the individual or community whose observance of traditional commandments are partial, or almost non-existent? What of the Muslim who eats during Ramadan—but only in private, in hiding, away from communal eyes? Is he secular or hypocritical? What of she who does not eat during Ramadan, but does drink wine occasionally? What of those communities in Central Asia who celebrate the Id by drinking vodka? Are these people secularists or sinners or ignorant? Or are they, as are so many, engaged in the never-ending movements, interpretation, and transformation of their own traditions, always continually being negotiated and negotiated anew by communities and individuals over the course of time?

I would in fact claim that secularism is a very particular moment in the Western Christian process of negotiating its own tradition—as was the Protestant Reformation and as is the phenomenon of Christian fundamentalism. All are particular moments in the way the concrete practice of tradition mediates, transforms, and negotiates the tradition of practices that define any civilizational endeavor. That a particular moment of this negotiation in Western Christianity is understood in terms of secularism has much to do with the privileging of belief over practice, of faith over works, and of *innerlischkeit* over external practice that has been part of Christianity from its origins (as evinced in its rejection of Jewish Law and its unique allegorical way of reading and interpreting scripture) and that received particular emphasis during the Protestant Reformation of the 16th century. Secularism as unbelief is thus the complement of tradition, understood primarily in terms of belief rather than practice. Moreover, the contemporary rejection of tradition in Western Europe is itself intimately tied up with the overwhelming terms of collective identity. In fact, both phenomena may very well be related. The Peace of Westphalia and the concept of *cuius regio eius religio* may be central here. Western Europe, which was Christian, became rather a continent of nation-states; and in different ways, traditional practices pertaining to the sacred were subsumed within a new set of practices organized around national identities. Consequently, the relevance for any binary distinction between secular and religious realms becomes much more difficult to maintain in Eastern Orthodoxy, Judaism, Islam, and other religiously oriented civilizations. This then has significant implications for how religious instruction can be developed in schools, especially in terms of the relation of religion to the respective nation-building (and hence civic) projects of countries with different Eastern Orthodox, Jewish, and Muslim majorities.

These more theoretical or perhaps metahistorical reflections bear on quite a few of the cases here; whether we think of the ideological positioning of religious Zionists in regard to democracy and education as studied by Fischer; the interweaving of religion and national identities in Cyprus, studied by Latif; or the role of Islam in Malaysia and the confluence of ethnic and religious identities that Liow analyzed; as well as the rather ambivalent and contradictory attitudes taken to Islam and Islamic education in Turkey that Kuru presents; or even of those Jewish schools in France as studied by Arkin—all are examples of traditions negotiating new realities, with new results in newly emergent forms of civil sociability and new understandings of the relations between what we so narrowly think of as religious and secular life in the civic sphere (though of course, not all of them are salutatory). The juxtaposition of Israel and Malaysia is in fact of particular interest, as both seek to build a civic project around one particular national and religious collectivity, while still proclaiming liberal visions of citizenship, though, to be sure, Malaysia also explicitly espouses a multicultural ideal (though often, as we shall see, falling far behind in practice), while such an ideal is in fact an anathema to the religious and national elites currently supervising civic education in the state of Israel.

The point of these remarks is thus to emphasize that religious and civil identities do and sometimes do not come together in various ways, and we must be very wary of positing a one-to-one relationship between them, or of reducing the one to the other. As sacred traditions and civil identities interweave (or don't) in the contemporary world, the existence of multiethnic, multiconfessional states and societies characterized by deep pluralism presents a challenge to more traditional notions of civic identity. In some cases, a move toward integrating such religious-based identity claims with the habitus of citizenship does seem possible (if taking unexpected paths and forms). On the other hand, and to take but one salient example, the cases of the Chinese and Indian students in Malaysian schools (discussed by Liow) and the intolerance shown to them clearly expresses both the challenges of such pluralism and the failure of the state to rise to such a challenge. It is, moreover, precisely this challenge that has, to a great extent, come to define our contemporary world. It is this problem, of different communities of belonging and their relation to a shared civic and public sphere, that so many of the contributions to this volume struggle with. In a word, it is the problem of difference.

The Problem of Difference

We should begin by noting that in many ways the problem of difference stands at the root of democratic politics, which are, after all, predicated on a politics of interests—that is on a politics of different individuals and groups pursuing their particular interests (within an agreed upon set of "rules of the game" of course). Democracy in fact tends to highlight difference, to stress what makes us different, at least as far as our interests are concerned.

Democratic regimes exist in an abiding tension between a politics of interest—pushing its citizens to focus on what divides them, and a politics of consent—pushing citizens to affirm what unites them. This tension—or at least the high level of such tension—is not, I hasten to add, a characteristic of all political and social systems. Totalitarian systems, fascist regimes, communist societies, theocracies, and, on the other side of the coin, empires do not all betray the same tensions—the former can abide much less amount of difference, and the last, a much greater amount than democracies. Even within democracies, there are various differences between what have been termed liberal and republican versions, where the former allows a much greater institutional recognition of difference that the latter. The founding fathers of the United States recognized this tension and worked out mechanisms to accommodate it. The famous wall of separation between Church and State in the United States—that most religious of countries—is predicated precisely on the founders' recognition that it is better that peoples' politics be divided by their different material interests (which would then play out in the political sphere of the legislature), than by their religious differences (which could have potentially ruinous effects on social and political life). If current practice in places like the Balkans, the Middle East, the Indian sub-continent, and parts of the Republican Party in the United States are any guide, people like James Madison were stupendously correct in their assessment. That these accommodations may end up simply exacerbating individual differences, highlighting individual goods (as opposed to shared, public goods), and voiding the polity of a shared sense of belonging is a subject discussed in the paper of Berner and Hunter on civic education in the United States.

We should recall, that while the United States may well be (as Lipset 1964 claimed) the "first new nation," it is also a nation where certain sectarian Protestant assumptions on self and society were allowed to develop relatively free of the effects of the Counter-Reformation, and in general of the need to take into consideration the existence of the Catholic Church. The grand debate (often violent, to be sure) over the terms of Christian tradition that defined the Protestant Reformation and the Counter-Reformation in Continental Europe—and that eventuated in the development of secular polities and societies there—was, to a great extent, simply ignored in the New World and played but a minor role in the later history of the United States. There was no ultramontane party in 19th-century American politics, nor was there a State Church as in Sweden, nor was there a religious requirement for full citizenship rights over the course of the 19th century.

All of which does not mean that the United States was, or is, secular. Or rather it means that it was secular in the classical, circumscribed, and medieval usage of the term—referring to that area of public life that is outside sacerdotal regulation and ecclesiastical jurisdiction. Secularism then, in the United States, must be understood as a constitutional principle, rather than a moral position (as made more than clear in the chapter by Berner and Hunter included here), a principle embodied in that very separation of realms for which it is famous. This distinction, between secularism as moral position and as constitutional principle, is crucial to keep in mind when we come to understand the role of religion in public life, within the different social contexts dealt with by the papers here, especially given the different trajectories of nation formation that we find in Bulgaria, Israel, Cyprus, Malaysia, and Turkey, respectively.

Thus, in Bulgaria, the Bulgarian Orthodox Church plays an almost mythic role in the narrative of nation building and freedom from the "Turkish yoke." It is seen by many as being constitutive of national identity, but is also viewed with suspicion, both for its ties with the regime during the Communist era and also because Bulgaria is a very secular society; on the day-to-day level of lived life, there has always been a high degree of religious syncretism as well as intermarriage between different religious communities. Indeed, what can be seen from Schnitter and Kalkandjieva's paper is how the vicissitudes of nation formation were mirrored both in changing attitudes toward minorities as well as in changing state policy regarding religious education. The religious/secular dichotomy in fact comes to seem almost irrelevant, as religion is so clearly bound up with the sense of national belonging and identity (and hence too, the pervasive problems of minority religious groups therein). In Israel, too, religion and national identity are enmeshed in ways that totally defy the general categories we use for conceptualizing these issues. To be Jewish is, after all, both to be part of a people as well as part of a religious community stretching back for millennia. Eastern Orthodoxy (represented in our volume by the Bulgarian and Greek-Cypriot cases) and Judaism have therefore much in common in this sense, as does Islam. In all, the rather "taken-for-granted" assumptions that we have inherited from Western Christendom do not hold. Ethnic and national identities are tied up with religious histories, texts, traditions, and practices in a manner that makes any discussion of secularism as more than a constitutional principle exceedingly problematic. This is true (maybe even especially true) for a country like Turkey where even a formally secular public realm is highly mediated by the critical roles played by religious commitments and desiderata in defining national identity.

Consequently, what we see from all the papers in this volume is that the problems of dealing with constitutive difference in the public sphere are shared across the board. Moreover, the commonly proposed "liberal" solution to such differences would not seem relevant in most cases. Within the public sphere, according to the liberal reading, boundaries of difference are parsed into razor-thin edges and individuals interact not as members of groups, but as bearers of rights (citizen rights, social rights, human rights, and so on). Group identities have been, in the public sphere, replaced by individual identities, and the problem of tolerance of difference has been replaced by the legal recognition and entitlements of rights. Differences have become functional, rather than constitutive.

We know however that this has not been the case in all modern polities, and one may think of many of the cases presented here—Israel, Cyprus, Malaysia, Bulgaria, and Turkey—as having very different attitudes toward collective belonging. Indeed, as we see from Fischer's paper, in Israel there are effectively two different and coterminous terms of collective identity, one for Jews and one for non-Jews. Non-Jews are allocated a type of liberal membership in the collective, based on individual citizenship and rights where the classic formulation of Clermont-Tonnerre in 1789 about the Jews ("We must refuse everything to the Jew as a nation and accord everything to the Jew as an individual.") are repeated almost verbatim by leading Israeli jurists and educators (quoted in Berkovitz 1989, p. 71). But also and at the same time, there remains a retention of group rights for the Jewish people in a manner that would limit any "trump" of individual rights for non-Jews (e.g., Palestinian Arab citizens of Israel). As discussed years ago by Yoav Peled (1992), there are in Israel two competing definitions of citizenship: a "republican" definition of citizenship for Jews, and a "liberal individualist" one for non-Jews. Cyprus, too, is divided along the lines of such "thick" constituted communities, while Turkey denies the existence of any ethnic or ethno-linguistic community not defined as Turkish, and both Malaysia (Kraince 2009) and Bulgaria struggle to find the right language to address such pluralism within its citizenry. As we shall see in the following chapters, the educational system is, not surprisingly, one prime arena where such struggles are carried out.

However, even where the liberal paradigm is fully evoked, as in Western Europe, the United States, and beyond, a fundamental problem remains and has come to the fore over the last decades—individual rights do not provide for either recognition or a sense of belonging. And recognition—as political philosophers from Adam Ferguson to G.W.F. Hegel, and down to our own contemporaries, have reminded us—is the core of modern politics (Taylor 1992). After all, our demands for recognition and respect are not so much in those areas where we are the same as everyone else (that realm defined by rights), but precisely in those areas where we are unique and different (that is, in our specific and particularistic group identities and our sense of belonging). To claim that we are all fundamentally the same and to ensure these statuses in rights are, no doubt, crucial provisions for common life. But it does not at all address our demand to be approached and recognized in our separate and unique existence and identity (Tully 1995).

Indeed, what is "identity politics" if not the politics of recognition: ethnic, religious, gender, and other. Thus, new and old forms of group-based identity arise, to again make vocal and public demands for recognition. And this, in fact, is the social significance of such holidays as Kwanza, or of a Boston Rabbi lighting a Chanukah menorah on Boston Common, or a French Rabbi on the Champs de Mars. All betray the demand for recognition, for a recovering of one's identity and demanding public recognition for it as a space of belonging. Whether modern constitutional orders predicated on the equality of individual citizens organized collectively in *ideally* homogenous nation-states can in fact accommodate such demands is one of the principle questions in contemporary political theory (Tully 1996; Taylor 1992). For such demands challenge the very framework of the national state as providing the overarching sense of belonging needed by humans to grow and flourish. They also challenge the very fundamental ideas of selfhood that have informed political ethics in the Western Europe and North Atlantic communities since the revolutions of the 18th century.

Not surprisingly, these demands are often framed religiously. This is the case not only over prayer in school or placing the Ten Commandments in front of an Alabama courthouse, but also in many other instances. It is in fact not surprising that in contemporary America, the struggle over identity, community, class, and status (i.e., over recognition) often takes the form of a struggle over religious symbols. This is as true in Europe as well. The French ruling over the head scarf, the debates over the preamble to the European constitution—if it should refer to a shared Christian heritage—or the recent Dutch debate to outlaw full-facial veils in public all point to this phenomenon (Crouch 2006). A particularly interesting case is the 2008 denial of French citizenship to a "covered" Muslim woman from Morocco, where her dress, habit, and demeanor were defined as "radical religious practices" (*une pratique radicale de sa religion*) and so was seen as incompatible with "the essential values of French society" (or *valeurs essentielles de la communauté française*; Emon 2012).

Unfortunately, and along with such processes of legal exclusion, we are also witnessing a huge withdrawal of different groups into themselves, a closing of ranks against the outside world and a reticence to interact with those who are truly other or different. This has emerged paradoxically with the growth of human rights, as what Michael Ignatieff (2001) called a form of "idolatry," that is as a "trump" in every countervailing argument based on collective goods and demands for recognition. Such a "trump" will not in itself, however, counteract the growing separation of communities within the nation-state, which, in turn, will leave rights themselves as nothing but formal enactments of positive law, bereft of any ability to ensure civic engagement and commitment on the part of the citizenry—or indeed any shared sense of belonging amidst the very different religious and ethnic communities that increasingly define the nation-states of the 21st century.

Rights, Belonging, and the Civil Sphere

In fact, the maintenance of pluralistic forms of society and a tolerance of constitutive difference may paradoxically turn on our ability to re-engage with other (including perhaps some older, religious) traditions and eschew the "trump" of individual rights that has come to define the liberal political order. One of the major questions we face is if religious education can be a forum for such re-engagement, one which can lead to new understandings of pluralism and to the recognition of ethnic and religious minorities, or is it instead yet another force for exclusion and the circumscription of a sense of belonging within the nation-state. (The chapters of this volume provide no clear answer to this question.) To properly appreciate what is at stake, it would be wise to review briefly the terms of citizenship and indeed, of the constitutional order as these present themselves to us in contemporary democratic and liberal societies. These include, the secularization of the political realm, the privatization of religion, and the removal of substantive differences and divergent claims to the *Good* from the public arena.

In fact, and as we have come to find in recent years, the secular public sphere is not devoid of its own claims to the *Good*, and these claims are in fact, among the most contested ones in the contemporary world. Thus, and to take but one example, the secular-liberal vision of society rests on a particular understanding of mankind as made up of autonomous, self-defining moral reasoners. Precisely this idea of moral autonomy, however, is contested by billions of church, mosque, temple, and synagogue goers the world over. For these religiously committed individuals, people are not morally autonomous, but, rather, live under heteronomous-enacted and revealed laws. The secular, liberal claims for moral autonomy are not then as neutral as they present themselves to be—a point developed in Ahmet Kuru's paper on Turkey. Moreover, the debate between advocates of moral autonomy and what we may term, perhaps, moral heteronomy (a revealed law and morality) goes to the heart of what a civic education should be. What is important to recognize, however, is that such autonomy is not a necessary condition for acting responsibly or civilly in the public arena.

Beyond this problem with current visions of the public square is the fact that removing competing claims to the *Good* really serves more to displace the problem than to solve it. For—and as can be seen in many societies, and as discussed at length in Berner and Hunter's chapter—this situation leaves us with a "thinly" defined public sphere to which the commitment of many individuals and communities are highly mediated. On the other hand, and hidden within or at the boundaries of this public sphere, are very "thick" moral communities, many with highly rigid definitions of the *Good* as well as clear boundaries of membership and loyalties. Thus, removing moral claims from the shared sphere of our interaction does not in fact seem to work, in terms of leaving us with a "usable" space for our common life. In fact, it seems to leave us with two separate spheres of shared interaction: the one, defined to a great extent by the state and its institutions, is where we interact according to abstract and increasingly impersonal rules of justice that are, however, far removed from a more intimate and manageable sphere of public trust, mutual recognition, and the sense of belonging. A second sphere, however, also exists; it is where we grant one another a certain degree of moral credit, predicated on our shared communal, religious, ethnic, or racial pasts. The discourse of this second realm is the discourse of trust and solidarity, of care and compassion, of loyalty and commitment. The discourse of the first is that of rights and state sanctions.

Precisely, that public reason on which our liberal-constitutional social order is based has also left us bereft of a sense of belonging. By a sense of belonging, I refer to claims that can be made on us, or that we can make on others, that appeal to no sense of abstract justice or right, but solely on a shared sense of solidarity, trust, and mutuality. To give a sense of what I mean, I would like to quote the words of the local Boston ward-leader Martin Lomasny that he related to Lincoln Steffens (1931, p. 618) at the beginning of the 20th century: "I think," said Lomasny, "that there's got to be in every ward somebody that any bloke can come to—no matter what he's done—and get help. *Help, you understand, none of your law and justice, but help.*" This was famously quoted by Robert Merton to explain the perseverance of the political machine in American political culture. Legalized assistance, doled out by cold, bureaucratic organizations (welfare agencies, settlement houses, legal aid clinics, public relief departments, etc.) all were seen as involving a loss of self-respect. In an impersonal society, the political machine provided, in Merton's terms, for humanized and personalized manners of assistance that did not degrade the recipient. What the quote gets at is the chasm between enacting a regime of abstract rights and life in a human community of mutual care and shared belonging. As can be well imagined, each provides very different social spaces, experiences, and models of civil life and civic enculturation. These are, if you will, precisely the differences between the rights-based provisions for religious education in Europe, outlined in Silvio Ferrari's contribution on the one hand, and, on the other, the type of thick, community-based principles of belonging that we see exemplified (in their most problematic moments) in the papers on Israel, Cyprus, and Malaysia.

Human needs for empathy, trust, and solidarity are of course recognized today, as in the past, but they are—to a great extent—accepted aspects of the private realm, while the public arena is ruled by the dictates of an increasingly abstract reason. In more sociological terms, we may claim that the division of public and private realms (upon which so much in our conceptualization of citizenship rests) is, in many Western societies, parallel to a division between truth and trust, reason and empathy, justice and mercy. But of course, the extremely complicating variable in today's world is how religious communities have come to represent that side of the equation associated with: trust, empathy, and mercy. And whatever else they are, religious communities are decidedly not universal, which is precisely where they come up against the rules of an abstract and universal reason, and so give rise to a questioning of their relevance as models of civic identity, which is pretty much the situation where so many find themselves today.

We have an idea of the public order, which is (1) secular, (2) predicated on the idea of the morally autonomous individual, and (3) oriented toward the preservation of different sets of individual rights rather than the realization of an idea of the *Good*. At the same time, we have more and more communities within the nation-states made up of individuals who do not understand themselves to be morally autonomous (but see themselves as enacting different sets of God-given commandments), who are not at all secular, and who have very clear ideas of a public *Good*—indeed of a divine *Good*—that trumps the legal recognition and assurance of individual or citizen rights. The result is the establishment of two competing arenas of social interaction, expectations, mutuality, identity, and indeed civil commitment. These two competing arenas are presented below, the one defined by what I call "TRUST," and the other by what we could term "CONFIDENCE."

TRUST	CONFIDENCE
Shared dispositions	Multicultural values
Moral community	Community of rights bearers
Value of peace	Value of justice
Familiarity	Strangeness
Sameness	Difference
Shared moral dispositions	Disparate moral values
Shared experience	Dissimilar experience
Moral credit granted to communal members	No credit granted, knowledge demanded
Others experienced as risk	Others experienced as dangerous
Risk leaves room for doubt	Danger requires security
Our group	Other group

The problem with this bifurcation of our social world is that the first, the world of trust and of moral community, is predicated on sameness, on familiarity, on our assumptions of knowledge of our communal "other". Sameness, however, is always illusionary, always partial, incomplete, and given to disruption. If we predicate our moral community on sameness, we will always be disappointed. We will always find one group or another, existing somewhere on the margins, or the borders of this "sameness," who—especially in times of trial and tribulation—are seen to betray this sameness, to violate our shared moral code and to betray their real colors, of strangeness and difference. Indeed, over sixty years ago Sigmund Freud wrote of the "narcissism of the small difference"—of how we perceive the threats to our identity not in the totally different and far-off other, but in the near-other, he or she who is similar in so many ways, but not in this one attribute (whatever it may be), which then achieves an iconic standing as representing all that is different and threatening, and so must be destroyed.

As long as trust is restricted to those who are the same, we will continually be patrolling the borders of this sameness to check for deviations and differences. The boundaries will be points of continual contestation, of fear, and of opprobrium. In times of crises (when the next bomb goes off in the London transport, or the next Imam is arrested in Leicester, or even perhaps when the economy slumps and I can no longer pay my mortgage), those who are a bit like us, but also a bit not like us, will come to take on a new aspect—not at all like us. Rather, they will be looked upon suspiciously, as possibly (perhaps even probably) dangerous, and as such, we will invoke the laws of justice and the sanctions of the state and its security forces, rather than the moral credit of our shared communal experience. As we know, this was the experience of Jews in 19th- and 20th-century Europe. In some ways, it is repeating itself with the Muslim citizens of European societies today. Similar attitudes we can find in Bulgaria toward Jehovah's Witnesses, in Malaysia toward Indians and Chinese, in Israel toward Palestinians, in Turkey toward Kurds and Alevis—the list can go on indefinitely. The question the various chapters of this volume are attempting to address is if religious education can play a role in bridging not only the divides between different communities of trust, but also between such communities and that overarching community of confidence as defined by citizenship, rights, and the abstract principles of justice. There are, as we shall see, no easy solutions, no overall solutions, and much reason for concern—but reasons for optimism as well.

Conclusion

At the end of the day, the question thus becomes: How can we get beyond the dichotomous models outlined above, to create—in fact, to imagine— a new and creative way "to live together differently?" What would be the model for inter-communal, rather than intra-communal, action and initiative? Most of our cases, after all, delineate educational programs enacted by a state, often one identified with a particular religious (or ethnic) community. The few exceptions—of the United States and France—reflect the legal separation of Church and State in those countries. It is of interest to note that the United Kingdom (not addressed in our papers) presents a model of a State Church (Anglicanism) which, despite its confessional particularity remains inclusive and where the Anglican parish provides in effect a common space for all of the parish citizenry (of whatever religious tradition) to feel at home. Not surprisingly, this is reflected in the developments over the past thirty years in the teaching of religion in state schools (what is called RE, or Religious Education, in the United Kingdom; Jackson 2007). Sadly, this model is most probably not exportable outside of the United Kingdom.

It is also of interest to note that of the cases collected here, the only two cases where there is no state-sponsored religious education are the United

States and France. Both countries were constituted as nation-states in the 18th century. Surely this is not coincidental. (The Netherlands presents yet another case of early statehood correlating with no state-sponsored religious education per se, provided rather through the unique system of social "pillarization" that characterizes the Dutch polity [ter Avest et al. 2007].) They are also the two countries in our overlapping sets where the polity, the constitutive community of the *volunté générale,* or conscience collective (if we prefer Emile Durkheim's terminology) is not identified with a singular religious group (despite many Republican attempts to define the United States as a Christian nation). From these cases then, it becomes clear that the trajectory of nation-state formation is itself a crucial variable. Compare for example the United States and France to those latecomers to statehood, such as Cyprus and Israel, and how much more difficult is the negotiation of religion and citizenship there. (Malaysia, also a latecomer to nationhood, is however an avowedly multiethnic and multicultural entity, as well as being a constitutional monarchy, which may explain why the problems of democratic difference discussed above play out somewhat differently there.) Turkey and Bulgaria are, in these terms, somewhat middle range in terms of state formation, both coming to be in the early, rather than the middle, decades of the 20th century. Not surprisingly in both these cases, accommodation of religious and ethnic differences seem more promising than in latecomers like Cyprus and Israel. In fact, the comparison of cases such as Malaysia and Israel—which are so similar in their educational challenges around issues of religion, ethnic identity, and citizenship—is one of the major benefits of a work such as this.

In this context, one is reminded of the early work of the great Norwegian comparative political theorist, Stein Rokkan who formulated a correspondence between the coming of age of nationhood and statehood and the relative challenges of democratic accommodation and citizenship across different countries. For him, much was path dependent. Early linguistic and cultural integration and the relative role of the Church as part of the process of nation formation (as in Northern Europe) or not (as in France) were prime variables in the process of democratic accommodation. For him too, late-20th-century newcomers to state formation all faced greater challenges in the realms of cultural unification, participation, and distribution than their European predecessors (Rokkan 1975, pp. 598–600). In our own cases here, France and Turkey present prime cases of nation formation developing in a marked conflict with clerical elites and authorities, with strong laicist ideologies resultant in both cases; though in Turkey, the nation-building elite has attempted to control religion and religious education, while in France, it distanced the state from religious education (Kuru 2009). Rokkan's work was centered on Europe, but we can see the relevance of his variables across the cases we are considering here as well. And though 20th-century processes of nation formation were more telescoped than earlier Western European ones—not surprisingly, where religious elites played a role in nation formation (Bulgaria, Cyprus—especially Greek Cyprus, Israel, Malaysia), religious education has become part and parcel of citizenship enculturation within the nation-state.

The question, however, remains if religious education can indeed be a site for the reconciliation of abstract citizenship with very different communities of trust, belonging, and meaning. Or will it serve only to distance those not identified with the majority religion from feelings of membership in the collective. I emphasize "different communities"; that state-sponsored religious education provides such meaning to Jews in Israel is clear, but what of the 25 percent of the population who is not Jewish? The same problem exists among Chinese, Indians, and Tamils in Malaysia, Muslims and the somewhat derogatively connoted "new Christians" in Bulgaria, and Alevis in Turkey. In all, state-sponsored religious education clearly provides a site of meaning, trust, and belonging for the majority of the state's citizens. But what of the ever-increasing minorities? In Cyprus, the question is if religious education can play a conciliatory role between communities, or does it simply perpetrate the ethno-national intransience (and will the recent addition of Islamic high schools [the Imam-Hatip schools] in the North, together with a first Faculty of Theology, further those trends); these are major issues being debated today.

There are no easy answers to these questions. In Cyprus, we would do well to fear the transformation of an ethno-national conflict into a religious one, as indeed has happened in the Israeli-Palestinian struggle over the past forty years. On the other hand, the precursor of the Anan plan for communal unification was a bicommunal project across North and South Nicosia, joining their sewer systems. A healthy pragmatism may still be a viable approach to intercommunal relations, while any exercise in reimagining ontological meanings and the definitions of solidarity may prove to be less than central in bringing communities together. In Israel, the question very much remains if Judaism can provide the sort of broad, inclusive sociopolitical framework that a specific type of sectarian Protestantism has done in the United States and Anglicanism has in the United Kingdom. On the face of things, there would seem to be every reason to doubt such an outcome. Yet, on the other hand, only now is there a dawning awareness that such is necessary, and only very recently are there efforts in this direction. The work of Yesodot, described by Fischer, is one such effort. The intellectual work of the Hartman Institute in Jerusalem is another; and other, albeit extremely limited, examples do exist.

Bulgaria, too, may not face as negative a future as one may assume from an uncritical reading of the Schnitter and Kalkandjieva chapter. As they note, integration into the European Union will be a crucial factor in the developing trajectory of national belonging. Bulgaria also had a long history of religious syncretism, intermarriage, and what we could call a quotidian pragmatism. The role of the Bulgarian Church in saving Bulgaria's 56,000 Jews from deportation in World War II comes to mind. While both the Patriarchate and the Islamic authorities pursue their own political agendas, the long shadow cast by ancient shared traditional ways of life (including religious life) may prove just as powerful in the long run.[1] In fact, if we look at France and the continual conflicts over minority rights of religious expression in the public realm, we may very well come to the conclusion that state-sponsored religious education is not a crucial variable at all in terms of distancing different communities from feelings of active citizenship and membership in the collective. Other factors are at work. In both Malaysia and Turkey too, it would seem that the exclusionary moves are, mostly framed in ethnic and national terms, rather than religious ones (though in the former case, religious identities are, of course, immediately implicated).

While state-sponsored religious education may in fact not play a substantial role in distancing minority communities from feelings of participation, this still begs the question of their capacity to provide a cite of inclusion and belonging to the national collective for such communities. While many of the findings presented here would seem to negate such assumptions, a blanket rejection of such possibilities is also not in order. Again, we may think of the United Kingdom and how the City of Birmingham developed a new conception of RE that overcame the old dichotomous notions of either teaching about religion or teaching a religion (that distinction discussed by Silvio Ferrari in our first chapter, as learning "about" or "from" religious traditions). The starting point for their vision of RE was that:

> The curriculum for a maintained school satisfies the requirements of this section if it is a balanced and broadly based

curriculum which—Promotes the spiritual, moral, cultural, mental and physical development of pupils at the school and of society; and Prepares such pupils for the opportunities, responsibilities, and experiences of adult life. (Government of the United Kingdom 1988)

The aim of this 2005 New Agreed Syllabus Conference (Birmingham Agreed Syllabus 2007) was to define RE not in terms of either the promotion of religion or even the inculcation of information about religions, but rather to reformulate the whole enterprise in more pragmatic terms of what could be learned from religion(s) to help young people achieve their life goals. Fascinating in this project was the development of twenty-four "dispositions" that were seen as shared across the different faith communities in the city, and students were exposed to the manner in which each community taught and practiced these "dispositions."[2]

Such an approach that frames the religious experience of communities in more pragmatic and less ideational (what we can think of as creedal) terms is a far cry from what we find in many of the cases studied here. As we noted earlier, the British model may not in fact be reproducible elsewhere. But the principles of its approach, a certain type of pragmatic orientation to what it means to share a city (or a state) may indeed be generalizable, even if each country would develop the forms of such pragmatism in a specific and quite particularistic manner. The heritage of Bulgarian syncretism comes to mind as quite a different place to start, than that of the Cypriot municipal waste disposal, or the practical exercises in citizenship required in Israeli education curricula discussed by Fischer. It is, however, the nonideological starting place that is important, not its content. We will return to this point in the concluding Afterward to this volume.

NOTES

1. Let me illustrate with a personal anecdote. In 2010, I was in the Bulgarian city of Plovdiv during the Jewish holiday of Tu b'shvat (the New Year for the Trees). The community gathered for a meal and ceremony, and honored all the different segments of the community: the elders, the youth, the community worthies, and so on. They also proudly and publically honored the "non-Jewish members of the community." One could hardly imagine this happening in other countries. In the same city, after Friday night prayers, I asked the prayer leader why

he had skipped those prayers for which a quorum of ten men was needed, as I counted sixteen men in the service. His reply: "More than half of them are Muslims."

2. The twenty-four dispositions included the following: being imaginative and explorative; appreciating beauty; expressing joy; being thankful; caring for others, animals, and the environment; sharing and being generous; being regardful of suffering; being merciful and forgiving; being fair and just; living by rules; being accountable and living with integrity; being temperate, exercising self-discipline, and cultivating serene contentment; being modest and listening to others; cultivating inclusion, identity, and belonging; creating unity and harmony; participating and willing to lead; remembering roots; being loyal and steadfast; being hopeful and visionary; being courageous and confident; being curious and valuing knowledge; being open, honest, and truthful; being reflective and self-critical; being silent and attentive to, and cultivating a sense for, the sacred and transcendence.

REFERENCES

Berkovitz, J.R. *The Shaping of Jewish Identity in Nineteenth Century France*. Detroit: Wayne State University, Press, 1989.

Birmingham City Council. *The Birmingham Agreed Syllabus for Religious Education 2007*. Birmingham.

Eisenstadt, S. N. *Power, Trust and Meaning*. Chicago: University of Chicago Press, 1995.

Emon, Anver. *Religious Pluralism and Islamic Law: Dhimmis and Others in the Empire of the Law*. Oxford: Oxford University Press, 2012.

Ferrari, Silvio. "State regulation of religion in the European democracies: the decline of the old pattern." In *Religion and democracy in contemporary Europe*. Edited by Gabriel Motzkin and Yochi Fischer, 103–112. London: Alliance Publ. Trust, 2008.

Government of the United Kingdom. *1988 Education Reform Act*. London: National Archives. http://www.legislation.gov.uk/ukpga/1988/40/contents/enacted.

Ignatieff, Michael. *Human Rights as Politics and Idolatry*. Princeton, NJ: Princeton University Press, 2001.

Jackson, Robert, Siebren Midema, Wolfram Weisse, and Jean-Paul Willaime, eds. *Religion and Education in Europe*. Münster, Germany: Waxmann Verlag, 2007.

Jackson, Robert, and Kevin O'Grady. "Religions and Education in England: Social Plurality, Civil Religion and Religious Education Pedagogy." In *Religion and Education in Europe*. Edited by Jackson et al., 180–202. Münster, Germany: Waxmann Verlag, 2007.

Kraince, Richard. "Reforming Islamic Education in Malaysia: Doctrine or Dialogue." In *Making Modern Muslims: The Politics of Islamic Education in Southeast Asia*. Edited by R. Hefner, 107–140. Honolulu: University of Hawaii Press, 2009.

Kuru, Ahmet. *Secularism and State Policies towards Religion: The United States, France and Turkey.* Cambridge, UK: Cambridge University Press, 2009.

Lipset, Seymour M. *The First New Nation.* London: Heinemann, 1964.

Crouch, Gregory. "Dutch Consider Banning Islamic Garments in Public." *New York Times,* 18 November 2006: A3.

Rokkan, Stein. "Dimensions of State Formation and Nation-Building: A Possible Paradigm for Research on Variations within Europe." In *The Formation of National States in Western Europe.* Edited by C. Tilly, 562–600. Princeton, NJ: Princeton University Press, 1975.

Smith, Wilfred Cantwell. *The Meaning and End of Religion.* Minneapolis: Fortress Press. 1990.

Steffens, Lincoln. *The Autobiography of Lincoln Steffens.* By Lincoln Steffens, 618. New York: Harcourt, Brace and Co., 1931.

Taylor, Charles. *Multiculturalism and the Politics of Recognition.* Princeton, NJ: Princeton University Press, 1992.

ter Avest, Ina, Cok Bakker, Gerdien Bertram-Troost, and Siebren Miedema. "Religion and Education in the Dutch Pillarized and Post-Pillarized Educational System: Historical Background and Current Debates." In *Religion and Education in Europe.* Edited by Jackson et al., 203–219. Münster, Germany: Waxmann Verlag, 2007.

Tully, James. *Strange Multiplicity: Constitutionalism in the Age of Diversity.* Cambridge: Cambridge University Press, 1995.

Willaime, Jean-Paul. "Different Models of Religion and Education in Europe." In *Religion and Education in Europe.* Edited by Robert Jackson, Siebren Midema, Wolfram Weisse, and Jean-Paul Willaime, 47–65. Münster, Germany: Waxmann Verlag, 2007.

Yoav Peled. "Ethnic Democracy and the Legal Construction of Citizenship: Arab Citizens of the Jewish State." *American Political Science Review* 86.2 (1992): 432–443.

I

Teaching Religion in the European Union

A LEGAL OVERVIEW

Silvio Ferrari

Introduction

To understand the "map" of religious education in Europe today, an important legal distinction must be drawn between the obligations that European states have undertaken, in terms of international law and the choices they have made in their domestic laws.[1] In international law, the most important provision is Article 2 of the First Additional Protocol to the Convention for the Protection of Human Rights and Fundamental Freedoms adopted by the Council of Europe in 1952:

> No person shall be denied the right to education. In the exercise of any functions which it assumes in relation to education and to teaching, the State shall respect the right of parents to ensure such education and teaching in conformity with their own religious and philosophical convictions. (Council of Europe 1952)

Two rights derive from this provision: (1) the right to establish private schools with a religious or philosophical orientation,[2] and (2) the right of students to be exempted from the obligation to follow a denominational teaching of religion in public schools.[3] Most European states have, however, gone further in their domestic laws, taking affirmative action to

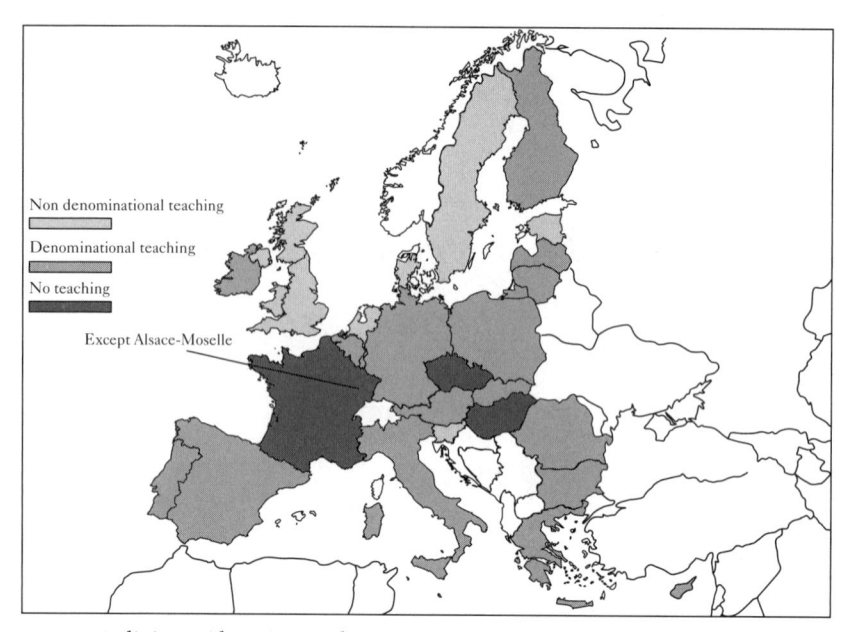

MAP I.I Religious Education in the EU Countries. This map reflects the European situation as of 2011.

ensure a religious education consistent with the convictions of the parents and their children.[4] Consequently, several states provide for (1) the public funding of private schools, whether religious or not;[5] and (2) the religious education in public schools, in denominational or non-denominational form. Concerning this second topic, religion is far from being absent from the EU public schools. Even in the few countries where there is no specific course devoted to religious education, references to religion—Christianity and Judaism, but also Islam and other religions—are necessary to teach history, philosophy, literature, and other school disciplines. But this "scattered" presence of religion in school education no longer seems to be sufficient. Today there is a growing consensus around the idea that the state (and its schools) must strengthen the knowledge of religion. At least four reasons are given: (1) the need to fight religious ignorance that prevents the comprehension and so ignorance of a central dimension of personal and collective life; (2) the need to understand and govern the new religious plurality, which requires the knowledge of different religions, for example, Islam; (3) the need to meet the demand for meaning, which became more acute after the collapse of the great secular ideologies; and (4) the need to educate to citizenship, to mutual tolerance and to the respect for the "other" that these values implies.[6] However, while there is broad agreement on this diagnosis, there is no unanimity on what to do, that is, on the best way to teach religion at school.

At least three different approaches have been followed by the EU states in this field:

1. Giving more space to the knowledge of religion in the study of other school subjects, without creating a specific course devoted to the denominational or non-denominational teaching of religion. This is the solution proposed in France by Régis Debray in a report published in 2002 (Debray 2002). Objections to this approach are that if no prior knowledge of the contents of a religion is provided to students, references to that religion in the course of history or literature may remain incomprehensible.
2. Strengthening the knowledge of religion through the non-denominational teaching of religions (what is frequently called teaching about religions). Some religious communities object that this approach is tainted by a relativistic drift that leads students to believe that all religions are equally true (or false),[7] and some experts criticize this approach as descriptive and often backward looking that generates a pedagogy which consists fundamentally in looking at religion from a distance.
3. Strengthening the knowledge of religion through courses devoted to the teaching of a specific religion (teaching of religion). This approach is based on the belief that a student needs to know his or her own particular religious tradition in order to enter into dialogues with other religions and cultures, and to answer the demand of meaning that characterizes our time. The criticism that has addressed this approach argues that knowing one religion is not enough in a religiously plural society (Neusner and Sonn 1999, 1; Ferlito 2005, 74–75), and that this system inevitably involves some discrimination against the religious communities that are not given the right to teach their religion at school. Each option can be modulated in different ways and combined with others in various forms. But what is the current situation in the EU countries?

Countries without the Teaching of or about Religion

Map 1.1 shows the countries where no teaching of or about religion is offered: these are France and, to a more limited extent, the Czech Republic and Hungary. France (with the exception of Alsace-Moselle, where a system of denominational teaching of religion is in place; see Messner 2011) is practically the only country in Europe that does not offer a specific course where the teaching of or about religion is provided: references to religion are contained only in the teaching of other school subjects like history, geography, language, arts, and philosophy. In the secondary schools, parents or students can ask for the creation of a chaplaincy, and, with the authorization of the school authorities, the chaplain may teach religion on the school premises to students who want to receive this teaching (Messner 2011). However, the teaching of religion is not part of the school curriculum, nor is it offered during school time.

In the Czech Republic, the denominational teaching of religion may be provided by some religious communities to pupils who demand it (at least seven pupils attending the same school must apply; Tretera and Horák 2011).[8] Religion classes are often given during Wednesday afternoons, which is a half day without classes. Teachers are paid by the school and have the same legal status as other teachers, but they cannot teach without the authorization of the concerned religious community (Tretera and Horák 2011).

In Hungary, the denominational teaching of religion can be given at the request of parents or students. The school provides the classrooms and an appropriate time that—according to local situations—can be placed within or outside school hours. The curriculum is defined by the religious authorities that also select and hire the teachers (the religious communities receive state funding for paying them; Schanda 2011).

Although the legal arrangements of these three countries are different, they share the fact that no teaching of or about religion is part of school curriculum.

Countries with a Non-Denominational Teaching about Religion

Geographic Distribution

The countries with a non-denominational teaching about religions are all located in the northern part of Europe, with the exception of Slovenia (see Map 1.1, note 1). These countries have a high percentage of citizens who do not profess any religion or are members of Protestant Churches,[9] and these two facts may have had an influence on the adoption of this system of teaching religion in schools. On the one hand, people who are not members of any religious community are more likely to accept a non-denominational teaching about religions than a denominational teaching of one or more religions in the public schools. On the other hand, in many of these countries the denominational teaching of religion has been transformed into a non-denominational teaching about religions through an internal process of secularization, favored by the closeness of State and Church. This is the case of the countries of Northern Europe, where, in accordance with the Lutheran system of State Church, the teaching of the state religion was considered to be a task of the state. The secularization of the state institutions gradually turned this denominational teaching into a non-denominational religious education. Thus, in Sweden, the teaching of the Lutheran religion was successively transformed into the "teaching of Christianity" (1919), the "science of Christianity" (1962), and the "science of religion" (1969) (Larsson 2007, 194). A similar development took place in Norway where this teaching was called "Christian Education" in the early 1970s, became "Christian Religious and Life Stance Education" in 1997, and is now entitled "Religion, Life Stances and Ethics" (Skeie 2007, 233–234).

Characteristics of the Teaching

Teaching about religions is organized, managed, and controlled by the state. In particular, state institutions are in charge of the training, selection, appointment, dismissal, and remuneration of teachers. Teachers do not need an authorization issued by religious authorities. Authorization by religious authorities is also not needed to define the curricula or syllabi, nor is it needed to approve textbooks—though in some cases, some of these activities are performed in cooperation with the religious communities (as is the case in the United Kingdom; McClean 2011).

This non-denominational teaching is compulsory[10]: in some countries, students have the right to opt out of it,[11] and no alternative education is provided to them.[12] The non-denominational character of this teaching does not exclude the possibility to pay special attention to Christianity (as is the case in Denmark[13] and the United Kingdom[14]). This point has been recently been discussed in a decision of the European Court of Human Rights, concluding that "in view of the place occupied by Christianity in the national history and tradition" of Norway, "the fact that knowledge about Christianity represented a greater part of the Curriculum for primary and lower secondary schools than knowledge about other religions and philosophies cannot, in the Court's opinion, of its own be viewed as a departure from the principles of pluralism and objectivity amounting to indoctrination" (Folgerø and Others v. Norway, 15472/02, at n. 89). The same principle has been repeated, this time with reference to Islam, in the decision of the case *Hasan and Eylem Zengin v. Turkey* (1448/04, at n. 63), notwithstanding the secular character of the Turkish state.

Countries with a Denominational Teaching of Religion

Geographic Distribution

Map 1.1 shows that the geographical distribution is more balanced, with countries evenly spread all over Europe. The majority of these countries have a strong presence of Catholic or Orthodox communities (with the exception of Finland), and the majority of the post-Communist countries (where religious education has been reintroduced in schools after 1989) are included in this group. In this case, too, the religious background of these States has had an impact on shaping the system of religious education. In Catholic countries, the Church has always claimed the monopoly of the teaching of religion in public schools, confining the state to the role of provider of the financial and logistic support for Church activity, while in the predominantly Orthodox countries—where the distinction between Church and State has always been weak—a process of secularization (along the lines of what happened in the Protestant countries) did not develop, nor was the shift from the denominational to the non-denominational teaching of religion encouraged, as had been in the Nordic countries of Europe.

Characteristics of the Teaching

Generally speaking, the denominational teaching of religion is organized, managed, and controlled by the religious communities (frequently in cooperation with the state), but the scope of their powers is different from country to country.[15] In most cases, religious authorities have the power to select the teachers. Even when the teacher is appointed and paid by the state, he or she cannot teach without the authorization of the concerned religious community, and the revocation of the authorization entails the obligation to abandon the teaching.[16] Whether this authorization can be revoked for reasons other than teaching incompetence is a debated point. Religious communities also play a role (which is different from country to country) in the definition of the curriculum and the syllabus[17] and in the adoption of the textbooks.[18]

Frequently, states have the obligation to offer denominational teaching of religion,[19] but students (or their parents) have the right to choose whether to attend such classes or not; in some cases, the teaching is compulsory and students have only the right to opt out.[20] In a few countries, students who do not follow the teaching of religion are required to attend an alternative teaching.[21]

Denominational religious instruction is frequently supported, from an economic and logistic point of view, by the state that pays the teachers and makes available the facilities and the school time.[22] However, this support is unevenly distributed: in Italy, for example, only the teachers of the Catholic religion are paid by the state.

Not all religions can be taught at school. In some states, this right is granted only to recognized or registered religious communities, and almost everywhere a minimum number of students applying for the teaching of a specific religion is required.[23] In some cases, these restrictions significantly limit the number of minority religions that can be taught in public schools[24]; in other cases, minority religious communities, although having the right to teach their religion, prefer not to make use of this opportunity.[25]

Evolution and Limits of Denominational Religious Education

Recently, some major changes have occurred in the countries where a denominational teaching of religion is imparted. These changes can be summarized in three points:

1. In some countries where, until twenty to thirty years ago, just one religion could be taught, it is now possible to teach a number of religions (for example in Italy, Spain, and Portugal).
2. In other countries (for example, Germany), there are increasing ecumenical and inter-denominational openings (Willaime 2007, 62–65). However, such a development (and this is its main limit) can take place

only in religiously plural countries; it is hard to imagine it in countries with a dominant religion like Poland or Italy.
3. The denominational teaching of religion is less and less limited to the knowledge of a single religion, and it frequently includes elements of general religious cultures and ethical issues. This is the case, for example, of Italy, Spain, and (in France) Alsace-Moselle (Willaime 2007, 65–66). However, the approach to these issues cannot be neutral (as it should be in the case of non-denominational teaching), as it reflects the point of view of the religion that is taught.

As a consequence of these changes, the subject matter of denominational and non-denominational teachings of religion has become closer, while the authorities in charge of organizing and controlling the educational subject matter (the religious communities in one case, the state in the other) remain distinct and separate entities.

Perspectives

Education scholars frequently distinguish between teaching of (or into a) religion,[26] teaching about religion,[27] and teaching from religion.[28] While the first two models are essentially descriptive and are associated with two different ways of organizing religious education, the third model is normative and indicates a purpose that can be reached through the teaching of religion as well as through the teaching about religion (particularly in light of what has been noted about the convergent trend of the two systems); this explains why this third model is not correlated to a specific legal system of organization of religious education.

The choice to provide a denominational or non-denominational religious education has its roots in the religious and cultural tradition of each country: countries with a Catholic or Orthodox background tend to adopt the first model, and those with a Protestant tradition—particularly where there is a Church of State—have a preference for the latter. Both systems are changing under the pressure of the transformation of the European religious landscape, characterized by a process of pluralization that is taking place both inside and outside each religion (Schreiner 2007, 13). On one hand, Europe is far less homogeneous, religiously speaking, than it was in a still-recent past, due to the increase of people who follow non-Christian religions or do not identify with any religion. On the other hand, the space for individual choices, preferences, lifestyles, and personal ways of interpreting religious faith has grown within each religious tradition. These two processes take place in a context of the desecularization and deprivatization of religion that has given new importance and visibility to religions in public space (Berger 1999; Davie 2000). For this reason, religious education has become a central topic in the discussions about how to foster democratic citizenship (Jackson 2007, 27–55) and social cohesion.

However, the European debate about religious education risks focusing on a false dilemma. On the one hand, the need to safeguard the denominational teaching of religion has been strongly reaffirmed, and any attempt to introduce science or history of religions into the teaching religion has been stigmatized as relativistic. The supporters of this approach recognize the need to provide students with knowledge and information regarding a plurality of religions, but insist that such demand must be answered from a particular point of view, that of the religion professed by each student. On the other hand, the contemporary religious plurality (and the opportunity to prepare students to understand it) has been invoked to replace the denominational teaching *of* religion with non-denominational teaching *about* religions, implying that public schools should have a preference for this latter system. Many Churches and religious communities (especially in the Catholic and Orthodox world) are in favor of the first model; some international organizations (in particular, the Council of Europe) support the second.[29]

Behind this debate, there are two different conceptions of the public school. In one case, the school is considered primarily as an institution serving the families and the students: if they make a request for education in a specific religious tradition, public schools must do everything they can to answer it. In the other case, the school is seen as an institution that has the task to serve society as a whole: if social changes require a wider knowledge of the different religions that exist in a country, the school must satisfy this need.

In fact, the two claims are not incompatible; on the contrary, they can complement each other. The need, resulting from the increased religious plurality, to learn about different religions requires more *information*: the central issue in this case is the ability of the teacher to provide sound and balanced knowledge that can help in understanding different religious experiences and in preventing the building of a religious stereotype of the "other." In this sense, teaching about religion should be (as much as possible) "neutral" toward the different worldviews that are presented. The request to deepen the knowledge of a specific religious tradition answers a need not so much of information, but of *formation*: the student is called to engage earnestly with the answers that a specific religious tradition has given to the central questions of existence and to verify how much they satisfy his or her personal search for meaning. Although the formative and informative dimensions are not absent, respectively, in the teaching about and in the teaching of religion, this distinction suggests terms for combining the two models to reach the ultimate goal of a good educational system that is to say, the raising of autonomous, responsible, and committed persons. In this context, The Netherlands can provide a good example (although each country has to find its own pattern): public schools are expected to provide not only a non-denominational teaching about religions, but also, when parents require it, a denominational teaching of a specific religion (Pépin 2009, 88–89).

Based on these observations, it is possible to adduce some conclusions concerning the legal models of religious education in Europe. First, it is helpful to emphasize that the European Union does not require uniform solutions in the area of teaching of or about religion. It demands only that religious instruction is received on a voluntary basis (or, if it is compulsory, that students have the right to be exempted from the teaching)[30] and, in the case of non-denominational teaching, that it "is conveyed in an objective, critical and pluralistic manner."[31] As all the legal systems in force in the European Union meet these limits, they are free to develop their religious education according to local traditions and preferences.

This being said, it is undeniable that in the countries with a denominational religious education, where just one religion is taught at school, the problem of learning about the different religions that exist in Europe has become acute. If the religious communities are not able to develop an interdenominational and interreligious education (and they are still far from that), the only viable alternative would be a non-denominational education about a plurality of religions. A model for such instruction has been indicated in the recommendation *Religion and Democracy* of the Parliamentary Assembly of the Council of Europe, which promotes a better knowledge of different religions through the teaching of comparative history of religions as well as the history and philosophy of religion.[32] In this perspective, non-denominational teaching about religions and non-religious conceptions of life and the world would become mandatory and would be organized and delivered according to the standards of other school teachings (that is without any control of religious authorities on teachers, programs, books, and so on), although some kind of cooperation and consultation with the different stakeholders (families, religious communities, associations of teachers, etc.) would be advisable.[33]

At the same time, it is equally undeniable that the denominational teaching of religion is part of the legal tradition of many European countries where the school is conceived as an institution responding to the various requests coming from civil society. Moreover, even if a non-denominational education about religions is introduced or if the knowledge of religions is embedded within various school disciplines (according to the French model), denominational religious teaching has a role to play in the process of students' education. But it requires to be seriously reformed: in particular, it is necessary to make it fully voluntary, to give the right to impart this teaching to several religions, and to ensure that the support provided by the state is not selectively granted to only some of them; according to different national situations, this teaching could be placed inside or outside the school hours, and the teachers could be paid or not by the state.

Once these conditions are met, the two systems of religious teaching can coexist and offer, through their integration, a contribution to the students' education that is adequate to the challenges posed by the religious transformations of Europe.

NOTES

1. In this text, the expression "teaching *of* religion" (or "*denominational* teaching") indicates the teaching of a specific religion from the internal point of view of the concerned religion, while the expression "teaching *about* religions" (or "*non-denominational* teaching") indicates the provision of knowledge and information about a number of religions from a point of view that is external to each of them (see also notes 34–36). "*Optional* teaching" means that students must choose between two or more alternative teachings, for example religion or ethics; "*voluntary* teaching" means that students can choose whether to follow that teaching, but no alternative teaching is provided in case they decide not to attend it. The notion of "*public* school" is particularly complex. The definition given in OSCE 2007, 20 will be adopted in this paper: according to it, public school means "a school whose organization, financing and management are primarily the responsibility of, or under the primary oversight of, a public body (state, regional, municipal, etc.)."
2. See also Article 13.3 of the International Covenant on Economic, Social and Cultural Rights (1966): "The States Parties to the present Covenant undertake

to have respect for the liberty of parents and, when applicable, legal guardians to choose for their children schools other than those established by the public authorities, which conform to such minimum educational standards as may be laid down or approved by the State," and similarly, Article 5.1.b of the UNESCO Convention against Discrimination in Education (1960). The issue of private schools will not be considered here. Suffice it to say that there are countries, Ireland and Belgium for example (see Colton 2011; Torfs 2011), where Catholic-oriented private schools make up the majority of schools, a fact that has a clear impact on the religious education offered in these countries.

3. See also Article 5.1 of the UNESCO Convention Against Discrimination in Education (1960): "The States Parties to this Convention agree that: [...] (b) [...] no person or group of persons should be compelled to receive religious instruction inconsistent with his or their conviction."

4. The need for such an action could be grounded in Article 13.3 of the International Covenant on Economic, Social and Cultural Rights (1966): "The States Parties to the present Covenant undertake [...] to ensure the religious and moral education of [the] children in conformity with their [of the parents] own convictions." See also Article 5.1.b of the Convention against Discrimination in Education (UNESCO 1960).

5. Public funding of private schools is recommended by the Parliamentary Assembly of the Council of Europe (see the resolution on academic freedom in the European Community, n. 1-1456/83 of March 14, 1984), but the European Court of Human Rights has always held that states are not obliged to provide such support.

6. See the Recommendation 2008/12 of the Committee of Ministers of the Council of Europe to member states on the dimension of religions and non-religious convictions within intercultural education, December 10, 2008, n. 4: "information on and knowledge of religions and non-religious convictions which influence the behaviour of individuals in public life should be taught in order to develop tolerance as well as mutual understanding and trust" (CM/Rec, December 2008).

7. For example, see Card 2009 (Congregation for Catholic Education), 3: "if religious education is limited to a presentation of the different religions, in a comparative and "neutral" way, it creates confusion or generates religious relativism or indifferentism."

8. According to the Act on Churches No. 3/2002, some religious communities have "the special right to provide religious teaching" at school; today there are twenty-one religious communities enjoying this right.

9. Citizens of Denmark and Sweden are mostly Lutheran (in 2002, respectively 84 percent and 80.8 percent). In Estonia, 77 percent of the population does not belong to any religious community, and 11 percent belong to the Lutheran Church. In the United Kingdom, 71.4 percent of the population declared

themselves Christian in 2001 (the vast majority identifying with the Church of England), and 15.94 percent declared not to belong to any religious community. Among these countries, The Netherlands, with 42 percent of the population reporting no religious affiliation, followed by 31 percent declaring themselves Catholic (2003), and Slovenia, which is predominantly Catholic (57.8 percent of the population in 2002), are the exceptions. For these data, see Robbers (2007).

10. There are two exceptions to this rule: Estonia (Kiviorg 2011) and Slovenia (Ivanc 2011), where religious education is optional.
11. In Denmark (Christoffersen 2011) and the United Kingdom (McClean 201), for example, but not in Sweden (Friedner 2011).
12. The right to be exempted from the non-denominational teaching of religion has been the object of two recent decisions of the European Court of Human Rights: Folgerø and Others v. Norway, 15472/02; and Hasan and Eylem Zengin v. Turkey, 1448/04 (particularly at nn. 71–76). See Relaño (2010).
13. In Denmark the "central field of knowledge is Christianity» but «pupils must also gain knowledge about non-Christian religions and life styles" (Christoffersen 2011).
14. S. 375 (3) of the Education Act, 1996, affirms that the syllabus must "reflect the fact that the religious traditions in Great Britain are in the main Christian whilst taking account of the teaching and practices of the other principal religions represented in Great Britain."
15. This control is justified by the religious communities in having the need to grant the orthodoxy of the teaching. See, for example, Card 2009 (Congregation for Catholic Education), 13–14: "it is for the Church to establish the authentic contents of Catholic religious education in schools. This guarantees, for both parents and the pupils themselves, that the education presented as Catholic is indeed authentic. [...] The Church identifies this task as its own, *ratione materiae*, and claims it for its own competence, regardless of the nature of the school (State-run or non-State-run, Catholic or non-Catholic) in which such teaching is given."
16. This is the case, for example, of Portugal (Folque 2011), The Netherlands (van Bijsterveld 2011; in the Dutch public schools, non-denominational and denominational religious education coexist), Poland (Krukowski 2011), the Czech Republic (Tretera and Horák 2011), Austria (Hammer and Franck 2011), Belgium (Torfs 2011), Spain (Motilla 2011), Italy (Ferrari 2011), Latvia and Luxembourg (only for the teachers of Catholic religion; Balodis 2011; Poirier 2011). On the contrary, in Finland the teachers are state employees who enjoy the same legal status of other teachers in public schools and do not need the authorization of the religious authorities; Kotiranta (2011).
17. It is so in Portugal (Folque 2011), Spain (Motilla 2011), Austria (Hammer and Franck 2011), The Netherlands (van Bijsterveld 2011), and Latvia (for the teaching of Catholic, Orthodox, and Lutheran religions; Balodis 2011). But there are

exceptions: in Cyprus, the curricula are prepared and textbooks approved by the Ministry of Education (Emilianides 2011); in Finland, the curricula are prepared by the religious communities, but need to be approved by the National Board of Education (Kotiranta 2011).

18. In some countries (for example Austria, Spain, Romania, Portugal, and Italy) only the textbooks that have been approved by the concerned religious authorities can be adopted by the school.

19. This system is in force in The Netherlands (van Bijsterveld 2011), Romania (Tăvală 2011), Poland (Krukowski 2011), Bulgaria (Kalkandjieva 2008, 169–172). In Portugal (Folque 2011), Spain (Motilla 2011), and Italy (Ferrari 2011), the state has the obligation to provide the teaching of the Catholic religion only. In Poland and in The Netherlands, schools have the obligation to provide also a teaching of ethics or non-religious beliefs.

20. In Greece and Cyprus, the teaching of the Greek Orthodox religion is compulsory; non-Orthodox students have the right to be exempted. It is discussed whether Orthodox students enjoy the same right. In Austria and Germany, the teaching of religion is compulsory for the students whose religion is taught at school, but they have the right to opt out. In Romania, the teaching is compulsory and the students can opt out from it (Pépin 2009, 1).

21. These include other educational activities in The Netherlands (van Bijsterveld 2011), philosophy of life in Finland (Kotiranta 2011), ethics in Latvia (Balodis 2011), moral and social education in Luxembourg (Poirier 2011), and values and norms or ethics in Germany (Heinig 2011). In Spain, students who opt out from the teaching of Catholic religion can (but are not obliged to) follow the teaching of "History and Culture of Religions."

22. Teachers of religion are paid by the state in Belgium, Finland, Poland, The Netherlands, the Czech Republic, Spain, Italy, Luxembourg, Romania, and other countries.

23. At least three students of the same school in Austria; seven in Poland and in the Czech Republic; ten in Portugal and Latvia; ten to fifteen (depending on the type of school) in Romania; three students of the schools of the same municipality in Finland; in Spain, if more than ten students require the teaching of a specific religion, the teacher is paid by the state. In Germany, the required number of students is different from Land to Land.

24. The religious communities that can teach their religion in the EU countries in which there are denominational teachings of religion include Austria with about fifteen recognized religious communities; Belgium: six recognized religious communities (Catholic, Protestant, Anglican, Orthodox, Jewish, and Muslim); Bulgaria: the Orthodox and Muslim communities; Greece and Cyprus: only one religious community (Greek Orthodox), with the exception of the part of Greece with a Muslim majority (Thrace) in which Islam is taught; Italy: the Catholic Church and six religious communities that have concluded

an agreement with the state (Lutheran, Adventist, Pentecostal, Valdensian, Assembly of God, and Jewish); Latvia: five religious communities (Lutheran, Catholic, Orthodox, Baptist, and Old Believers); Poland: twenty-four religious communities (the Catholic Church, Polish Autocephalous Orthodox Church, Evangelic-Augsburg Church, Methodist Church, Evangelic-Reformist Church, Polish Catholic Church, Free Christians Church, Church of Christ, Baptist Christian Church, Church of the Mariavites, Evangelical Christian Church, Seventh-Day Adventists Church, Church of Pentecost, New Apostolic Church, Church of God in Christ, Christian Reformed Church, Church of Evangelical Christians, Polish Church of Free Christians, Community of Christian Churches, Pentecost Communities, Evangelical Brethren Church, Christian League, Union of Jewish Confessional Communities, and Islamic League); Spain: the Catholic Church, and the Evangelical, Jewish, and Islamic Federations can teach religion at school, but outside school time.

25. This is the case, for example, of the small Protestant communities in Italy: see Schreiner (2007, 10).
26. "Educating into a religion deals with a single religious tradition, is taught by 'insiders' and often has the objective of enabling pupils to come to believe in the religion or to strengthen their commitment to it" (Jackson 2007, 29).
27. "Educating about religion confines itself to using descriptive and historical methods, and aims neither to foster nor to erode religious belief" (Jackson 2007, 29).
28. "Educating from religion involves pupils in considering different responses to religious and moral issues, so that they may develop their own views in a reflective way. Here the main objective might be seen as enabling pupils to develop their own point of view on matters relating to religion and values" (Jackson 2007, 29).
29. See supra, notes 6 and 7.
30. See the European Court of Human Rights decision 403119/98 in the case Saniewski v. Poland.
31. See the European Court of Human Rights decisions 15472/02, n. 84 in the case Folgerø and Others v. Norway; Eylem Zengin v. Turkey (1448/04, at nn.36 and 42).
32. Council of Europe, Recommendation 1396 of Parliamentary Assembly (1999) Religion and Democracy: 13. The Assembly consequently recommends that the Committee of Ministers invite the governments of the member states: [...] ii. to promote education about religions and, in particular, to: a. step up the teaching about religions as sets of values towards which young people must develop a discerning approach, within the framework of education on ethics and democratic citizenship; b. promote the teaching in schools of the comparative history of different religions, stressing their origins, the similarities in some of their values and the diversity of their customs, traditions, festivals,

and so on; c. encourage the study of the history and philosophy of religions and research into those subjects at university, in parallel with theological studies; d. co-operate with religious educational institutions in order to introduce or reinforce, in their curricula, aspects relating to human rights, history, philosophy and science; e. avoid—in the case of children—any conflict between the state-promoted education about religion and the religious faith of the families, in order to respect the free decision of the families in this very sensitive matter. [...] 14. The Assembly also recommends that the Committee of Ministers: i. lay down, as part of its projects on education for democratic citizenship and history teaching, guidelines for the introduction of educational syllabuses relevant to points 13.ii.a, b and c of this recommendation."

33. The opportunity to include different stakeholders in the organization of the non-denominational teaching of religion is strongly underlined in the recommendations of the OSCE (2007, 15). The arrangements for producing agreed syllabuses for religious education that are in force in England can offer interesting clues (Pépin 2009, 65).

BIBLIOGRAPHY

Balodis, Ringolds. "Religion in Public Education—Latvian Experience." Paper presented at the proceedings of the European Consortium for Church and State Research, held in Trier, Germany, November 12–13, 2010. In *Religion in Public Education*. Edited by Gerhard Robbers, 273–294. Trier, Germany: European Consortium for Church and State Research, 2011. Available online, www.church-state.eu/Meetings/Meeting-2010/1,000000270353,8,1.

Berger, Peter. *The Desecularization of the World*. Grand Rapids, MI: Eerdmans, 1999.

Congregation for Catholic Education, "Circular Letter to the Presidents of Bishops' Conferences on Religious Education in Schools." Congregation for Catholic Education, May 5, 2009.

Christoffersen, Lisbet. "Religion in Public Education—Denmark." Paper presented at the proceedings of the European Consortium for Church and State Research, held in Trier, Germany, November 12–13, 2010. In *Religion in Public Education*. Edited by Gerhard Robbers, 113–116. Trier, Germany: European Consortium for Church and State Research, 2011. Available online, www.churchstate.eu/Meetings/Meeting-2010/1,000000270353,8,1.

Colton, Paul. "Religion in Public Education in Ireland." Paper presented at the proceedings of the European Consortium for Church and State Research, held in Trier, Germany, November 12–13, 2010. In *Religion in Public Education*. Edited by Gerhard Robbers, 227–256. Trier, Germany: European Consortium for Church and State Research, 2011. Available online, www.churchstate.eu/Meetings/Meeting-2010/1,000000270353,8,1.

Council of Europe, Convention for the Protection of Human Rights and Fundamental Freedoms, 1952.
Davie, Grace. *Religion in Modern Europe: A Memory Mutates*. Oxford: Oxford University Press, 2000.
Debray, Régis. *L'enseignement du fait religieux dans l'école laïque*. Paris: Odile Jacob, 2002.
Emilianides, Achilles. "Religion in Public Education in Cyprus." Paper presented at the proceedings of the European Consortium for Church and State Research, held in Trier, Germany, November 12–13, 2010. In *Religion in Public Education*. Edited by Gerhard Robbers, 87–99. Trier, Germany: European Consortium for Church and State Research, 2011. Available online, www.churchstate.eu/Meetings/Meeting-2010/1,000000270353,8,1.
European Court of Human Rights, Folgerø and Others v. Norway, 15472/02.
European Court of Human Rights, Hasan and Eylem Zengin v. Turkey, 1448/04.
Ferlito, Sergio. *Le religioni, il giurista e l'antropologo*. Soveria Mannelli, Italy: Rubbettino, 2005.
Ferrari, Alessandro. "La religion dans l'education publique—les[è « le », not « les »] cas italien." Paper presented at the proceedings of the European Consortium for Church and State Research, held in Trier, Germany, November 12–13, 2010. In *Religion in Public Education*. Edited by Gerhard Robbers, 257–273. Trier, Germany: European Consortium for Church and State Research, 2011. Available online, www.churchstate.eu/Meetings/Meeting-2010/1,000000270353,8,1.
Folque, André. "Religion in Public Portuguese Education." Paper presented at the proceedings of the European Consortium for Church and State Research, held in Trier, Germany, November 12–13, 2010. In *Religion in Public Education*. Edited by Gerhard Robbers, 399–424. Trier, Germany: European Consortium for Church and State Research, 2011. Available online, www.churchstate.eu/Meetings/Meeting-2010/1,000000270353,8,1.
Friedner, Lars. "Religion in Public Education—Sweden." Paper presented at the proceedings of the European Consortium for Church and State Research, held in Trier, Germany, November 12–13, 2010. In *Religion in Public Education*. Edited by Gerhard Robbers, 493–502. Trier, Germany: European Consortium for Church and State Research, 2011. Available online, www.churchstate.eu/Meetings/Meeting-2010/1,000000270353,8,1.
Hammer, Stefan, and Johannes Franck. "Religion in Public Education—Report on Austria." Paper presented at the proceedings of the European Consortium for Church and State Research, held in Trier, Germany, November 12–13, 2010. In *Religion in Public Education*. Edited by Gerhard Robbers, 39–62. Trier, Germany: European Consortium for Church and State Research, 2011. Available online, www.churchstate.eu/Meetings/Meeting-2010/1,000000270353,8,1.
Heinig, Hans Michael. "Religion in Public Education." Paper presented at the proceedings of the European Consortium for Church and State Research, held in

Trier, Germany, November 12–13, 2010. In *Religion in Public Education*. Edited by Gerhard Robbers, 167–194. Trier, Germany: European Consortium for Church and State Research, 2011. Available online, www.churchstate.eu/Meetings/Meeting-2010/1,000000270353,8,1.

Ivanc, Blaž. "Religion in Public Education—Slovenia." Paper presented at the proceedings of the European Consortium for Church and State Research, held in Trier, Germany, November 12–13, 2010. In *Religion in Public Education*. Edited by Gerhard Robbers, 455–472. Trier, Germany: European Consortium for Church and State Research, 2011. Available online, www.churchstate.eu/Meetings/Meeting-2010/1,000000270353,8,1.

Jackson, Robert. "European Institutions and the Contribution of Studies of Religious Diversity." In *Religion and Education*. Edited by Robert Jackson, Siebren Miedema, Wolfram Weisse, and Jean-Paul Willaime, 27–56. Münster, Germany: Waxmann, 2007.

Kalkandjieva, Daniela. "Religious Education in Bulgarian Public Schools: Practices and Challenges." In *Education and Church in Central and Eastern Europe at First Glance*. Edited by Gabriella Pusztai, 173–184. Debrecen, Hungary: CHERD, 2008.

Kiviorg, Merilin. "Religious Education in Estonia." Paper presented at the proceedings of the European Consortium for Church and State Research, held in Trier, Germany, November 12–13, 2010. In *Religion in Public Education*. Edited by Gerhard Robbers, 117–138. Trier, Germany: European Consortium for Church and State Research, 2011. Available online, www.churchstate.eu/Meetings/Meeting-2010/1,000000270353,8,1.

Kotiranta, Matti. "Religious Education in Finland." Paper presented at the proceedings of the European Consortium for Church and State Research, held in Trier, Germany, November 12–13, 2010. In *Religion in Public Education*. Edited by Gerhard Robbers, 139–154. Trier, Germany: European Consortium for Church and State Research, 2011. Available online, www.churchstate.eu/Meetings/Meeting-2010/1,000000270353,8,1.

Krukowski, Józef. "Religion in Public Education—Poland." Paper presented at the proceedings of the European Consortium for Church and State Research, held in Trier, Germany, November 12–13, 2010. In *Religion in Public Education*. Edited by Gerhard Robbers, 383–398. Trier, Germany: European Consortium for Church and State Research, 2011. Available online, www.churchstate.eu/Meetings/Meeting-2010/1,000000270353,8,1.

Larsson, Rune. "Religious Education in Sweden." In *Religious Education in Europe*. Edited by Elza Kuyk, Roger Jensen, David Lankshear, Elizabeth Löh Manna, and Peter Schreiner, 193–198. Oslo, Norway: IKO, 2007.

McClean, David. "Religion in Public Education—United Kingdom." Paper presented at the proceedings of the European Consortium for Church and State Research, held in Trier, Germany, November 12–13, 2010. In *Religion in Public Education*. Edited by Gerhard Robbers, 503–520. Trier, Germany: European Consortium for Church and State Research, 2011. Available online, www.churchstate.eu/Meetings/Meeting-2010/1,000000270353,8,1.

Messner, Francis. "Religion et éducation en France." Paper presented at the proceedings of the European Consortium for Church and State Research, held in Trier, Germany, November 12–13, 2010. In *Religion in Public Education*. Edited by Gerhard Robbers, 155–166. Trier, Germany: European Consortium for Church and State Research, 2011. Available online, www.churchstate.eu/Meetings/Meeting-2010/1,000000270353,8,1.

Motilla, Augustin. "Religion in Public Education—Spain." Paper presented at the proceedings of the European Consortium for Church and State Research, held in Trier, Germany, November 12–13, 2010. In *Religion in Public Education*. Edited by Gerhard Robbers, 473–492. Trier, Germany: European Consortium for Church and State Research, 2011. Available online, www.churchstate.eu/Meetings/Meeting-2010/1,000000270353,8,1.

Neusner, Jacob, and Tamara Sonn. *Comparing Religions through Law: Judaism and Islam*. London and New York: Routledge, 1999.

OSCE. *Toledo Guiding Principles on Teaching about Religions and Beliefs in Public Schools*. Warsaw, Poland: OSCE/ODIHR, 2007.

Pépin, Luce. *Teaching about Religions in European School Systems: Policy Issues and Trends*. London: Alliance Publishing Trust, 2009.

Poirier, Philippe. "La religion dans l'enseignement publique au Luxembourg." Paper presented at the proceedings of the European Consortium for Church and State Research, held in Trier, Germany, November 12–13, 2010. In *Religion in Public Education*. Edited by Gerhard Robbers, 319–362. Trier, Germany: European Consortium for Church and State Research, 2011. Available online, www.churchstate.eu/Meetings/Meeting-2010/1,000000270353,8,1.

Relaño, Eugenia. "Educational Pluralism and Freedom of Religion: Recent Decisions of the European Court of Human Rights." *British Journal of Religious Education* 32.1 (January 2010): 19–29.

Robbers, Gerhard. *State and Church in the European Union*. Baden-Baden, Germany: Nomos, 2007.

Schanda, Balázs. "Religion in Public Education in Hungary." Paper presented at the proceedings of the European Consortium for Church and State Research, held in Trier, Germany, November 12–13, 2010. In *Religion in Public Education*. Edited by Gerhard Robbers, 217–226. Trier, Germany: European Consortium for Church and State Research, 2011. Available online, www.churchstate.eu/Meetings/Meeting-2010/1,000000270353,8,1.

Schreiner, Peter. "Religious Education in the European Context." In *Religious Education in Europe*. Edited by Elza Kuyk, Roger Jensen, David Lankshear, Elizabeth Löh Manna, and Peter Schreiner, 9–16. Oslo, Norway: IKO, 2007.

Skeie, Geir. "Religion and Education in Norway." In *Religion and Education in Europe*. Edited by Robert Jackson, Siebren Miedema, Wolfram Weisse, and Jean-Paul Willaime, 221–241. Münster, Germany: Waxmann, 2007.

Tăvală, Emanuel P. "Religion and Public Education in Romania." Paper presented at the proceedings of the European Consortium for Church and State Research, held in Trier, Germany, November 12–13, 2010. In *Religion in Public Education*. Edited by Gerhard Robbers, 425–442. Trier, Germany: European Consortium for Church and State Research, 2011. Available online, www.churchstate.eu/Meetings/Meeting-2010/1,000000270353,8,1.

Torfs, Rik. "Religious instruction in public education in Belgium." Paper presented at the proceedings of the European Consortium for Church and State Research, held in Trier, Germany, November 12–13, 2010. In *Religion in Public Education*. Edited by Gerhard Robbers, 63–72. Trier, Germany: European Consortium for Church and State Research, 2011. Available online, www.churchstate.eu/Meetings/Meeting-2010/1,000000270353,8,1.

Tretera, Jiří Rajmund, and Záboj Horák. "Religion in Public Education in the Czech Republic." Paper presented at the proceedings of the European Consortium for Church and State Research, held in Trier, Germany, November 12–13, 2010. In *Religion in Public Education*. Edited by Gerhard Robbers, 99–112. Trier, Germany: European Consortium for Church and State Research, 2011. Available online, www.churchstate.eu/Meetings/Meeting-2010/1,000000270353,8,1.

van Bijsterveld, Sophie. "Religion in Public Education." Paper presented at the proceedings of the European Consortium for Church and State Research, held in Trier, Germany, November 12–13, 2010. In *Religion in Public Education*. Edited by Gerhard Robbers, 363–382. Trier, Germany: European Consortium for Church and State Research, 2011. Available online, www.churchstate.eu/Meetings/Meeting-2010/1,000000270353,8,1.

Willaime, Jean-Paul. "Different Models for Religion and Education in Europe." In *Religion and Education*. Edited by Robert Jackson, Siebren Miedema, Wolfram Weisse, and Jean-Paul Willaime, 57–66. Münster, Germany: Waxmann, 2007.

2

Religion and Ethical Education in Divided Societies

THE CASE OF CYPRUS

Dilek Latif

THE "CYPRUS CONFLICT," which has been characterized as one of the world's most intractable problems of ethno-communal conflict, is still unresolved. The Greek and Turkish Cypriots, Cyprus's two major ethnic groups, are divided along linguistic, historic, ethnic, and religious lines. The first interethnic strife in the island began in the mid-1950s against British colonialism, and soon turned to a violent struggle with much bloodshed and division of the two communities a few years later. The years 1963, 1974, 1983, and 2004 can all be pinpointed as turning points of the conflict. In 1960, when Cyprus became independent from Britain, the Turkish and Greek Cypriot communities founded the Republic of Cyprus, but within three years, ongoing intercommunal strife led to the collapse of constitutional rule.

The eventual partition of the two communities and the physical division of the island took place after a Turkish military intervention following a coup d'état by Greek army officers in 1974 that attempted to unite the island with Greece. Since then, Cyprus has been split into the "Turkish Cypriot" north and the Greek Cypriot south, divided by a demilitarized zone. In 1974, the UN General Assembly requested the withdrawal of foreign troops, restoration of human rights, and a return to the 1960 constitutional order under the Republic of Cyprus. The United Nations also coordinated a number of unsuccessful talks aimed at the reunification of the island as a federal state. Due to the failure of negotiations for a solution to the Cyprus conflict, the Turkish Cypriot community declared the Turkish Federated State of Cyprus in 1975 to pave the way for a federal settlement on the island. This administration was upgraded to the Turkish Republic of Northern Cyprus (TRNC) in 1983, which is recognized only by Turkey.

The last UN attempt at a resolution—the "Basis for a Comprehensive Settlement of the Cyprus Problem"—was proposed by then-UN Secretary General Kofi Annan, negotiated by the parties, and produced in five different versions (Annan I, II, III, IV, and V). The final plan failed after being rejected by the great majority of Greek Cypriots (76 percent) in the April 2004 referendum. After the referendum, the Republic of Cyprus entered the European Union (EU) on May 1, 2004, as the only "legitimate state" on the island. Currently, the EU Constitution applies only to the areas under direct Republic of Cyprus control and is suspended in the areas administered by Turkish Cypriots. Representatives of both communities continue to negotiate, but with no fruitful outcome as yet.

Establishing the Historical Context and the Parallel Educational Institutions

A historical examination of the case shows that, owing to its geographic location and strategic importance, Cyprus was conquered and ruled by various nations throughout its long 10,000 years of history. Ancient civilizations in Cyprus included the Mycenaeans/Phoenicians, Hittites, Egyptians, Assyrians, and Persians. Cyprus was ruled as well by Romans, Byzantines, Lusignans, Venetians, Ottomans, and the British, respectively. As a consequence, Cyprus has been religiously and culturally diverse since medieval times, with Greeks, Turks, Maronites, Armenians, Latins, Orthodox Christians, Muslims, Catholic Christians, Jews, Gypsies, and Lino-bambaki coexisting with their different identities. However, the development of ethnic national ideologies also led to the rigid, exclusive, and separate identities adhered to by Greeks, Turks, Maronites, Armenians, Latins, and Gypsies. The religiously and culturally diverse, but somewhat integrated, society of the island during the Catholic Frankish Lusignan dynasty of the 12th to 15th centuries lasted until the end of Venetian rule in 1571.[1]

Ensuing rule by the Ottoman and British Empires, respectively, led to the division of the inhabitants along Orthodox Christian and Muslim religious lines. Under the Ottoman "millet system," which was used to administer the island from 1571 to 1878, Ottoman subjects could identify themselves according to their religion. They were divided into religiously oriented communities and permitted to use their own lands and institutions to regulate behavior and conflicts under their particular religious leaderships. Each "millet" possessed a large degree of autonomy regarding its own social, cultural, and legal affairs. This system encouraged the establishment of separate communal institutions, such as schools and hospitals. It also made possible the creation of a significant base for the exercise of political and economic power as well as religious influence.

Orthodox Christians were acknowledged as a separate "millet" in Cyprus, with the Orthodox Archbishop serving as their political leader.[2] The other religious communities then gradually integrated and/or assimilated into the larger Greek Orthodox society. Under Ottoman rule, Christian schools were allowed, but state aid and recognition of education were limited to Muslims. The head of the Greek Orthodox Church was the supreme authority in all matters pertaining to Christian education. There were three types of schools, all supported by voluntary contributions:

1. Greek schools in the three cities of Nicosia, Larnaka, and Limassol, which were the pioneers of higher education and also kept religious and national feelings alive;
2. Community elementary schools in cities and villages; and
3. Private schools in cities and villages.[3]

The Turkish Muslim community of Cyprus, which was brought from Anatolia following the Ottoman conquest of the island in 1571, was subject to Islamic law. Religious education was provided for the Muslims in *medreses* (educational institutions) and *tekkes* (religious places of the Sufi orders) in rural areas. Mainly, Islamic *waqfs* (pious endowments) funded the establishment of *medreses*, libraries, and other religious buildings in Cyprus. Just sixty-five Muslim schools, mostly elementary, were in operation when the British took over the administration of the island in 1878, and the only Muslim high school in the whole of Cyprus was the "Idadi" school.

The distinct separation prevailing between Christian and Muslim since Ottoman times was maintained by the British colonial administration and has remained a sound principle and practice for school administration to the present day in Cyprus. Nevertheless, by implementing their own policies of ethnicity and race, the British contributed to the shift from the inhabitants' previously religious identity to an ethnic national identity.[4] As a result, Orthodox Christian Cypriots and Muslim Cypriots were transformed into Greeks and Turks, respectively. During the first fifty years of colonial rule, the British pursued a relatively liberal policy toward the nationalist orientations of the respective education systems for Turkish and Greek Cypriots.[5] After the Greek Cypriot riot against the British in 1931, however, the development of a local Cypriot identity promoting patriotism was encouraged by the British authorities, and schooling became an instrument of ideological control.[6] Educational rules for creating a Cypriot identity faced resistance, especially among the Greek Cypriots. The Church of Cyprus promoted nationalist ideas, known as Helleno-Christian Orthodox ideology, in the face of British attempts to "de-Hellenize" the island, as this was also seen as an identity threat.[7] The fear of losing their own identity alienated the two major communities on the island from one another, contributing to the rise of nationalism and ethnic clashes.

Following long and arduous negotiations, the leader of the anticolonial struggle, Archbishop Makarios, finally accepted the establishment of an independent Republic of Cyprus in 1960. A bicommunal republic, formed under the guarantorship of the two motherlands of Greece and Turkey and the former colonial power Britain, incorporated a delicate power-sharing mechanism. The Greek and Turkish communities were to be equal partners, though the cofounders of the republic comprised 80 percent and 20 percent of the population, respectively. The strong bicommunal character of the constitution was reflected in all sections; and many of the rights, freedoms, and obligations of the citizens were derived from membership in one of the communities (Article 6–28). Two communal chambers exercised legislative powers with regard to all religious, educational, and cultural matters and issues of personal status; the courts dealt with civil disputes and religious matters (Part IV, Articles 61–85 and 86–111). The autonomy of the Turkish Cypriots's religious institutions—finally attained toward the end of British rule—was maintained and strengthened with independence.

The education system was beyond the responsibility and control of the central government. The fact that the Greek and Turkish communal chambers looked toward their respective motherlands in shaping their education policies, objectives, and orientations suggested the existence of two competing communities, rather than one new Cypriot state.[8] The president of the Greek Cypriot chamber embodied a Helleno-Christian Orthodox ideology, and in 1962, expressed the view that its education policy should avoid any action that could contribute to the formation of Cypriot identity.[9]

The Republic of Cyprus survived only three years before violent clashes between the two communities in 1963 led to the collapse of constitutional rule and the withdrawal of Turkish Cypriots from the government. As a result, in 1965 Greek Cypriots took full control of the administrative institutions of the Republic of Cyprus. Henceforth, the unilaterally established Ministry of Education both expressed the ideological needs of the Greek Cypriots as Orthodox Hellenes living in Cyprus and manifested a dogma that excluded Turkish Cypriots from participation in the decision-making processes of the Republic of Cyprus.[10] Meanwhile, from 1964 to 1974, Turkish Cypriots operated their own administration in armed enclaves and organized their own educational affairs. As a consequence of the Kemalist reforms, operative in Turkey since the 1920s, the Turkish Cypriot education system had been adamantly secular. During the 1960s, only one hour per week was allocated to divinity classes from the second to fourth years of primary schools, while neither lower nor upper secondary schools taught any religion at all until 1976.[11]

July 1974 marked a crucial turning point in the history of Cyprus. The Greek coup, organized by the military junta in Greece and their EOKA B collaborators, aimed to unite Cyprus with Greece, thus precipitating a Turkish military operation in response that led to the current de facto division of the island. Since then, the subject of education on both sides of the island and the popular discourses it has generated have become organic parts of the Cypriot conflict.

Impact of Education and Competing Narratives on Divided Cyprus

The education systems, national curricula, and textbooks on both sides of the Cyprus conflict reflect the ongoing ethnic division and suffer from ethnocentrism. Both the Greek and Turkish Cypriot communities use school curricula to legitimize their respective political positions in such a way that future citizens are prevented from developing a critical approach.[12] In particular, the official historical accounts of the Greek and Turkish Cypriot communities mirror each other in a way that puts the blame on the other as well as denies their opponent's suffering. They also delegitimize the historical existence of the "other" and ignore those processes of socio-cultural interaction that had occurred over time. The conflicting historical narratives of each community take for granted that Cyprus "belongs" to each of them, based on historical grounds. Each community relays and justifies its interpretation of events in the light of current political discourses, using predominantly history education and the textbooks. With regard to religion and ethics education, each side has followed completely different approaches, as we will see subsequently.

The Greek Cypriot Historiography and Education System

Before the division of Cyprus in 1974, official Greek Cypriot history and narrative focused on endorsing the demand for the unification of Cyprus with Greece. In this respect, Greek Cypriot textbooks stressed the continuity of Hellenism in Cyprus since the time of ancient Greece. Until Cyprus became independent in 1960, the syllabuses, curricula, and textbooks in Greek Cypriot schools came from Greece. Even after 1960, only a few books were locally produced and published, and the majority of the textbooks continued to come from the Greek Ministry of Education. According to a study in education on international misunderstanding in Cypriot school history textbooks, "the significant fact concerning the history textbooks is the proportion of space (about one third) given to the conflict between Greeks and Turks."[13] The study shows that in the book for Class VI, 109 pages out of 168 were allocated to the wars between Greeks and Turks. In this context, the Turks were portrayed as historical enemies, whereas the Greeks were viewed as insurgents fighting to preserve their language and identity.

However, after the 1974 division of Cyprus, the Greek Cypriot narrative changed, leading to the revision of the version of history presented in textbooks hitherto. The desire to reunite the island drove Greek Cypriots to highlight the past peaceful coexistence of the Greek and Turkish Cypriot communities in Cyprus. The new historical perception, however, was not reflected in education practices. There have hardly been any references to coexistence and cooperation, whereas Turkish Cypriots are presented as "Turks" who are historical enemies or opponents of the Greeks.[14]

The proposed education reforms of the late 1970s in favor of a more Cypriot-centered approach were criticized by the right-wing parties and the Church. When the Republic of Cyprus applied for EU membership, the harmonization process created pressure for an inclusive education policy and multiculturalism. Nevertheless, the right-wing government in the 1990s followed the "Greece-Cyprus Unified Education" policy, explicitly aimed at orientation to the Greek identity and Orthodox Christian tradition.[15]

After Cyprus joined the European Union in 2004, the Republic of Cyprus Committee for Educational Reform (August 31, 2004) was established with a mandate from the Greek Cypriot Minister for Education and Culture to analyze the Greek Cypriot education system. According to the committee's report, the entire Greek Cypriot education system was "Helleno-ethnocentric and religious in character" and culturally monolithic. The committee suggested that narrow ethnocentric monocultural elements of education should be discarded and that a European dimension with the principles of "inclusive democracy," embracing the Turkish Cypriots, be incorporated instead.[16] Nevertheless, there have been no serious attempts on the Greek side to reform the education system.

The former Minister of Education, Andreas Demetriou, distributed a circular to all state schools before the start of the new academic year in 2008, in which he outlined two principal aims as "the development of innovation and creativity in schools" and "the cultivation of a culture of peaceful coexistence, mutual respect, and co-operation between Greek Cypriots and Turkish Cypriots." Shortly after, Archbishop Chrysostomos II accused the minister of attacking the nation's Hellenic identity and warned the government that if "they don't take their hands off education" and abandon their intentions, the Church would "react vigorously."[17]

The Turkish Cypriot Historiography and Education System

The Turkish Cypriot education system is an ideological organization aimed at legitimizing the division of Cyprus on the basis that "the two communities in Cyprus cannot live together." Hence, the demonization of the "other" lay at the very heart of this system. On account of the ethnocentric approach that presented the Turkish Cypriot national community as an organic part of the "Great Turkish Nation," school curricula focused on Turkey rather than on Cyprus. The essence of the education program is primarily the teaching of reforms and the revolution of Atatürk in order to motivate the students to sustain secular, democratic, national, and contemporary values as well as create a historical consciousness and a sense of past, present, and future. Teaching the basic components and processes of Turkish history encouraged the formation and protection of the national identity.[18] Whenever the Greek Cypriots were mentioned, they were presented in such a way as to emphasize that the division of Cyprus and the separation of the two communities were only "natural."

To counterbalance the Greek Cypriot official narrative stressing the Greek and Hellenic origins of Cyprus since time immemorial, the Turkish Cypriot official narrative and national history emphasized instead the Ottoman/Turkish nature of the island. The period of intercommunal tension from 1964 to 1974 was presented as a "dark period" for the Turkish Cypriots, for which "the whole responsibility lies on the Greek Cypriot side." The "happy ending" for the Turkish Cypriot community arrived in 1974 when Turkey undertook a military intervention and divided Cyprus geographically and demographically into two: North and South. Thereafter, "the Turkish Cypriots are living safely and happily in North Cyprus." The narrative in the textbooks goes on, "with the declaration of Turkish Republic of Northern Cyprus (TRNC), the Turkish Cypriot people, who have been fighting against all sorts of oppression and cruelty for years, founded their own State after hundreds of years, in which they will eternally live in freedom and independence."

Overall, the official narratives across the divide are not helpful in creating an understanding of the "other" and for encouraging the peaceful coexistence of the two communities. Foreign peace mediators raised this issue in the past, questioning how any settlement would work given the nationalistic content of school history books.[19] During the Annan Plan negotiations, Council of Europe member Valt Svimer, after a meeting between the two parties to consider the Council's contribution to the settlement of the Cyprus issue, stated that "the Council would take initiatives in promoting the revision of history books by both communities so as to wipe out any allusion to hatred or any misinformation with respect to either sides."[20] The goal of such initiatives has been to redefine and reidentify "us" and "them." However, reconceptualizing national identity, and thus paving the way to reconciliation between the conflicting parties, requires political will to emerge from the wider society.

Despite the Council of Europe's eagerness to cooperate with both the Turkish and Greek Cypriots in revising the secondary school history books during the Annan Plan negotiations, the outcome has been only partially successful. On the Greek side, although the Republic of Cyprus Committee for Educational Reform proposed suggested changes in a 2004 report, the Greek Cypriot Minister for Education and Culture did not announce any such revision of Cyprus history textbooks. On the Turkish side, after the proreconciliation Republican Turkish Party (CTP) came to power in 2003, a visible change took place both in the education system and in the history textbooks. The ethnocentric and ethnonationalist Cyprus history textbooks that had been in use continuously since 1971 were rewritten in 2004, following the Annan Plan referenda.

The revised Cyprus history textbooks presented a view far from the previous ethnocentric perception of history, disavowed any obvious indication of a national enemy or the "other," and adopted a multicultural and student-centered approach.[21] After the reformation on history education, mainly right-wing circles initiated a fierce debate on the content and approach of the new textbooks and warned of the danger of the erosion of national identity and the end of national consciousness. Shortly after the National Unity Party (UBP) came to power following the general election in April 2009, the revised Cyprus textbooks were replaced by brand new ones. This further change in the textbooks is regarded as a step backward, toward the old-style textbooks along the lines of the current Turkish Cypriot history textbooks. Although the change in the Turkish Cypriot history textbooks in 2004 was used to stimulate a debate over the revision of Greek Cypriot history textbooks, the latest change in the textbooks in the Turkish North lifted the pressure on the Greek South.

In parallel with the Council of Europe attempts, the failed Annan Plan proposed the establishment of an impartial Reconciliation Commission to foster communication and understanding between Turkish and Greek Cypriots. The commission would promote dialogue regarding the past, prepare a report on the history of the Cyprus problem as experienced and interpreted, and also make recommendations including guidelines for publications and school textbooks. However, since the rejection of the plan, no substantive improvement took place regarding education toward reconciliation, except the funding of a few education projects by the EU Commission and UNDPACT.

Religious and Ethical Education across the Divide

The 1960 Constitution of the Republic of Cyprus provides for freedom of religion and prohibits religious discrimination. Due to the bicommunal nature of the republic, provisions are made for both the Greek Orthodox Church of Cyprus and the institution of *waqf* and the Laws and

Principles of *awqaf* (Ahkamül Evkaf). The Constitution specifies that the Autocephalous Greek Orthodox Church of Cyprus and the Evkaf, the Muslim institution that regulates religious activity for Turkish Cypriots, have exclusive rights to regulate and administer their internal affairs and property in accordance with their laws and principles. Three other constitutionally recognized religious groups —Maronite Catholics, Armenian Orthodox, and Latins (Roman Catholics)—are afforded the same rights regarding religious matters as they had before the Constitution came into force. With respect to education and cultural matters, the Constitution gives these smaller religious groups assurances that they will not be disadvantaged in the allocation of public funds.

Historically, the role of religion, religious institutions, and religious leaders among the Turkish and Greek Cypriots was very different. The Ottoman millet system allocated a leadership position to the archbishops and the Orthodox Church, whereas no Islamic religious figure held any political power. Hence, the Church played a great part in promoting Greek nationalism and campaigned for Enosis (union with Greece). The leader of the Greek Cypriot struggle for independence in the 1950s was the head of the Greek Orthodox Church, Archbishop Makarios III, who became president from 1960 until his death in 1977. This shows the initial association between the Church and the Republic of Cyprus.

In contrast, Islam did not play any influential role in Turkish Cypriot nationalism, whose key building block was instead the Kemalist views of the founder of the modern Turkish republic, Mustafa Kemal Ataturk. In the northern part of the island, the Turkish Cypriot basic law makes reference to the secular nature of the TRNC and does not specify any recognized religion or state religion. Religious leaders have no role in politics. Although religious instruction is available in primary schools, it is not obligatory in secondary schools. Religion among Turkish Cypriots is regarded as a personal matter, relating more to custom and tradition than national identity.

Overall, there has been a convergence of attitudes with respect to the manipulation of history education and official narratives on both sides of the divide for the purpose of creating divergent *identities*. However, the Turkish and Greek Cypriot administrations followed completely different paths in terms of religious and ethics education in Cyprus.

Religious and Ethics Education in the Greek Cypriot South

Since 1963, the Greek Cypriot–controlled governments have required children in public primary and secondary schools to take instruction in the Greek Orthodox religion. Religious education is a compulsory preprimary, primary, and secondary subject that is taught two hours per week.[22] In secondary school, it is taught by teachers who specialize in religious education, but preprimary and primary educators teach religious education without being specialists in theology.[23] Parents who practice another religion are entitled to ask that their children be exempted. These children then do not attend the practice session (religious services), but still need to take the theoretical instruction.

The national curriculum of the Republic of Cyprus covers the subject of religious education under the heading "Christian Orthodox Education." As stated, the main goal is to teach students "to realize that they are members of the Christian Orthodox Church, to learn the fundamental truths of Christianity and to experience a loving relationship with God."[24] Besides, the national curriculum presents the scope of Orthodox education as follows:

> To begin with, pupils should be enabled to understand the presence of God throughout the history and the apocalypse of God as an answer to the fundamental questions of human existence.
>
> Children must also experience the figure, the teachings and the work of Jesus Christ, as the highest contribution of God for the multilateral fulfillment of man.
>
> Children need to experience the Christian way of love towards all people, regardless [of] color, religion and race.
>
> Children should be introduced to the basic aspects of other religions and develop a critical attitude towards them. In this way, they will become able to understand and respect the religious beliefs of other people. "Orthodox Education" provides pupils with the skills to appreciate the meaning of the Orthodox ethics, traditions, prayer and to make them part of their everyday life.
>
> Pupils should also appreciate the beneficial influence of the Orthodox Church [in] the development and progress of civilization.
>
> Apart from these, "Orthodox Education" also develops children's understanding of the collective worships of the Church and encourages them to participate in these worships.
>
> Children have to respect the value and importance of the various ecclesiastical monuments.
>
> Finally, "Orthodox Education" needs to promote children's responsibility for the continuation of the Orthodox faith and way of life.[25]

The religious education textbooks used are edited by both the Ministry of Education of Cyprus and the Ministry of Education of Greece. Teachers need to use the textbooks and the teacher's handbook in their entirety, as their content is mandated in the national curriculum of Cyprus guidelines and objectives.[26] There are six textbooks, one for each year, for use in religious education in the primary schools. The textbook for the first grade is titled *With the Grace of Christ: Orthodox Christian Education*, and some of the main subjects include the meaning of the cross, the birth and resurrection of Christ, Orthodox Easter, the Holy Spirit and holy water, prayers, the power of love, and the holy sacrament of Eucharist.[27] The second-grade textbook, *With the Love of Christ: Orthodox Christian Education*, covers love, the meaning of the Orthodox Church and icons, children of God, the meaning of forgiveness, and information on Christ and the Virgin Mary.[28]

The third-grade textbook, *The Life with Christ: Orthodox Christian Education*, has similar content to the previous textbooks. The next one, *Christ's Path: Orthodox Christian Education*, includes information on Orthodox Christianity in northern Europe, eastern countries, America, Africa, and other Christian communities.[29] The fifth-grade textbook, *With Christ in the Struggle: Orthodox Christian Education*, includes Jesus' struggle, saints and martyrs who died for the Christian faith, justice in the world, and the meaning of peace.[30] The last primary school textbook, *Christ is the Truth: Orthodox Christian Education*, examines the topics of searching for the truth, worshiping, when Greeks met Christ, the Bible, the meaning of forgiveness, the path of Christian truth, and spiritual health.[31]

As can be seen, the main topics of religious education in the primary schools revolve around Orthodox Christianity. All the textbooks include stories about the life of Jesus Christ, his parables, stories about the many saints of the Orthodox Church and the Virgin Mary, and an emphasis on the role of the Orthodox Church.[32] Compulsory religious education also occupies a prominent position throughout the lower secondary (gymnasium) and upper secondary (lyceum) levels. The first year of the lower secondary school, Grade 7, focuses on the Old Testament and the encounter of Judaism with Hellenism; the Grade 8 curriculum consists of the New Testament and the life of Jesus Christ; and Grade 9 classes concentrate on the formation of the Church as an institution and the Christians during the Roman, Byzantine, Latin, Ottoman, and British periods.[33] Grade 9, the last year of lower secondary school, also covers other Christian denominations, the spreading of Christianity to Western and Eastern Europe, and the historical conflict between the Roman Catholic and the Orthodox Church.

The catechistic-denominational character of religious studies in the Greek Cypriot education system is more evident in the upper secondary school curriculum. Grade 10 focuses on Orthodox Christian worship, but also aims to inform the students about the main parareligious phenomena and movements, while maintaining their individual freedom.[34] In addition, students are expected to find out how these movements diverge from Orthodox Christianity and to criticize and reject them by maintaining and repeating Orthodox Christian arguments against them.[35] The same approach is repeated in Grade 11 with regard to the other Christian denominations, especially Roman Catholicism and its theological mistakes vis-à-vis Orthodoxy. Similarly, the curriculum covers Judaism, Islam, Hinduism, and Buddhism, as well as African, Chinese, and Japanese religions, with the aim of critiquing their views from an Orthodox Christian perspective.[36] The Grade 12 curriculum also discusses ethics from an Orthodox Christian perspective.

Throughout the religious education undertaken in upper and secondary schools, a strong link between Orthodox Christianity (Christian theology) and Greek national identity is evident. On the other hand, the way in which other religions are presented contributes to the sense of "us" and "them." Religious education is one of the major subjects of the centralized education system of the Greek South that adopts the same national curricula and official textbooks in all schools at the same level. Following the European Union's decision on religious education, in 2006 the Ministry of Education proposed reducing the number of hours of religious instruction in public schools from two to one per week. Due to the strong objections of the Church and other religious organizations to the proposal, however, the Ministry postponed its implementation.

Informal Religious Education

The Orthodox Christian Church is free to provide religious education, called "Sunday school," which takes place mostly on Saturdays. This program is instituted on a parish-by-parish basis, meaning that there are differences from area to area. The priest of each district organizes it with volunteer teachers or priests who want to teach. Religious education offered by the Church is free of charge and voluntary; only children whose parents want them to attend or themselves want to attend are enrolled.

Apart from including the discussion of a religious topic, these classes are informal and often include indoor and outdoor play.

Education of the Cypriot Religious Minorities

When the Armenians, Maronites, and Latins were asked in 1960, as constitutionally recognized religious groups, to choose to belong to either the Greek or the Turkish community, they all opted to join the Christian Greek Cypriot community. There is a legal and institutional framework for the rights and protection of the three religious groups, and the relationship between the Greek Cypriot Orthodox Church and the other three religious communities has been courteous. Although all of the groups have their own distinct churches and associations, they face problems of political representation and native language education as being predicated merely on religious group membership. Only the Armenians have public primary schools providing education in the Armenian language. These schools follow the official Greek Cypriot school curriculum and provide additional instruction in Armenian, Greek, and English, as well as extracurricular programs in Armenian history, geography, and traditional dance.[37] There is no education provided in Maronite Arabic, making it extremely difficult for the Maronite community to preserve their ancestral language. Latins, the smallest religious group, also do not have native-language education, and their children attend either Greek Cypriot or Roman Catholic schools.

Religious and Ethics Education in the Turkish Cypriot North

Article 1 of the TRNC Constitution, approved by the Turkish Cypriots in 1983, stresses the secular nature of the state. The Constitution also guarantees freedom of faith and conscience. The main historical Muslim institution was reconstituted by Evkaf as the Evkaf Administration (currently called Evkaf and Religious Affairs Office). Meanwhile, the Mufti—once the spiritual leader of the Turkish Cypriot community as well as influential in legal and educational matters—lost his historical title and privileges in the 1980s and became the Director of Religious Affairs (DRA) under the control of the Evkaf Administration.[38]

With regard to religious education, Article 23 (4) of the Constitution states that "education and instruction in religion shall be conducted under state supervision and control." According to this article, the state provides religious education and asserts that legally there can be no religious schools, after-school religious instruction, or extracurricular religious education. Religious Culture and Morality (Ethics) was a compulsory course in primary and secondary schools until 2005. When the leftist CTP came to power in 2004, new regulations the following year enabled each secondary school to decide whether to provide religious instruction. For the next four years, many schools either decided not to include religion lessons in their curricula or made these lessons optional. However, this has changed with the UBP government in 2009.

The general objective of the Religious Culture and Morality (Ethics) lessons is to provide knowledge, particularly of Islam (Hanafi branch of Sunni Islam), as well as other world religions and ethical issues. In addition, these lessons focus on promoting religious understanding and tolerance, and therefore include citizenship issues. Religious education is taught for two years, to ten—and eleven-year-old students in the fourth and fifth grades of primary school, and for three years, to twelve—to fourteen-year-olds in secondary school. The course is taught one hour per week with the same official Turkish Ministry of Education textbook used in Turkey.

There was no written syllabus or teaching program for religion and ethics education until 2006. At that point, and according to the curriculum (which is identically adopted from Turkey), five basic concepts of religious education were taught, which included respect for humans, respect or thought, respect for freedom, respect for ethical values and respect for cultural heritage. There were also six justifications for the necessity of religious education, which are listed as anthropological-humane, societal, cultural, universal, philosophical, and legal bases. The current primary school Religious Culture and Morality curriculum is based on seven learning spheres: faith, worship, the Prophet Muhammad, the Qur'an and its interpretation, morality, religion, and culture. The fourth-grade curriculum includes knowledge about religion and morality; the life of the Prophet Muhammad; acknowledgment of the Qur'an; love, friendship, and brotherhood; and family and religion. The fifth-grade curriculum comprises faith in prophets and sacred scripts/books, worship rituals (namaz), the Prophet Muhammad, basic teachings of the Qur'an, prohibited behaviors and manners in Islamic faith, and Turks.

Likewise, the secondary school curriculum covers knowledge of Islam and morality, national unity and solidarity, customs and traditions, Turkish and Islamic culture and civilization, Atatürk and our religion, and other religions. It also includes instruction about Islam and other world religions such as Christianity, Judaism, Buddhism, and Hinduism. The approach of the textbooks is to encourage more tolerant attitudes toward the followers of other religions, underlining the points of agreement among religions rather than conflicts over ethical values.[39]

The general nature of education in the North is such that teachers have great autonomy in class to present materials as they wish. On the other hand, because there are no training colleges for religious teachers in the TRNC, at the lower secondary level, the religious course is generally taught by history, philosophy, social studies, or even music teachers.[40] Furthermore, the teachers themselves do not take any classes on religion during their undergraduate education. As a result, most schools lack competent teachers, and the religious courses have often been neglected.[41] There is no compulsory religious education for high school and university students in the North. Before 2011, there were also no faculties of theology, Imam-Hatip (public Islamic) schools, or any institutions of higher education for training imams.

In an extremely secular state such as the TRNC, the religious education curriculum concentrates on teaching the factual knowledge of Islam, other world religions, and the culture of religions and ethics, while denying the political and social dimensions of Islam. In practice, however, the curriculum is not being implemented in schools; specialized teachers in religious education are lacking, and religious instruction is considered the least important subject and is generally disregarded. A broad knowledge of Islam, reading of the Qur'an, and prayers and practices in the mosques are not part of the official religious education program.

Recent Tension over Religious Education within the North

The goal of government-controlled religious education in the North is to prevent the misuse of religion through an incorrect interpretation that could lead to social polarization. Therefore, the Constitution prohibits children from participating in any religious classes that are not authorized by the government. Overall, parents approve of the government's non-faith-based approach to religious education.[42] Nevertheless, there is currently growing tension between parents who want their children to learn more about Islam and its requirements and the various trade unions—especially the teachers' unions, some NGOs, political parties, and nonreligious circles.

In the past, primary and secondary school teachers used to take their students to the mosques on Fridays for the Friday sermon. This practice was forbidden by the Turkish army after the military operation in 1974.[43] In summer, imams offer courses in religion and the Qur'an in local mosques for children whose parents want them to receive broad religious instruction. Over the last few years, summer courses in religion have been a source of controversy and have been banned twice, in 1996 and 1997, as teaching religion outside school is not permitted. In effect, "imams in mosques are allowed to preach but not to teach."[44]

Following a change of government in April 2009, an effort was made to change religious education in lower secondary schools from optional to compulsory. Although compulsory religious education for one hour a week was reintroduced, it has not been implemented yet due to the strong reaction against it by the teachers' unions and other associations, including Alawites. The teachers' unions instead proposed adding an optional course on the history of religions, culture, and ethics to the curriculum. In addition, the current UBP government signed a protocol with the Directorate of Religious Affairs for the provision of a summer course titled "Religion, Culture, and Ethics" as well as Qur'an lessons. This protocol was strongly rejected by the fundamentally secularist Turkish Cypriot circles, including the teachers' unions; some of their members even broke into the Qur'an courses organized in two village primary schools and a local mosque. Growing opposition to these courses, which are regarded as religious expansionism on the part of the Turkish AK Party government, led to their cancellation.

Dr. Yusuf Suicmez, the Director of Religious Affairs at that time, expressed the view that misuse of religion can be prevented only through accurate and contemporary religious education. He warned that if religious education is not properly planned according to the needs of the society, religion will spill out into the streets with unpredictable results.[45] As a consequence, families (mostly Turkish immigrants living in Cyprus) who wanted their children to take summer courses in religion and Qur'an education applied to the Directorate of Religious Affairs for their children to be sent to Turkey. The number of Turkish Cypriot students participating in religious education in Turkey was 400 in 2008 and 500 in 2009.[46] The dispute over summer courses in religious education is still continuing without any resolution.

Religious Institutions and Associations in the North

In addition to the TRNC's Directorate of Religious Affairs (under the control of Evkaf), there is a religious affairs counselor at the Turkish

Embassy in the North. Along with these official institutions are two unofficial associations: the Association of Universal Love and Brotherhood and the Cyprus Turkish Islam Association, which organizes some activities, mainly for university students from Turkey. The first group advocates an understanding of Islam that emphasizes universal peace. The second promotes the Turkish-Islamic Synthesis, which calls for the union of Turkish nationalism and Islam. It is assumed that the Cyprus Turkish Islam Association has close ties to Turkish Cypriot Sheikh Nazım Kıbrısi (Nazim al-Qubrusi), the leader of the Naqshbandi *tariqa* in North Cyprus and the Naksibendi order in Europe. Although Sheikh Nazım has many followers in Europe and the Americas and receives many disciples visiting from abroad, he does not appeal to the locals.

Besides the Sunni Muslim institutions, there are two Alawite associations of immigrants from Turkey and a Rumi Institute in the North. The larger Alawite association, Hacı Bektaşi Veli Derneği, organizes rituals, cultural activities, and gatherings in addition to teaching the religious musical instrument *saz* to its followers' children. The chair of the Hacı Bektaşi Veli Association, Ozdemir Gül, pointed out that Alawite children cannot learn anything about Alawism within the official school curriculum and also called for legal regulation of the Directorate of Religious Affairs concerning the position of Alawies.[47] The recently founded Rumi Institute at Near East University embraces Sufism and organizes academic conferences on the teachings of Mawlana Jalal al-Din Rumi as well as cultural activities; in addition, it presents a short theatrical play on Sufism at state schools on a rotating basis, authorized by the Ministry of Education.[48] It is worth mentioning that neither of these unofficial religious associations and institutions in the North is influential in shaping society's general beliefs and perceptions, nor do they play a significant role in religious instruction.

Interreligious Dialogue

When intercommunal strife began in 1963, contact between the religious leaders of the Greek Orthodox and Turkish Muslim communities of Cyprus was minimal. Lack of access to the other side of the divide following the 1974 war made it impossible for religious leaders to engage in a dialogue. No religious leaders participated in the internationally sponsored bicommunal meetings at the buffer zone or outside the island until 2003.[49] Even following the partial opening of the border in 2003, Orthodox and

Muslim religious leaders had little contact with each other. Some bishops and priests refused to cross over the border for political reasons, and only the Bishop of Morphou has been active in reconciliation activities.

The first meeting in the past thirty-three years between the two communities' religious leaders, Church of Cyprus Archbishop Chrysostomos II and the Turkish Cypriot Head of Religious Affairs, Ahmet Yonluer, took place at the buffer zone in February 2007 and was regarded as a positive development by both sides. Although the previous and current heads of Religious Affairs have had a few unofficial meetings with Orthodox representatives, nothing concrete has been achieved in terms of interreligious dialogue. During his most recent visit to Cyprus in February 2011, Chair of Elders Archbishop Desmond Tutu urged Archbishop Chrysostomos to play a role in facilitating efforts toward a solution on the island. Tutu later explained that the two religious leaders talked about "the possibility of an inter-religious council in Cyprus to address issues of mutual concern and the role of religion in helping to promote a settlement."[50] Despite Archbishop Chrysostomos's expressed eagerness to emulate Tutu's role in South Africa, there is little room for optimism, especially considering the historically obstinate position of the Orthodox Church in the Cyprus conflict.

Conclusion

Cyprus is divided as a consequence of the rising ethnonationalisms of the two major communities on the island, the Greek and Turkish Cypriots—not because of religious differences. Education has been used as an instrument on both sides of the divide to further political goals, legitimize official narratives, and solidify the ethnic identities defined vis-à-vis the other. Whereas there has been a convergence of attitudes regarding the manipulation of history education as a way of perpetuating the conflict, each side followed a different pattern with respect to religious and ethical education.

Orthodox Christians focused on religious and ethics education, but the strong link between Orthodoxy and Greek national identity alienated minorities and followers of other religions in the South. The principal aim of the Republic of Cyprus's education system to promote Greek identity by definition excludes the promotion of a more inclusive civic identity. On the other hand, the secularization of the Turkish Cypriot administration and its advancement of the Kemalist legacy in Turkey since the 1930s have led to the secularization of society as a whole in the North. The religious education provided under the state-controlled system facilitated this process, and in this context, religious instruction has been largely ignored.

The recent tension and heated discussion over mandating currently optional religious and ethics education in lower secondary schools, combined with the cancellation of religious summer courses, demonstrates the need for a societal consensus concerning the nature of religious and ethics instruction in the northern part of the island. Can religious education play a role in mediating the divisions in Cyprus? The diverse patterns of religious and ethics education across the divide have produced significantly different types of problems and tensions within the respective communities. Nonetheless, the Greek Cypriot national curriculum is currently under revision, and questions regarding the nature of religious instruction among the Turkish Cypriots remain unanswered. These conditions could provide an opportunity to restructure religious education in the direction of a more inclusive society within and across the border.

The crucial question of what role religious education can play in reconciling the Greek and Turkish Cypriot communities has not been genuinely explored by the religious leaders, scholars, or peace activists on the island; yet Cyprus has the potential to be transformed through a possible resolution of the conflict, into an exceptional model of a working federation, shared and ruled by Muslim and Christian communities in partnership. Such a model would be a beacon for other divided societies in different parts of the world, as well as a welcome alternative system to the current clashes over religion, culture, and ethics.

NOTES

1. Andrekos Varnava, "The State of Cypriot Minorities: Cultural Diversity, Internal-Exclusion and the Cyprus Problem," *Cyprus Review* 22.2 (Fall 2010): 207.
2. Altay Nevzat, *Nationalism amongst the Turks of Cyprus: The First Wave* (Oulu, Finland: Oulu University Press, 2005), 62.
3. William Wilbur Weir, *Education in Cyprus, 1893–1900* (Nicosia, Cyprus: Cosmos Press, 1952), 24.
4. Andrekos Varnava, *British Imperialism in Cyprus, 1878–1915: The Inconsequential Possession* (Manchester, UK: Manchester University Press, 2009), 152–201.
5. Panayotis Persianis, "British Colonial Higher Education Policy-Making in the 1930s: The Case of a Plan to Establish a University in Cyprus," *Compare* 33.3 (September 2003): 251–368.

6. Chara Makriyianni and Charis Psaltis, "The Teaching of History and Reconciliation," *Cyprus Review* 19.1 (Spring 2007): 50.
7. Varnava, *British Imperialism in Cyprus*, 51.
8. Andreas Karagiorges, *Education Development in Cyprus, 1960–1977* (Nicosia, Cyprus: A. G. Garagiorges, 1986), 152.
9. Mary Koutselini-Ioannidou, "Curriculum as Political Text: The Case of Cyprus (1935–1990)," *History of Education* 26 (1997): 400.
10. Makriyianni and Psaltis, "The Teaching of History and Reconciliation," 52.
11. Altay Nevzat and Mete Hatay, "Politics, Society and the Decline of Islam in Cyprus: From the Ottoman Era to the Twenty-First Century," *Middle Eastern Studies* 45.6 (November 2009): 923.
12. Dilek Latif, "Dilemmas of Moving from the Divided Past to Envisaged United Future: Rewriting the History Books in the North Cyprus," *Special Issue: Legitimation and Stability of Political Systems—The Contribution of National Narratives*, Edited by Ingo Richter, *International Journal for Education Law and Policy* (Special Issue 2010): 35–46.
13. Barbara Hodge and Geoffrey L. Lewis, *Cyprus School History Textbooks: A Study in Education for International Misunderstanding* (London: Education Advisory Committee of the Parliamentary Group for World Government, 1966), 11.
14. Yannis Papadakis, "Nationalist Imaginings of War in Cyprus," in *A Cruel Necessity? The Bases of Institutionalised Violence*, edited by R. Hinde and H. Watson (London: I. B. Tauris Academic Studies, 1995), 54–64.
15. Ministry of Education and Culture of Cyprus, *The National Curriculum of Cyprus: Primary Education* (Nicosia, Cyprus: Department of Primary Education, 1996), 17.
16. Stavroula Philippou and Chara Makriyanni (eds.), *Multiperspectivity in Teaching and Learning History*. Presentations from seminars and workshop materials of the Council of Europe, held in Nicosia, Cyprus, November 24–27, 2004.
17. Stefanos Evripidou, "A Struggle for the Future of Cyprus," *Friends of Cyprus* 52 (Summer 2009): 24.
18. Education Planning and Programme Development Department, "Essence of the Education Program," TRNC Ministry of National Education and Culture, 2009.
19. *Cyprus Mail*, August 8, 2006.
20. *Cyprus Mirror*, July 8, 2003.
21. Hakan Karahasan and Dilek Latif, *Education for Peace III: Textual and Visual Analysis of the Upper Secondary School Cyprus History Textbooks* (Nicosia, Cyprus: POST Research Institute, 2010).
22. Alexandros Tapakis, *Religious Education in Primary and Pre-Primary Schools: A Guidebook for Primary and Pre-Primary School Teachers* (Nicosia, Cyprus: Holy Monastery of Kykkos, 2003), 13.
23. Maria Krasia, "The Aims of Religious Education in the National Curriculum of Cyprus," *European Forum for Teachers of Religious Education*, 2004. Available online, http://www.mmiweb.org.uk/eftre/index.html.

24. Ministry of Education and Culture of Cyprus, *The National Curriculum of Cyprus: Primary Education* (Nicosia, Cyprus: Department of Primary Education, 1996), 128.
25. Ministry of Education and Culture of Cyprus (1996), 128.
26. Maria Krasia, "Religious Education in Cyprus," *European Forum for Teachers of Religious Education*, 2004. Available online, http://www.mmiweb.org.uk/eftre/index.html.
27. Ministry of Education and Culture of Cyprus, *With the Grace of Christ: Orthodox Christian Education*, First Grade of Primary School (Nicosia, Cyprus: Department of Primary Education, 1999).
28. Ministry of Education and Culture of Cyprus, *With the Love of Christ: Orthodox Christian Education*, Second Grade of Primary School (Nicosia, Cyprus: Department of Primary Education, 1998).
29. Ministry of National Education and Religions, *Christ's Path: Orthodox Christian Education*, Fourth Grade of Primary School (Athens, Greece: OEDB and Pedagogical Institute, 2000).
30. Ministry of National Education and Religions, *With Christ in the Struggle: Orthodox Christian Education*, Fifth Grade of Primary School (Athens: OEDB, Pedagogical Institute 2002).
31. Ministry of National Education and Religions (2002).
32. Maria Krasia, "Religious Education in Cyprus," *European Forum for Teachers of Religious Education*, 2004. Available online, http://www.mmiweb.org.uk/eftre/index.html.
33. Stavroula Philippou, "National Report 'Europe' in the Secondary School Curricula of the Republic of Cyprus," PAM-INA WP3 School Curricula Analysis (Nicosia, Cyprus, June 2010), 21.
34. Ministry of Education and Culture, *Curricula for Grade 10 of the Unified Lyceum* (Nicosia, Cyprus: Curriculum Development Service, Directorship for Secondary Education, 2000), 3.
35. Philippou, "National Report," 22.
36. Philippou, "National Report," 23.
37. Julia-Athena Spinthourakis et al., "Country Report: Cyprus," Educational Policies that Address Social Inequality (November 2008), 4. Available online, http://www.epasi.eu/CountryReportCY.pdf.
38. Ali Dayioglu and Mete Hatay, "Cyprus," in *Yearbook of Muslims in Europe*, vol. 1, edited by Jørgen S. Nielsen (Leiden, The Netherlands: Brill, 2009), 79.
39. Hakan Arslan, "Religious Education in a Secular Education System," in *Secular Education in a Muslim Society: Conversations from Northern Cyprus*, edited by Raymond Zepp (Famagusta, Cyprus: Eastern Mediterranean University Press, 2006), 16.
40. Interview with Dr. Yusuf Suicmez, Former Director of Religious Affairs and Deputy Dean of Faculty of Divinity of Near East Univeristy, April 15, 2011.

41. Talip Atalay, *Kuzey Kıbrıs'ta Yaygın Din hizmetleri: Kurumsal Yapılanma ve Din Görevlileri* [Widespread religious education and mosque services in North Cyprus: Institutional formation and religious staff] (Istanbul: Seçil Ofset, 2007), 240.
42. Arslan, "Religious Education in a Secular Education System," 15–24.
43. Interview with Gokalp Kamil, Chairman of Near East University Rumi Institute, April 18, 2011.
44. Ali Dayioglu and Mete Hatay, "Cyprus," in *Yearbook of Muslims in Europe*, vol. 1, p. 83.
45. *Cyprus Star*, "A Conversation with the Director of Religious Affairs Dr. Yusuf Suiçmez," July 13, 2009.
46. *Cyprus Star*, "Religious Education is not banned in TRNC." November 3, 2010.
47. Interview with Özdemir Gül, Chair of the Hacı Bektaşi Veli Association, May 16, 2009.
48. Interview with Gokalp Kamil, Chairman of Near East University Rumi Institute, April 18, 2011.
49. Ali Dayioglu and Mete Hatay, "Cyprus," in *Yearbook of Muslims in Europe*, vol. 2, edited by Jørgen S. Nielsen (Leiden, The Netherlands: Brill, 2010), 137–138.
50. Stefanos Evripidou, "Tutu Urges Archbishop to Play a Greater Role," *Cyprus Mail*, February 9, 2011.

BIBLIOGRAPHY

Arslan, Hakan. "Religious Education in a Secular Education System." In *Secular Education in a Muslim Society: Conversations from Northern Cyprus*. Edited by Raymond Zepp, 15–24. Famagusta, Cyprus: Eastern Mediterranean University Press, 2006.

Atalay, Talip. *Kuzey Kıbrıs'ta Yaygın Din hizmetleri: Kurumsal Yapılanma ve Din Görevlileri* [Widespread religious education and mosque services in North Cyprus: Institutional formation and religious staff]. Istanbul: Seçil Ofset, 2007.

"Conversation with the Director of Religious Affairs Dr. Yusuf Suiçmez," *Cyprus Star*, July 13, 2009.

Cyprus Mail. August 8, 2006.

Cyprus Mirror. July 8, 2003.Dayioglu, Ali, and Mete Hatay. "Cyprus." In *Yearbook of Muslims in Europe*. Vol. 2. Edited by Jørgen S. Nielsen, 125–140. Leiden, The Netherlands: Brill, 2010.

Dayioglu, Ali, and Mete Hatay. "Cyprus." In *Yearbook of Muslims in Europe*. Vol. 1. Edited by Jørgen S. Nielsen, 75–88. Leiden: Brill, 2009.

Education Planning and Programme Development Department. "Essence of the Education Program." Nicosia, Cyprus: TRNC Ministry of National Education and Culture, 2009. Accessed June 8, 2009, http://www.mebnet.net/Daireler/Talim veTerbiyeDairesi/.

Evripidou, Stefanos. "A Struggle for the Future of Cyprus." *Friends of Cyprus* 52 (Summer 2009): 24.

Evripidou, Stefanos. "Tutu Urges Archbishop to Play a Greater Role." *Cyprus Mail*, February 9, 2011.

Hodge, Barbara, and L. Geoffrey Lewis. *Cyprus School History Textbooks: A Study in Education for International Misunderstanding*. London: British Parliamentary Group for World Government, 1966.

Interview with Özdemir Gül, Chair of the Hacı Bektaşi Veli Association, May 16, 2009.

Interview with Gokalp Kamil, Chairman of Near East University Rumi Institute, April 18, 2011.

Interview with Dr. Yusuf Suicmez, Former Director of Religious Affairs and Deputy Dean of Faculty of Divinity of Near East University, April 15, 2011.

Karagiorges, Andreas. *Education Development in Cyprus, 1960–1977*. Nicosia, Cyprus: A. G. Garagiorges, 1986.

Karahasan, Hakan, and Dilek Latif. *Education for Peace III: Textual and Visual Analysis of the Upper Secondary School Cyprus History Textbooks*. Nicosia, Cyprus: POST Research Institute, 2010.

Koutselini-Ioannidou, Mary. "Curriculum as Political Text: The Case of Cyprus (1935–1990)." *History of Education* 26 (1997): 395–407.

Krasia, Maria. "The Aims of Religious Education in the National Curriculum of Cyprus." Tielt, Belgium: European Forum for Teachers of Religious Education, 2004. Accessed April 12, 2011, http://www.mmiweb.org.uk/eftre/index.html.

———. "Religious Education in Cyprus." Tielt, Belgium: European Forum for Teachers of Religious Education, 2004. Accessed April 12, 2011, http://www.mmiweb.org.uk/eftre/index.html.

Latif, Dilek. "Dilemmas of Moving from the Divided Past to Envisaged United Future: Rewriting the History Books in the North Cyprus." *Special Issue: Legitimation and Stability of Political Systems—The Contribution of National Narratives*. Edited by Ingo Richter. *International Journal for Education Law and Policy* (Special Issue 2010): 35–46.

Makriyianni, Chara, and Charis Psaltis. "The Teaching of History and Reconciliation." *Cyprus Review* 19.1 (Spring 2007): 43–69.

Ministry of Education and Culture. *Curricula for Grade 10 of the Unified Lyceum*. 1st ed. Nicosia, Cyprus: Curriculum Development Service, Directorship for Secondary Education, 2000.

Ministry of Education and Culture of Cyprus. *The National Curriculum of Cyprus: Primary Education*. Nicosia, Cyprus: Department of Primary Education, 1996.

Ministry of Education and Culture of Cyprus. *With the Love of Christ: Orthodox Christian Education*. Second Grade of Primary School. Nicosia, Cyprus: Department of Primary Education, 1998.

Ministry of Education and Culture of Cyprus. *With the Grace of Christ: Orthodox Christian Education*. First Grade of Primary School. Nicosia, Cyprus: Department of Primary Education, 1999.

Ministry of National Education and Religions. *Christ's Path: Orthodox Christian Education*. Fourth Grade of Primary School. Athens, Greece: OEDB and Pedagogical Institute, 2000.

Ministry of National Education and Religions. *With Christ in the Struggle: Orthodox Christian Education*. Fifth Grade of Primary School. Athens, Greece: OEDB and Pedagogical Institute 2002.

Nevzat, Altay. *Nationalism amongst the Turks of Cyprus: The First Wave*. Oulu, Finland: Oulu University Press, 2005.

Nevzat, Altay, and Hatay Mete. "Politics, Society and the Decline of Islam in Cyprus: From the Ottoman Era to the Twenty-First Century." *Middle Eastern Studies* 45.6 (November 2009): 911–933.

Papadakis, Yannis. "Nationalist Imaginings of War in Cyprus." In *A Cruel Necessity? The Bases of Institutionalised Violence*. Edited by R. Hinde and H. Watson, 54–67. London: I. B. Tauris Academic Studies, 1995.

Persianis, Panayotis. "British Colonial Higher Education Policy-Making in the 1930s: The Case of a Plan to Establish a University in Cyprus." *Compare* 33.3 (September 2003): 251–368.

Philippou, Stavroula. "National Report 'Europe' in the Secondary School Curricula of the Republic of Cyprus." PAM-INA WP3 School Curricula Analysis. Conducted in the context of the Comenius Project PAM-INA. Nicosia, Cyprus, June 2010.

Philippou, Stavroula, and Chara Makriyanni, eds. *Multiperspectivity in Teaching and Learning History*. Presentations from seminars and workshop materials of the Council of Europe, held in Nicosia, Cyprus, November 24–27, 2004. Strasbourg, France: Council of Europe, 2005.

"Religious Education is not banned in TRNC," *Cyprus Star*, June 7, 2010.

Spinthourakis, Julia-Athena, Eleni Karatzia-Stavlioti, Georgia-Eleni Lempesi, Ioanna Papadimitriou, and Chrysovalante Giannaka. "Country Report: Cyprus." Patras, Greece: Educational Policies that Address Social Inequality, 2008. Accessed April 15, 2011, http://www.epasi.eu/CountryReportCY.pdf.

Tapakis, Alexandros. *Religious Education in Primary and Pre-Primary Schools: A Guidebook for Primary and Pre-Primary School Teachers*. Nicosia, Cyprus: Holy Monastery of Kykkos, 2003.

Varnava, Andrekos. *British Imperialism in Cyprus, 1878–1915: The Inconsequential Possession*. Manchester, UK: Manchester University Press, 2009.

Varnava, Andrekos. "The State of Cypriot Minorities: Cultural Diversity, Internal-Exclusion and the Cyprus Problem." *Cyprus Review* 22:2 (Fall 2010): 205–218.

Weir, William Wilbur. *Education in Cyprus, 1893–1900*. Nicosia, Cyprus: Cosmos Press, 1952.

3

Teaching Religion in Bulgarian Schools

HISTORICAL EXPERIENCE AND POST-ATHEIST DEVELOPMENTS

Maria Schnitter and Daniela Kalkandjieva

THE ISSUE OF religious instruction emerged in Bulgarian society after the collapse of communism. The return of religion to the public square, however, was not a uniform process. On the one hand, it was driven by a move to restore continuity with the pre-Communist past, while on the other, it was expected to meet the principles of freedom of religion and civic pluralism that was characteristic of Western democracies. This latter goal has not been easily met. Thus for example, the Bulgarian Constitution of 1991 declared Eastern Orthodox Christianity to be the traditional religion of Bulgaria—causing serious objections by the country's minorities. These were withdrawn only when the Constitutional Court (in 1998) ruled that the practical significance of "traditional religion" was only in terms of official holidays. The court, however, maintained the "cultural and historical role [of the Eastern Church] for the Bulgarian State." (Nenovski 2002)

The agreement reached on the public character of Orthodoxy did not guarantee a smooth introduction of religious teaching in public schools, which soon became a serious challenge for Bulgarian society. Many people expressed concerns after the study of religion was introduced as an elective discipline in Bulgarian public schools in 1997. Especially strong was the resistance to the request of the Synod of the Bulgarian Orthodox Church and of the Chief Mufti's Office for mandatory religious education.

According to a survey conducted in 2006, only 14.1 percent of the population supported such reform of the study of religion in public schools, while 18.4 percent opted for confessional indoctrination. Meanwhile, the majority of interviewed in this survey was in favor of general introductory lessons that would inform children about different religious traditions (Survey 2006). Despite the heated debates in society, no consensus was reached. The reasons for this state of affairs are complex. They are rooted not only in the Communist past, but also in the previous historical experience of Bulgarian society, the post-atheist dynamics in the religious demography of Bulgaria, and the weaknesses of the academic training of teachers of religion.

Historical Models of Teaching Religion in Modern Bulgarian Society

The teaching of religion in modern European schools is usually determined by the mainstream churches and state authorities in a given country. The Bulgarian case is somewhat different, as the advance of modern education there began in the 1830s, when Bulgarians had neither their own state nor their own church. They were, in a sense, a nation without a state. As part of the Rum millet, that is, the community of the Orthodox subjects of the Sultan, they were subject to the Patriarchate of Constantinople, whose rights encompassed more than the realm of religion. As chief administrator of all Orthodox subjects in the Ottoman state, the Patriarch was free to impose the Greek language in place of the Bulgarian "Slavonic" one[1]—not only in liturgy, but also in all Orthodox schools of the empire. This ruling was challenged when Bulgarians, inspired by the rise of nationalism, began to set up their own national churches and schools independent of the Patriarchate of Constantinople. In 1870, they were also allowed to establish an Exarchate, which, within the framework of the millet system, became more than a mere religious institution—it began to represent the Orthodox Bulgarians as a separate nation in the Ottoman Empire. As such, the Bulgarian Exarchate established a network of national schools where it took care of both religious and secular education of the Orthodox Bulgarians under its jurisdiction.[2] At the same time, Bulgarians who did not belong to Eastern Orthodoxy[3] studied separately in schools supervised by the corresponding religious administrations—for example, Catholic missions or Muslim muftis. This confessional separatism in the organization of religious and secular education was determined by the Ottoman millet system. As a result, despite the great confessional diversity, the different religious communities developed an attitude of exclusion toward the "religious other." Thus, while the confessional autonomy of the millet system (especially of personal law) evinced a unique form of "illiberal tolerance," its legacy for intercultural relations following national independence was very mixed (and not only in Bulgaria).

After the Liberation of Bulgaria in 1878, the new state preserved the principle of confessional separatism in the sphere of religious teaching, but added some modifications. The Tarnovo Constitution (1879) granted freedom of religion to all citizens who belonged to non-Orthodox Christian denominations or to non-Christian faiths (Article 40). It also granted the right of autonomous self-government to all non-Orthodox denominations (Article 42), as required by Article 5 of the Treaty of Berlin (July 1878). On the same basis, the 1880 "Provisional Regulations for Religious Governance of the Christians, the Muslims and the Jews" was promulgated. At the same time, the Tarnovo Constitution omitted to guarantee freedom of religion and proclaimed Orthodoxy as the dominant religion of Bulgaria (Article 37). It also obliged the Bulgarian ruler to confess the majority religion (Article 38) and granted internal autonomy to the Bulgarian Orthodox Church, according to Article 39,

> In ecclesiastical terms, the Bulgarian Principality constitutes an inseparable part of the Bulgarian Church territory and is subordinated to the Holy Synod—the supreme authority of the Bulgarian Church wherever this authority is situated. (Tarnovo Constitution, 1879)

The reason for this specific wording was rooted in the discrepancy between the territories of the Bulgarian state and the Church. By 1878, the territory of the Bulgarian Exarchate embraced the present-day territory of Bulgaria, together with those of the FYR of Macedonia and the region of Edirne in present-day Turkey. Moreover, it overlapped with the territory negotiated as Bulgarian by the Treaty of San Stefano, signed on March 3, 1878. This "San Stefano Bulgaria," however, ceased to exist in July 1878, when the Great Powers divided it into three parts at the Congress of Berlin. These parts consisted of the tributary Principality of Bulgaria (presently northern Bulgaria, including the region of Sofia), the autonomous Ottoman province of Eastern Rumelia (the southern territories of present Bulgaria), and the regions of Macedonia and Edirne, which were returned to the direct control of the Sublime Porte. Article 39 of the Tarnovo Constitution was thus an attempt to preserve Bulgarian unity through the Exarchate. In parallel, the restoration of "San Stefano Bulgaria" became the major policy goal of all Bulgarian governments until the end of World War II. In 1885, the Bulgarian Principality united with Eastern Rumelia, but all attempts by Sofia failed to join Macedonia and Edirne in Thrace to Bulgaria. The Bulgarian Exarchate preserved its headquarters in Istanbul, refusing to abandon its jurisdiction over the dioceses in Macedonia and Edirne until 1945, when it finally moved them to Sofia.

This situation influenced the post-1878 development of religious teaching in Bulgarian schools: those that were situated in the free lands of Bulgaria were administered by the Bulgarian Ministry of Education, while those outside the state borders remained under the supervision of the Exarch's office in Istanbul. This situation in turn had deleterious consequences for the quality of Orthodox faith instruction, especially in free Bulgaria, where it was additionally impeded by a series of conflicts between pro-Western Bulgarian governments and the pro-Russian Sofia Synod, which was responsible for the religious affairs in the country. As a result, the state promoted secularized education in its schools and forbade clerics from teaching religion there. Until World War II, the *verouchenie* classes, that is, Orthodox faith instruction, were usually studied for one hour per week until the third grade. In 1909, the Law of Education guaranteed the right of religious minorities to establish their own private schools, where faith instruction was supervised by the religious leadership of that faith. These minority schools were maintained entirely by their own communities. The Bulgarian state rejected all attempts by the Orthodox Church to spread religious instruction beyond elementary school (first through fourth grade) until after the outbreak of World War II.[4] In 1939, the Ministry of Education promised the Holy Synod of the Bulgarian Orthodox Church to stipulate one hour of religious instruction a week in the pro-gymnasium (junior high school), a condition stated in the future Law of Education (Proceedings 1939). The Law of Education, however, disappointed the Bulgarian Orthodox Church, which requested that only theologians be eligible for the position of teacher of religion (Proceedings 1941). After much debate and for the first time in Bulgarian history, when the school year 1941–1942 began, Orthodox religious teaching was instituted at all stages of school education—elementary, pro-gymnasium, and gymnasium. The Orthodox Church planned to use this innovation as a means to liberate the young generation "from the delusions of negative materialistic and atheistic teachings that are [the] result of the collected knowledge in the field of natural scientific disciplines, still dominating the school curricula" (*Tsarkoven vestnik*, October 1942). At the same time, this expansion of religious instruction provoked some concerns among the state authorities. In March 1942, the Ministry of Education instructed teachers to avoid "thoughtless conflicts between science, religion, school and church" and to look for a harmonious integration of religion into other school disciplines. It also required teachers of history, geography, Bulgarian language, philosophy, and music to cooperate with teachers of religion in order to develop in their pupils "faith in Divine providence, strong love for Bulgaria and creative turn to the tradition and religious and moral grounds of their people" (Proceedings 1942).

The spread of religion classes coincided with the wartime territorial expansion of Bulgaria. In 1940, Bulgaria reintegrated Southern Dobrudzha, which had been taken by Romania after Bulgaria's defeat in World War I; a year later, as the ally of Nazi Germany, it was allowed to establish its civil, military, and church authorities in the conquered areas of Macedonia and Aegean Thrace. This development was perceived by the Bulgarian political and Church elite as a rebirth of "San Stefano Bulgaria." It seems that the introduction of Orthodox religious instruction in 1941 was part of the government's strategy to create a homogeneous nation. According to the above-noted instruction of the Ministry of Education, the icon of Christ had to be placed in school buildings next to the portraits of Bulgarian kings, patriarchs, and heroes so that youth could "be inspired by religious impulses, by readiness to self-sacrifice, courage and boldness, by deep respect to the merits of people who contributed to the progress of the Bulgarian church, people and state and by all-hearted service for the progress of spiritual culture and the achievement of the new ideals of united and great Bulgaria" (Proceedings 1942).

To be sure, nationalist motives also influenced the attitude of Bulgarian governments with regard to religious teaching in the schools that were privately run by religious minorities. In their case, however, attitudes toward religion were determined by the role they were expected to play in the national consolidation process. Generally, small ethnoreligious groups such as the Jews and Armenians, who were not able to rely on assistance from a foreign state, were allowed to organize the religious instruction of their pupils as they pleased. In the more complicated case of Muslim schools, the state developed different policies for those situated in areas with a concentrated Turkish population as well as those in regions with Bulgarian-speaking Muslims, termed Pomaks (Mancheva 2001, 358). This differentiation was influenced by the 19th-century Bulgarian national ideology that had created an image of the Turk as "oppressor." Indeed, the idea of the "Turkish yoke" had been a prime element in the Bulgarian national myth since the mid-19th century and continues today to structure public consciousness and attitudes toward Turks and Islam in general (Hranova 2011). One result of this national myth has been the exclusion of the Turkish ethnic group from the body of the Bulgarian nation, while the Pomaks have been regarded as Bulgarians who were cut off from the body politic by forcible conversions to Islam during Ottoman rule. On these grounds, Bulgarian governments tried to reincorporate the Pomaks into the nation and to keep them away from the non-Bulgarian Muslims, while conducting a policy aimed at maintaining the ignorance and illiteracy of the Turks in order to make them controllable (Mancheva 2001, 356). Worst of all was the state attitude toward Muslims of Roma origin, who were included in the Turkish Muslim structures but were not allowed to take part in the elections of provincial and chief muftis or the government of the properties of the Muslim community (by the 1895 "Provisional Regulations for Religious Governance of the Muslims in Bulgaria" and the 1919 "Statutes for the Religious Organization and Government of the Muslims in Bulgaria"; Dzhambazov 2011, 171–172).

With failed attempts at forcing a mass conversion of the Pomaks to Orthodoxy during the Balkan Wars (1912–1913), due to the Bulgarians' defeat, the national governments developed alternative ways to "reincorporate" them. They were additionally motivated by the rise of Kemalist Turkey, perceived as a serious threat to Bulgaria's sovereignty. Therefore, the state took measures to isolate the Pomaks from the non-Bulgarian part of the Muslim community. Muslim private schools situated in the Pomak regions were henceforward incorporated into the system of state education. Special textbooks that avoided Christian symbols and texts that might alienate the Pomaks were designed for this purpose (Mancheva 2001, 364–369). The idea was to teach the Pomaks "to distinguish between religion and nationality and to convince them that their Bulgarian nationality (language and origin) did not conflict with their religion" (Mancheva 2001, 360). At the same time, the Muslim private schools in the Turkish areas remained in private control, and lessons there were taught in the mother tongue of this minority.

The Bulgarian state policy in relation to the local Muslim communities was also influenced by the Kemalist reforms that introduced Turkish language into the mosques in Turkey. To keep the local Turks away from any Kemalist influence, Bulgarian authorities preserved the use of Arabic in Turkish Muslim schools, while deciding to translate the Qur'an into Bulgarian in order to meet the needs of mosques in Pomak villages. In parallel, fewer muftis of Turkish origin were appointed, and training courses for Bulgarian-speaking muftis were organized. All these measures were meant to "prepare Pomak teachers and ulema to replace Turkish teachers and ulema in the Pomak regions" (Mancheva 2001, 369). At the same time, the Nuvvab religious school in Shumen, established in 1922 with the aim of training Islamic theologians to serve the entire Muslim community in Bulgaria, began to prepare teachers for the Turkish private schools (Evstatiev and Makariev 2010, 646). In the end, however, all these attempts simply enhanced the Bulgarian Muslims' perception of the Pomaks as "others." Accepted by neither Christian Bulgarians nor Muslim Turkish minorities, the Pomaks either described themselves solely in religious terms (as Muslims) or, in large urban centers, tended to merge with the majority Christian population.

The coup d'état on September 9, 1944, brought to power the "Fatherland Front," a coalition of parties that also included the Communists. Until the summer of 1947, however, the latter hid their plans for building socialism. In this period, the Communist Party took advantage of the underdeveloped condition of religious teaching in the state schools, in order to end it. On October 6, 1944, the Ministry of Education ordered the exclusion of religious instruction from school curricula. The ministry stated that the Fatherland Front considered the study of religion in school reactionary and an impediment to the scientific development of education (Kalkandjieva 1997, 74). It also forbade lay teachers to teach religion, while Sofia University ceased to train such teachers. Facing this situation, the Holy Synod of the Bulgarian Orthodox Church tried to save religious instruction for children by organizing courses for the pedagogical training of priests. On January 15, 1946, however, the Ministry of Education issued a ban on any study of religion in state schools, with the argument that religious teaching was a source of conflict in schools (Kalkandjieva 1997, 74–97). The final blow to the Church's efforts to save religious instruction in the form of Sunday schools was caused by the Constitution adopted in December 1947. It separated Church from State—for the first time in Bulgarian history (Article 78.2)—and granted exclusive rights for the upbringing of youth to the state (Article 77).

The situation was somewhat different in the Bulgarian private schools run by religious minorities, where the state had not interfered with religious instruction before the adoption of the 1947 Constitution. In 1948, the closure of the private schools of foreign foundations brought religious teaching in local Catholic and Protestant schools to an end. The issue of Jewish religious teaching was "solved" by the exodus of about 45,000 Jews to Israel in the late 1940s, while the Armenians' situation was resolved through their affiliation with Soviet Armenia (Kalkandjieva 1997). More specific was the policy developed with regard to the religious teaching of Muslims. The Communist regime preserved the previous differentiation between Pomaks and Turks. In the case of the Pomaks, who had already been incorporated into the state system of education, it assisted the establishment of a special Pomak high school. In 1946, the Bulgarian Parliament passed a bill establishing a gymnasium for Bulgarian Muslims, that is, Pomaks. It was opened in Plovdiv after a delay of two years. Meanwhile, the initial plan for this school as an institution to prepare imams and faith teachers for this ethnoreligious group was abandoned, and its curricula became fully secular (Stoyanov 1998, 96–98).

All of the private schools serving the Turkish minority, including the imam school "Nuvvab" in Shumen and the Turkish pedagogical institute in Stara Zagora, were now brought under state control (Kalkandjieva 1997, 254). As a result, in 1946 the five existing Turkish medreses were transformed into secular junior high schools; students were allowed to study the Qur'an and their native tongue. By 1948, the religious high school Nuvvab was also changed into a secular gymnasium for ethnic Turks (Stoyanov 1998, 96–98). At the same time, all existing private Qur'an courses attended by Muslim pupils were closed (Gruev 2003, 91–100). In this way, all forms of religious teaching disappeared—not only from the state schools, but also from the public sphere. It survived mostly in families where the grandparents were able to transmit their religious knowledge to children.

Post-Communist Attitudes to Teaching Religion in Public Schools

Being unable to freely confess their faith for more than forty years, most Bulgarian citizens have developed dubious attitudes to it. Although they tend to perceive religion as opposed to Communism, they still resist the idea that religion is at all compatible with a modern, scientific orientation. Under the influence of the first vision, any form of nonreligiosity—from militant atheism to modest agnosticism—is associated with the Communist past and thus not welcomed by society (Schnitter 2007, 24). Therefore, the leaders of the main groups dominating the political scene after 1989—the Union of Democratic Forces and the former Communists, who swiftly changed their name to the Bulgarian Socialist Party—immediately appeared at church services during the important Orthodox holidays. The representatives of the Movement for Rights and Freedoms that initially represented the Turkish minority in the country also demonstrated their affiliation with the traditional religion of these people—an attitude that spread to the Pomak and Roma Muslims as well. In general, the notion of religion as a victim of Communism also inspired a tendency to return to the pre-Communist role of religion in the public sphere, which was regarded as a restoration of the continuity with that past. This tendency was quite strong in the Union of Democratic Forces, especially during its second government (1997–2001), as well as among the leadership of the National Movement Simeon and its government (2001–2005).

Requests by the Orthodox Church to introduce religious teaching in public schools were rejected by the first post-Communist Bulgarian governments, which were under the de facto control of the Socialist Party. Initiated by the Union of Democratic Forces, this process was not free from the impact of the political struggle between former Communists and new democrats and their debates over the totalitarian past. If the former resisted the study of religion in school, the latter perceived its introduction into school curricula as a restoration of the continuity with an imagined pre-Communist past that was far from the actual historical experience in this area. To some degree, the attitude of the democrats was nurtured by an idealistic vision of the era before Communism, as a time when religion was a traditional part of the school curricula. This idealized past was nurtured by the lack of research on the study of religion in the state and private schools of pre-Communist Bulgaria.

In the spring of 1997, the provisional government of Stefan Sofiianski from the Union of Democratic Forces established a "Commission on Religion" at the Ministry of Education. Comprising representatives of the (Orthodox) Faculty of Theology of Sofia University, the commission's task was to prepare a concept for the study of religion in public schools (Denev 2004, 20–21). The result was to turn this new school discipline into traditional faith instruction in Eastern Orthodox Christianity. Although the commission claimed that this religious teaching would not constitute Orthodox indoctrination (Concept 1997, Part 2, § 4 and § 7), it permitted only graduates of the theological faculties to teach the new discipline (Part 3, § 13). The training of these teachers was entirely dominated by Orthodox theology because the licensed faculties provided no knowledge of other religious traditions. As a result, in September 1997, "Religion" was introduced as a discipline in the second, third, and fourth grades of elementary schools. In the 1997–1998 school year, these lessons were taught weekly for one hour in 464 schools (out of about 3,000 in the country) and were attended by 16,700 students (Ilchevski 2007, 103). During the next school year, teaching was expanded to all middle school grades (fifth to eighth), and the number of pupils who studied religion, that is, Orthodox Christianity, reached 25,000. This growth, however, was stopped by the escalating struggles within the Bulgarian Orthodox Church, which had further deteriorated in 1992 with the splitting of its leadership into two synods. As a result, the number of students who attended religious instruction began to decline over the years, eventually falling to 10,827 in 2010 (Roditeli 2011).

Meanwhile, Muslims living in regions with Turkish and Pomak populations also demanded courses in the study of Islam, which were introduced into the local schools in 1999. This development seems to have been determined less by attempts to enhance civil pluralism in Bulgaria than by a collective sense of guilt for the "Renaissance Process" of the 1980s, when the names of Bulgarian Turks were forcefully changed and the state made a concerted effort to erase Bulgarian Muslim identities.

In essence, confirming the confessional approach to religious education in contemporary schools reestablished the pre-Communist models of separate religious education for different religious groups. The new model also drew new divisions between the students in mixed regions, with Christians taking lessons in classrooms designed with icons and other Christian items, while their Muslim classmates studied in other rooms, organized in accordance with Islam. Consequently, these classes enhanced the students' knowledge of their own faith and their differences from the others, but did not provide them with skills for interreligious communication with their fellow citizens from other faith communities.

After the adoption of the first post-Communist Denominations Act (2002), the Ministry of Education made an attempt to improve the social effect of religious classes in public schools. It issued special regulations that reorganized the study of religion as a "mandatory-optional" and "free-choice optional" discipline (Article 4, §3; Regulations 2003). In the first case, "Religion" was studied as a minor discipline, and the annual mark for it was included in the average score of the students' diplomas, whereas in the second case it was not. At the same time, the study of religion was expanded and included in the entire school curriculum from the first to the twelfth grades. The 2003, regulations also attempted to overcome the narrow confessional orientation of the lessons in religion. They required religion(s) to be studied in terms of philosophy, history, and culture through the educational material allocated to different school disciplines (Article 4, §2). This intercultural or interdisciplinary approach remained a dead letter, however, due to the resistance of the respective leaderships of the Bulgarian Orthodox Church and the Chief Mufti's Office. Under pressure from them, in June 2003, the Minister of Education issued Instruction No. 2, requiring the lessons to be organized on the basis of the concepts of teaching "Religion" for the Christian students and "Religion-Islam" for the Muslim believers (Article 3, §3). The document stipulated that only graduates of the faculties of Orthodox theology and the Higher Islamic Institute would be eligible to teach these disciplines (Article 11; Instruction 2003). In this way, instruction not only confirmed the confessional separation of classmates within the public school as initially established, but also promoted faith indoctrination in schools in a way that contradicted national legislation and its principles of secular education. At the same time, it did not increase interest in the discipline. In 2006–2007, 16,667 students attended "Religion" and "Religion-Islam" classes—less than 2 percent of all Bulgarian students.

The third stage in the development of religious teaching was initiated when Bulgaria joined the European Union. In 2007, the Minister of Education appointed a commission of experts to develop a new concept of religious education. It differed from the previous commissions, which had consisted entirely of representatives of the Orthodox Church. As a result, the Commission on the Affairs of Religious Teaching in School—named "Bakalov's Commission," after its chairman—offered a new approach to religious teaching. As an interdisciplinary body that included historians, theologians, philologists, schoolteachers, and specialists in religious studies, the commission attempted to place the issue of religious education in the broader context of the problem of civil education in contemporary Bulgaria. Its concept, announced in 2008, was the first one that took into account the legal framework in which religious teaching in public schools had to take place, that is, it paid attention not only to national legislation, but also to the international acts ratified by Bulgaria (Concept 2008). The concept offered a new unified discipline, "Religion," whose curricula were pursued through a study of world religions rather than the confessional study of religion, as previously. According to Bakalov's Commission, schools, as public institutions, should teach a balanced knowledge of religion by presenting the main world religions in a way that respects human rights and the secular principles of the Bulgarian state. Its members considered that it was the duty and right of the various religious organizations to organize their own "Sunday schools," where children were to be instructed in their faith. This new conceptualization of religious education was rejected, however, by both the Orthodox and Muslim leaderships. According to the counterconcept proposed by the Bulgarian Orthodox Church, "the upbringing of a free, moral and initiative personality is impossible without the cultivation of the Orthodox Christian faith of our ancestors" (Church's Concept 2008). This document claimed that as "the guardian" of Orthodox Bulgarians throughout the centuries, this Church had to receive special rights to religious teaching in public schools. Especially radical was the position of Metropolitan Nikolay, who declared that Orthodoxy should dominate religious teaching and accused Bakalov's concept of breaking "the principles of tolerance and faith toleration by making all religions in Bulgaria equal" (Subasheva 2007). In addition, the Synodal Concept of 2008 insisted on the exclusive rights of Orthodox faculty graduates to teach religion. It further required that teachers of religion would be paid from the state budget. At the same time, the Church's proposal allowed some diversity by suggesting three major disciplines—"Religion-Orthodoxy," "Religion-Islam," and "Religion" (secular religious studies)—and recommending that, under certain conditions, other religious communities could organize their own religious classes in public schools. According to the Church, religious classes had to be taught twice a week and were mandatory for all twelve grades, plus kindergarten. The proposal promulgated the study of Orthodox rituals, prayers, and holidays in elementary school; Orthodox Church history in middle school; and Orthodoxy's history and philosophy in high school. Other world religions could be studied only in twelfth grade.

Among other issues, the Church's proposal suffered from a lack of realism. It could not garner support in a society in which only 4 percent of the people regarded religion as the most important morality-building factor; only 7 percent were regular churchgoers; and 24 percent had never entered a church, mosque, or other house of prayer (Survey 2008).

Moreover, because the demands for mandatory religious lessons called to mind the compulsory study of Marxism-Leninism before 1989, people strongly opposed such lessons. While this resistance can be explained by the memory of Communism, negative attitudes toward non-Orthodox religious traditions, particularly Islam and the new religious movements, appear to be a more complex problem related directly to the culture of civic pluralism and multicultural peace in contemporary Bulgaria. After 1989, Bulgaria was "flooded" with various preachers from all over the world, espousing new and varied religious doctrines. Interest in Krishna, Mormonism, Jehovah's Witnesses, and others gave way, however, to fears of these new movements, designated as "sects," which were thought to corrupt traditional values, even so far as to be labeled as "antidemocratic." The general turn away from these new religious movements also chilled any initial enthusiasm to the introduction of religious study in schools.

On the other hand, and in a curious way, the radical nationalists attacked both Bakalov's concept and its antithesis advanced by the Synod. They found the Church leadership guilty of allowing the study of Islam and accused Bakalov's Commission of undermining the Orthodox identity of the Bulgarian nation. To a large extent, this position reflects one of the most serious problems in contemporary Bulgarian historiography: the need for a critical rethinking of the past. Although the post-1989 "purification" from the legacy of Communist ideology heralded an abandonment of the previous class-based approach to history, it left untouched many nationalist theses from the period of late socialism—for example, the vision of Turks and Islam as destructive to Bulgarian national unity. Meanwhile, the drive for restoring continuity with pre-Communist times revived old nationalist ideas. As a result, today the idea of the Bulgarian Orthodox Church as guardian of the nation throughout the centuries enjoys great popularity, not only among the synodic hierarchs and extreme nationalists, but also among historians. The propagators of this sentiment seem to see no contradiction between this statement on the perennial role of the Church as protector of the Bulgarian nation and the 19th-century Bulgarians' struggle for the establishment of their national Orthodox Church. (It would, after all, be illogical to fight for something that already exists.) Such ahistorical theses have been included in school textbooks and popular narratives and have been learned as axioms by generations of Bulgarians. A more critical approach to their own history is needed, both to overcome the extreme nationalist behavior of some rightist parties and to foster debate over the study of religion in public schools.

The acutely negative attitudes toward Islam among some parts of Bulgarian society are a result not only of the historically constructed image of this religion and its association with the centuries of Ottoman rule, but also of its contemporary links to terrorism, especially after the attacks on the World Trade Center in New York on September 11, 2001. These fears were additionally nurtured by the more intensive religious revival that took place among the Muslim sectors of Bulgarian society, as compared to that of the Orthodox ones. In the last twenty years, the Orthodox community has experienced a serious decline: from 85.7 percent of the registered population according to the 1992 census, to 59.4 percent in 2011. Meanwhile, the second-most numerous religious community—Muslims—dropped from 13.1 percent to 7.9 percent over the same period (Census 1992; Census 2011). The significant discrepancy between the figures registered for both faiths in 1992 and 2011 is attributable to the use of different survey methods and visions of "religion": in 1992, religious affiliation was defined as "the historically determined belonging of an individual or his/her parents and forefathers to a particular group with specific religious views," and all citizens were obliged to declare their confession (Census 1992); in 2011, by contrast, they were free either to answer this question or not. In any case, the dynamic of religious demography reveals an even sharper decline in religious affiliation among Orthodox believers than among Muslim believers. As a result, some Bulgarians, including nonbelievers, view the intensity of the religious life of Muslims and other faith minorities as dangerous to a national identity that has been traditionally linked with Orthodoxy. According to statistics, Muslims have been more active than Orthodox Christians in mapping their religious space. It has been estimated that 750 new Orthodox churches and chapels were built from 1990 to 2006 (*Standart*, June 21, 2006), whereas the corresponding figure for mosques is 320 (*Trud*, July 3, 2006); given the difference in populations, this is a significant finding. Participation in religious instruction classes in state schools by members of the two respective faiths reveals a similar situation. In 2006, 10,000 Orthodox children attended such classes, compared with 4,000 Muslim children (*Standart*, September 5, 2006). Notwithstanding the relative proportion of adherents of Orthodoxy and Islam in Bulgaria, though, the Muslim community seemed to have a much more intensive religious life.

Attitudes of suspicion and fear of Islam have been widespread, sometimes with the consent of the Orthodox Church, and at other times led by nationalist parties. Although the collaboration of the Holy Synod with the Chief Mufti's Office with regard to the introduction of mandatory confessional lessons in public schools indicates some sense of interreligious dialogue, each party zealously defends its domain against the new religious movements that have appeared in Bulgaria since 1989. On some occasions, the rhetoric of the representatives of the Bulgarian Orthodox Church mixes religious fundamentalism with extreme nationalism. For example, in 2009, the Metropolitan of Veliko Tarnovo delivered a sermon against the planned construction of a Jehovah's Witnesses' prayer house and blessed a petition initiated by the Youth Division of the VMRO (Internal Revolutionary Macedonian Organization). According to him, the activities of this religious group presented a threat to the Bulgarian Orthodox Church as "the actual master of this country" and "Bulgaria is not a Taliban society" that should allow them. In the end, the Metropolitan blessed the fight against the false teaching of the sect (VMRO 2009). In most cases, however, the assaults against new religious movements have been initiated by the VMRO. In the spring of 2011, its activists attacked the Jehovah's Witnesses' prayer house in Burgas, together with soccer fans, yelling "Turks" and "Pomaks" (VMRO 2011). Such references reveal that for these people, Islam has come to signify a national enemy that makes possible the end of secular politics.

At the same time, Muslims continue to be an object of harassment, mostly by the party Ataka (Attack), rather than the VMRO.[5] This anti-Muslim focus became obvious during the protests against the use of loudspeakers for ezan (the Muslim call for prayer), organized by Ataka in several cities. As a result, some of the loudspeakers were removed from the mosques or their volume was decreased (Kalkandjieva 2008, 427). Despite these accommodations, an Ataka political rally, held at the Sofia mosque in May 2011, ended in violent clashes between the praying Muslims and the Ataka activists.

From such a perspective, the debate over religious teaching—both as the study of religion and as the study about religion—faces a difficult future. The plan for a new education bill has provoked yet another attempt by the Orthodox Church to impose its vision for mandatory confessional lessons. On September 24, 2010, the Church organized a procession of clerics and laymen from all dioceses. It supported a petition to the Bulgarian president, the chairman of the National Parliament, prime minister, and minister of education, in which the late Patriarch Maxim[6] called on "the church, family, school and state" to work together to transform Bulgarian children into "noble and harmonious personalities." The document declared "the opportunity for mandatory religious teaching" a defensible right of the Orthodox majority of Bulgarian children to be taught in the spirit and values of their faith tradition. On these grounds, the Orthodox Church insisted on taking part in the creation of the future law on education in order to guarantee that children in kindergarten "will obtain a moral strength strongly to resist the sin in themselves and the evil in the world around" (Chairman of the Holy Synod2010). This request also found support among the leaderships of other religious organizations, who expected the children of their followers to be able to study their own traditions in public schools as well. Once again, then, we see the continuing heritage of differentiated confessional teaching of religion in the public schools. The majority of Bulgarian society, however, did not support the petition.

The Academic Training of Teachers of Religion and the Challenge of Civic Pluralism

The academic training of teachers of religion has not undergone any special analysis from the point of view of civic pluralism since the introduction of religious teaching in public schools.[7] It is thus only fitting to end this study with a brief review of this situation. Bearing in mind the lack of solid traditions in this field and decades of militant atheism, one should expect serious weaknesses in both the theological and pedagogical training of these teachers. The political change wrought in 1989 made possible the revival of the academic study of theology. In 1991, the Orthodox Ecclesiastical Academy was transformed into a theological faculty, which was reintegrated into Sofia University. In the ensuing years, such units were also established at the universities in Veliko Tarnovo, Shumen, and Plovdiv. The academic study of Islam experienced a similar revival. In 1991, it was restored in the Semi-Higher Islamic Institute, which in 1998 was elevated to the Higher Islamic Institute. In 2001, the Evangelical churches in Bulgaria also established the Higher Evangelical Theological School, with four faculties organized along denominational lines. Although the non-Orthodox higher institutions are allowed to award only bachelor's degrees, they managed nonetheless to negotiate a continuation of the academic studies of their graduates at the New Bulgarian University and other Bulgarian academic institutions.

At first glance, the academic study of Orthodoxy seems to be in a better situation. The faculties where it takes place have accreditation to grant master's degrees, while the recently adopted Law for the Development of the Academic Staff of the Republic of Bulgaria (2010) allows schools in Sofia and Veliko Tarnovo to grant doctoral degrees as well. The introduction of religious teaching in public schools, however, represented a serious challenge for Orthodoxy. In order to teach in Bulgarian schools, one has to meet the requirements of the Regulations for Unified State Standards, adopted by the Ministry of Education and Science in 1995, concerning the higher education degree that confers the professional qualification "teacher" (Regulations for Unified State Standards 1995). This normative document contains a mandatory list of disciplines and exams that everyone who wants to become a teacher must pass—pedagogy, psychology, and so on. The faculties of Orthodox studies and the Higher Islamic Institute did not have such experts, however. Initially, they also had difficulty fulfilling the mandatory three-month teaching practice requirement for future teachers. To solve this problem, the Orthodox faculties and the Islamic Institute developed different approaches: adding courses, integrating theology with humanistic studies, or—as in the case of the University of Plovdiv—including theology in the Faculty of Philosophy and History. Although acquiring the qualification of "teacher" is not mandatory, the number of students who prefer this option has been growing in recent years. Most likely, this move is influenced by the local Metropolitan Nikolay, who zealously supports the introduction of Orthodox religious instruction as a mandatory discipline in public schools.

The real problem in the academic training of future teachers of religion, however, remains the quality and scope of the theological studies they receive in university. It is an often-neglected fact that the scientific degrees and ranks that the teaching staff of the former Ecclesiastical Academy received with the blessing of the Holy Synod were recognized as equal to those of the academic staff of Sofia University during the restoration of the Faculty of Theology in 1991, though their training was far from that of a strictly academic professoriate. A short review of their works reveals that only a few of them have been published in well-established academic journals, national and international. Some of these "doctors" and "professors" then became leading figures in other theological faculties. Another painful problem associated with the academic training of young theologians, including those who have chosen to become teachers of religion, is the narrow confessional curricula most faculties offer. The oldest one in Sofia gives its students extremely limited opportunities to learn about anything outside Orthodoxy; for example, the non-Orthodox

Christian denominations are taught as an optional discipline, in the form of "apologetics." This marginalization of non-Orthodox religions is "justified" with arguments about the lack of "free space" in the program and "the traditional lack of will among the students to study such topics" (Schnitter 2011).

At the University of Plovdiv, young theologians study "History of Religions" (45 hours) and "Non-Christian Religious Teachings" (45 hours). The latter, together with an optional course on "Non-Orthodox Christian Denominations" (60 hours), is taught from the perspective of Orthodox apologetics. In this way, the knowledge that students receive about the "religious other" does not leave space for dialogue, but rather is aimed at full rejection. A similar situation pertains regarding the theology curricula in Shumen, where non-Orthodox religious traditions are studied as optional disciplines. They include the history of Catholic missions in Bulgaria, relations between Jews and Christians, and intercultural communication. At the same time, there is serious neglect of Islamic studies in a region where the Muslim population is significant (about 84,000 Orthodox and 52,000 Muslims, according to the 2011 census).

The only place where students seem to receive broader academic training in theology is the Orthodox Faculty of Theology in Veliko Tarnovo, which offers mandatory courses on "History of Religions" (60 hours) and "Non-Orthodox Christian Denominations" (60 hours). Students also have an opportunity to expand their knowledge of world religions by taking optional courses on "Islam, Judaism and Iconoclasm in Byzantium," "History of the Roman Catholic Church, 1054–1517," "History of the Relations of the Orthodox Church with Roman Catholics and Protestants," "Western Christian Theology and Spirituality" and "Non-Christian Religious Teachings." At first glance, this curricula leaves the impression that the graduates of the Veliko Tarnovo Orthodox Faculty of Theology acquire good competence[8] in the sphere of interreligious relations. According to the Bulgarian University Ranking System for 2012, however, the University of Veliko Tarnovo received 0 (zero) points for publications and citations in scientific journals in the field of religion and theology (Bulgarian University Ranking System 2012). This state of affairs raises questions about the academic potential of the teaching staff of the Orthodox Theological Faculty and the qualifications of its alumni.

The training of teachers of religion at the Higher Islamic Institute bears some similarities to that undergone by their Orthodox colleagues.

Although the institute still has not received institutional accreditation from the National Agency for Assessment and Accreditation to develop master's studies, it offers courses that provide pedagogical training for its bachelor's students. As a rule, these students are taught by guest lecturers from other universities (Yusufova 2011, 223). In this way, its graduates can take optional courses on "Pedagogy" (90 hours), "Pedagogical Psychology" (60 hours), "Methods of Religious Teaching" (60 hours), "Child Psychology" (45 hours), and "General Psychology" (45 hours) Teaching Programs and Curricula). At the end of their studies, students are obliged to take two major exams: one in the field of Islamic theology and another (for the future teachers of "Religion-Islam") in social and pedagogical disciplines. The institute also meets the requirement for pedagogical practice in selected schools (Yusufova 2011, 223). The general level of education there, however, remains low by Bulgarian standards and suffers from a lack of qualified teaching staff (Evstatiev and Makariev 2010, 650). At the same time, students acquire knowledge of other major religions during the mandatory course on "History of Religions" (60 hours) (Teaching Programs and Curricula).

It seems that graduates of both the Orthodox faculties and the Higher Islamic Institute face difficulties finding employment as teachers of religion. Although their situation was improved by Instruction No. 2/2003 of the Ministry of Education, those who teach Islam in public schools are not paid by the state budget, but rather by the Muslim community and private foundations (Yusufova 2011, 226). In an interview broadcast on Bulgarian National Television (Channel 1) on September 24, 2011, a representative of the Chief Mufti's Office mentioned that 170 groups of students currently studied the school discipline "Religion-Islam." Meanwhile, some graduates of the institute have found jobs as teachers in the religious Muslim schools in Ruse, Momchilgrad, and Shumen, or teach Qur'an courses organized by mosques' boards or religious foundations (Yusufova 2011, 232). In some cases, the lack of transparency about the financial resources behind these courses provokes fears that they could inspire religious fundamentalism, prompting heated debates in Bulgarian media and society.

In conclusion, religious teaching in Bulgaria today suffers from several major problems. The first is the absence of a clear state vision about the goals, content, and forms of this school discipline. The Bulgarian Orthodox Church and the Chief Mufti's Office continue to exert considerable influence on state policy in this field. The Orthodox Church continues to treat religious teaching in public school as *verouchenie* (faith instruction) and does not take the necessary steps to secure the religious upbringing of the Orthodox children through its own network of Sunday schools. At the same time, the activities of the Muslim community and other religious minorities in this direction provoke tensions in the sphere of interreligious relations. In its turn, probably under EU influence, the state has gradually abandoned its initial idea of religious instruction in public schools and has taken the side of the majority of its citizens who consider that religious teaching there should impart knowledge about religions rather than actual faith instruction. A lack of knowledge of the historical traditions of religious teaching, however, nurtures old prejudices and short-term interests among some groups in society, thus threatening interreligious peace in the country. In addition, such ignorance limits the state's opportunities to develop well-thought-out strategies that can accommodate the past, as well as the needs of present-day Bulgarian society and its future perspectives in an age of pluralism and globalization.

Another weakness is caused by the lack of consensus in Bulgarian society. Although the majority of citizens agree that religious teaching is useful, they are divided as to whether the discipline should be optional or mandatory, who should teach it, what should be its curricula, and so on. A no-less-important factor is the atheist upbringing of the present generation of parents, who also have serious hesitations about the religious leadership due to their collaboration with the Communist regime. Moreover, the files of religious figures who have served as state security agents were opened in January 2012. According to their preliminary study, already in 1982, eleven of the fifteen metropolitans of the Bulgarian Orthodox Church, along with twelve members of the teaching staff of the Ecclesiastical Academy, were registered as state agents (Leviev-Sawyer 2012; Metodiev 2011, 32). In 1991, the latter was transformed into a theological faculty and integrated into Sofia University. In June 2012, several major figures in the teaching staff of the Orthodox Theological Faculty of the University of Veliko Tarnovo were also announced as agents (Decision No. 2-16 2012). The declassified documents from their files reveal that they used to work against Christian churches in the West without regard of their denomination—Orthodox, Catholic, or Protestant.[9] The facts raise the questions: Who teaches the future teachers of religion? And what kind of tolerance will they learn from such "professors"?

Further impeding the study of religion in public schools is the lack of well-trained teachers of religion. Despite the considerable number of graduates with diplomas in theology who hold the qualification "teacher of religion," not many of them are ready to meet the challenges of the complex Bulgarian reality, in which they have to deal not only with their own religion, but also with other faiths. Therefore, the existing university programs in theology need to be rethought in order to produce more socially responsible and effective training for teachers of religion. This change needs also to take into consideration the requirements of the European legislation. At the same time, the discipline "Religion" is monopolized by theologians, who resist the broader intercultural and interdisciplinary approach proposed by their colleagues from the humanities and social sciences (Evstatiev and Makariev 2010, 656).

The last, but not least, significant issue concerns the extremist behavior of some religious and nationalist groups and the type of knowledge they propagate. Knowledge of Bulgarian national history in general—and its religious history, in particular—needs to overcome the rhetoric of extreme nationalism, communist clichés, and religious exclusivity in order to achieve a more balanced vision of the past and respond to the current pluralistic reality—all without losing the sense of national, group, or individual identity. Yet the difficulty of such a move can be understood from a survey conducted in the 1990s finding that most interviewees identified Jesus Christ as a bearer of "rightist" ideas and ideals (conveniently forgetting the messages of social justice to be found in the "Sermon on the Mount," for example). There is, then, a long way to go, and the difficulty of teaching religion remains a function of the more complex issue of religious pluralism. Many Bulgarians, for example, continue to limit the idea of freedom of religion to the freedom to express only the majority religion publicly, while placing restrictions on religious minorities and often ignoring the freedom to change one's religious affiliation by one's own free will. Beyond these issues lie the continuing crises of the Bulgarian family and its seeming inability to provide the foundations of ethical values and orientations, which cannot, however, be ceded to the state without severe consequences. Yet the future remains open, with the process of EU integration sure to play a crucial role in the coming decades in the development not only of religious education, but also of civic values in general within Bulgarian society. Beyond this influence lies the legacy of a more generalized 19th-century and Enlightenment curiosity, as well as a desire for knowledge that is still alive among the Bulgarian people; this is one factor in orienting religious education toward a generalized understanding of different world religious traditions, as opposed to a form of faith indoctrination. Nevertheless, the continuing importance of the Orthodox Church in Bulgaria (and the Balkans in general) remains a crucial variable in all such developments, one of which the consequences cannot be calculated.

NOTES

1. The correct term is "Church Slavonic." This was the language used in liturgy and in old textbooks (before the mid-19th century) by Bulgarians as well as by other Slavs who belonged to Orthodoxy, e.g., Russians and Serbs. At the same time, Church Slavonic differed from the colloquial Bulgarian.
2. Some Orthodox Bulgarians remained under the jurisdiction of the Patriarchate of Constantinople and studied in Greek schools.
3. This can be confusing. Eastern Orthodox Church is an entity that embraces all Orthodox Churches, including the Patriarchate of Constantinople, Bulgarian Exarchate, and the Russian Orthodox Church. Therefore, it is better to use the term "Eastern Orthodoxy."
4. The debate between the Bulgarian government and the Synod of the Bulgarian Orthodox Church on lessons of religious instruction during World War II is presented in light of newly accessible archival documents studied by D. Kalkandjieva, in the framework of her research project "Religion and Education," administered by the Scientific Department of Sofia University.
5. In 2013, this situation changed. Now, Ataka launched its attacks against the Western monopolies in Bulgaria and silently gave support to the newly formed government of Bulgaria, which consists of representatives of the Bulgarian Socialist Party and the Movement for Rights and Freedoms (known as the Turkish Party).
6. Patriarch Maxim was born on October 29, 1914 and died on November 6, 2012.
7. The data below is from a survey conducted by Maria Schnitter in the summer of 2011.
8. This is due to the results from the Bulgarian University Ranking System (http://rsvu.mon.bg) announced in the summer of 2012. I should admit that my personal experience with this university confirms the low level of the teaching staff in the Faculty of Theology in Veliko Tarnovo. There are only few real scholars there.
9. This is based on my research on these files in the second half of 2012 (D.K.). There are plenty of new information there, but I think this is relevant to our subject.

BIBLIOGRAPHY

"750 novi tsarkvi postroeni za 16 g" [750 new churches built over 16 years], *Standart*, June 21, 2006: 22.

Bulgarian National Census Database. Census 1992. Available online, www.nsi.bg/Census/StrReligion.htm.

Bulgarian National Census. Census 2011. Available online, http://censusresults.nsi.bg/Reports/2/2/R10.aspx.

Bulgarian University Ranking System 2012. Results available in English, via http://rsvu.mon.bg/.

Chairman of the Holy Synod Max Bulgarian Patriarch. "Citizen's Petition of the Participants in the National Church Processions 'Education for the Spiritual and Good Future of our Children.'" Published on the official website of the Bulgarian Orthodox Church, September 24, 2010. Available online, http://bg-patriarshia.bg/news.php?id=29232.

Concept of the Holy Synod of the Bulgarian Orthodox Church announced in 2008. Available online in Bulgarian, http://www.mitropolia-varna.org/index.php?option=com_content&task=view&id=869&Itemid=29.

Concept of the Commission on the Issue of Religious Teaching in Bulgarian Public Schools, 2008. Available on the website of the Ministry of Education, Youth, and Science, http://www.minedu.government.bg/opencms/export/sites/mon/documents/08-01-28_concept_religion.pdf.

Concept on religious education in Bulgarian public schools. Sofia, 1997. Personal archive of Daniela Kalkandjieva.

Constitutional Court's Judgment no. 2, February 18, 1998. Case no. 15/1997. Published in *Darzhaven vestnik* [State Herald], no. 22, February 24, 1998.

Decision No. 2-16 of the Committee for disclosing the documents and announcing affiliation of Bulgarian citizens to the State Security and intelligence services of the Bulgarian National Army, issued on June 14, 2012. Retractable from http://www.comdos.bg/p/language/en/.

Denev, Ivan. "Religioznoto obrazovanie v Balgaria" [Religious education in Bulgaria]. Paper presented at the International Symposium on Religious Education, held at the University of Sofia, October 2004. In *Religious Education within the Context of the Common European Home*. Edited by Ivan Denev and Engelbert Gross, 11–22. Sofia, Bulgaria: University of Sofia, 2004.

Dzhambazov, Ismail. "Stremezhat na totalitatnia rezhim da razedeni myusyulmanite na etnicheska osnova" [The striving of the totalitarian regime to divide the Muslims alongside ethnic lines]. *Godishnik na Visshia Isliamski Institut* [Annual of the Higher Islamic Institute] 3 (2011): 167–184.

Evstatiev, Simeon, and Plamen Makariev. *Hristianstvo i islam: Osnovi na religioznata toleratnost* [Christianity and Islam: Bases of religious tolerance]. Sofia, Bulgaria: Center for Intercultural Studies and Partnership, 2007.

Evstatiev, Simeon, and Plamen Makariev. "Islam and Religious Education in Bulgaria: Local Tradition vis-à-vis Global Change." In *Yearbook of Muslims in Europe*. Vol. 2. Edited by Jorgen S. Nielsen, 635–661. Leiden, The Netherlands: Brill, 2010.

Godishnik Sofiiski universitet [Annual book of Sofia University]. vol. 37, Sofia, Bulgaria: Sofia University, 1941.

Godishnik Sofiiski universitet [Annual book of Sofia University]. Vol. 39 Sofia, Bulgaria: Sofia University, 1943.

Gruev, Mihail. *Mezhdu petolachkata i polumesetsa: Balgraskite myusyulmani i politicheskia regime (1944–1959)* [Between the five-pointed star and the crescent: The Bulgarian Muslims and the political regime (1944–1953)]. Sofia, Bulgaria: IK "Kota," 2003.

Hranova, Albena. "Zivotat na tri poniatia v balgarskata kultura—vazrazhdane, srednovekovie, robstvo" [The life of three notions in Bulgarian literature—revival, Middle Ages, and yoke]. In *Istoriografia i literatura: Za sotsialnoto konstruirane na istoricheski poniatia i Golemi razkazi v balgarskata kultura XIX–XX vek* [Historiography and culture: Concerning the social construction of historical notions and Grand narratives in Bulgarian culture]. Vol. 2. Edited by Boyan Znepolski, 350–502. Sofia, Bulgaria: Prosveta, 2011.

Ilchevski, Stefan. "Prepodavaneto na religia v balgarskite uchilishta: Istoricheski osobenosti i savremenno sastoianie" [Religious teaching in Bulgarian schools: Historical peculiarities and contemporary situation]. *Strategii na obrazovatelnata i nauchna politika* [Strategies for policy in science and education] 15.2 (2007): 100–109.

Instruction no. 2 on the study of the discipline on "Religion" in public schools, issued by the Ministry of Education and Science on June 23, 2003. *Darzhaven vestnik* [State Herald], no. 60, July 4, 2003.

"Izselnitsi davat pari za dzhamii" [Emigrants (from Bulgaria to Turkey) donate money for mosques], *Trud* [Labor], July 3, 2006: 3.

History of the Higher Islamic Institute. Available online, http://www.islamicinstitute-bg.org/main.php?sec=2&page=2.

Kalkandjieva, Daniela. *Balgarskata pravoslavna tsarkva i darzhavata, 1944–1953* [The Bulgarian Orthodox Church and the State]. Sofia, Bulgaria: Albatros, 1997.

———. "Politikata na Balgarskata komunisticheska partia kam nepravoslavnite religiozni obshtnosti (1944–1953 g.)" [The policy of the Bulgarian Communist Party to the non-Orthodox religious denominations (1944–1953)]. *Trudove na katedrite po istoria i bogoslovie* [Studies by the Departments of History and Theology at the University of Shumen, Bulgaria] 2 (1998): 252–264.

———. "'Secular Orthodox Christianity' versus 'Religious Islam' in Postcommunist Bulgaria." *Religion, State and Society* 36.4 (December 2008): 423–434.

Leviev-Sawyer, Clive. "Men in Black: What Did Bulgarian Orthodox Church Clergy Do while Spying for the Communist State?" *Sofia Echo*, January 18, 2012. Available online, http://www.sofiaecho.com/2012/01/18/1747679_men-in-black-what-did-bulgarian-orthodox-church-clergy-do-while-spying-for-the-communist-state.

Mancheva, Mila. "Image and Policy: The Case of Turks and Pomaks in Inter-War Bulgaria, 1918–44 (with special reference to education)." *Islam and Christian-Muslim Relations* 12.3 (July 2001): 355–374.

Metodiev, Momchil. "Darzhavna sigurnost v Duhovnata akademia" [State Security in the Ecclesiastical Academy]. *Hristianstvo i kultura* [Christianity and Culture] 7 (2011): 29–44.

Metodiev, Veselin, and Lachezar Stoyanov (eds.), *Balgarski konstitutsii i konstitutsionni proekti* [Bulgarian constitutions and drafts of constitutions]. Sofia: d-r P. Beron, 1990.

Nenovski, N. "Our Church Is 'Registered' by the Constitution," *Trud* [newspaper "Labor"] from December 23, 2002, p. 26.

Proceedings of the Holy Synod No. 36, December 21, 1939.

Proceedings of the Holy Synod No. 5, June 17, 1940.

Proceedings of the Holy Synod No. 28, May 27, 1941.

Proceedings of the Holy Synod No. 15, March 15, 1942.

Public Opinion on the Introduction of "Religion" as Educational Discipline in the Bulgarian Schools. Survey of the National Center for the Study of Public Opinion, February 28–March 5, 2006. Personal Archive of Daniela Kalkandjieva.

"Regulations for the Application of the Law of People's Education," *Darzhaven vestnik* [State Herald], no. 15, February 24, 2003. Available online, http://rio-lovech.hit.bg/index_files/PPZNP.htm.

"Regulations for the Unified State Standards about the Obtaining University Degree with Qualification "Teacher." Decree 12 of 1995, SG. 9 of 27.01.1995, suppl. no. 50 1.06.1995. Available online, http://www.minedu.government.bg/opencms/export/sites/mon/left_menu/documents/process/nrdb_95_pr_kval_uchitel.pdf.

Roditeli. "Pitat roditelite kak detsata da uchat religiya," [Pareants are asked how children to study religion], [newspaper] *Trud* [Labor], January 11, 2011. Available online, http://www.trud.bg/Article.asp?ArticleId=758178. Last use on September 15, 2011.

"Samo 14 000 detsa v chas po religia" [Only 14,000 children study religion], *Standart*, September 5, 2006: 5.

Schnitter, Maria. "Fundamentalism and Eurointegration." *Studia Religiologica* 40 (2007): 21–30.

Schnitter, Maria. Survey on the academic study of theology in Bulgaria, conducted in the summer of 2011. Personal Archive of Maria Schnitter.

Stoyanov, Valeri. *Turskoto naselenie v Balgaria mezhdu polyusite na etnicheskata politika* [The Turkish population in Bulgaria between the poles of ethnic policy]. Sofia, Bulgaria: LIK, 1998.

Subasheva, Daniela. "Plovdivskia mitropolit: MON niama politicheska volia za vavezhdane na pravoslavno verouchenie" [Metropolitan Nikolay of Plovdiv: The Ministry of Education has no political will to introduce Orthodox faith instruction]. *Darik News*, November 15, 2007. Available online, http://dariknews.bg/view_article.php?article_id=198651.

Survey of the National Center for Studying Public Opinion. Sofia, Bulgaria, March 2008. Personal Archive of Daniela Kalkandjieva.

Teaching Programs and Curricula of the Higher Islamic Institute. Available online, http://www.islamicinstitute-bg.org/main.php?sec=2&page=6.

Tsarkoven vestnik, no. 40, October 30, 1942, p. 457.

"VMRO napada Svidetelite na Yehova (dnes.bg)" [VMRO attacks Jehovah's Witnesses (dnes.bg)], YouTube video, [time], posted by "asengenov," April 18, 2011, http://www.youtube.com/watch?v=c3JLweq6mkA.

"VMRO-MO. Protest sreshtu "Svidetelite na Yehova" [VMRO-MO. Protests against Jehovah's Witnesses], YouTube video, 4:49, posted by "vmroyouth," March 7, 2009, http://www.youtube.com/watch?v=_pQL3gOoyhg.

Yusufova, Gyulyumser. "Isliamskoto religiozno obrazovanie v prehoda kam demokratsia" [Islamic religious education during the transition to democracy]. *Godishnik na Visshia Isliamski institut* [Annual of the Higher Islamic Institute] 3 (2011): 215–235.

4

The Vanishing State

RELIGIOUS EDUCATION AND INTOLERANCE IN
FRENCH JEWISH SCHOOLS

Kimberly A. Arkin

UNLIKE MANY OF the countries that provide case studies for this volume, France does not offer religious education in public schools. As Silvio Ferrari notes (in chapter 1 of this volume), the state tolerates the discussion of religion in courses devoted to other topics (it would be virtually impossible, for example, not to talk about Islam when discussing the 7th-century conquest of the Arabian peninsula, or Christianity when talking about European art). But it does not permit either the teaching of or about religion.[1] Furthermore, French political leaders and the French Department of Education have been deeply reluctant to entertain the idea that teaching about (let alone the teaching of) religion might be a way to address some of the issues of deep pluralism that all European countries face at the moment (Debray 2002). For many politicians, public intellectuals, and educators, religion and religious education are seen as the source of France's problem with social pluralism in the 21st century—just witness the widespread accusations that pious Muslims, and even Islam itself, are homophobic, misogynistic, and anti-Semitic (Brenner 2002; Brenner 2004; Fourest 2005; Finkielkraut 2003; Hirsi Ali 2007; Taguieff 2005; on this issue in relation to veiling, see Bowen 2007) and the deep discomfort with the growth of Islamic education (Landrin 2006, 12; Agence France Presse 2006).

This, however, has not always been the case (see Baubérot 2004). And there is a long-standing exception to France's increasingly "assertive" form of secularism (Kuru, chapter 6 of this volume). In seemingly flagrant violation of the 1905 law that separated Church and State by ending government support for "established" religions, the state funds private religious schools that meet certain legal criteria. It began doing so in 1959 and, despite appearances, the logic behind the move was (at least arguably) staunchly Republican. As we will see, the authors of the 1959 law intended it to help (re)produce the state's vision of autonomous, tolerant, democratic French citizens by combining the national curriculum with independent religious education. The practice, however, has been quite different.

This paper will focus on the unintended consequences of a particular aspect of this practice—the state's decision to finance, but not regulate, Parisian Jewish day schools. The 1959 law intended that day school students in government-funded institutions see themselves as simultaneously French *and* Jewish, just as Catholic school students were to be Catholic and devoted to French Republicanism. But scores of Jewish day school students in the mid-2000s imagined "Frenchness" and "Jewishness" as mutually exclusive alternatives, separate "nations" that could never comfortably coexist. As one high school student noted: "Everyone knows the Jews will not be safe as long as they live with Christians!" I will argue that, despite the fears motivating contemporary public hostility toward religious education, it was not necessarily the content of religious schooling that prevented day school students from generalizing their trust beyond other Jews. Rather, it was the context of Jewish schooling that allowed Jewish students to understand themselves as incommensurably different from and existentially threatened by "the French." By funding and ignoring day schools, the state made this context and thus the separation of religious and Republican identities possible.

Religious Schooling and the Republic

This was not supposed to happen. For the French state, the creation of appropriately Republican citizens has long been tied to education, and most particularly the replacement of religious education (and thus particularistic religious values) with an ever-changing state vision of morality (Stock-Morton 1988; for a mature articulation of this, see Durkheim 2002). It is thus not a surprise that the fledgling Third Republic (1870–1940) attempted to consolidate its power by attacking the Catholic Church's considerable role in early childhood education. Beginning in the early 1880s, the government enacted the so-called Ferry laws—named after then-Minister of Education, Jules Ferry—thereby making previously church-administered elementary education free, secular (*laïque*), and mandatory. This process of secularization included the replacement of the particularistic and metaphysical morality that had been taught by priests (or, in rarer cases, pastors or rabbis) with a philosophical morality Republicans thought necessary for turning a religiously and politically divided public into a cohesive national community (Stock-Morton 1988). It did not, however, include the secularization of children themselves. In fact, public schools at the time—and to this day—created space for embodied Catholic piety: weekly time off for catechism, fish on Fridays, and vacation on significant holy days. A few decades later, the 1905 legal separation between Church and State simply confirmed, accelerated, and extended this process of institutional (rather than individual) secularization beyond elementary education (Baubérot 2004).

But in 1959, the French government seemed to undermine its own position by passing a law that allowed state financing of private religious schools under certain conditions. Called the *loi Debré* after its sponsor, Gaullist Prime Minister Michel Debré, the measure was intended as a compromise, a way of ending the ideological battle between Catholic and secular schooling. Faced with a demographic explosion in the school-aged population, politicians were struggling with ways to quickly expand school capacity (Battut et al. 1995). Some on the Left argued for state absorption of all existing private institutions, thus eliminating *libre*, or independent, education altogether (Journal Officiel 1959). On the Right, some politicians demanded that the state fund private education unconditionally in the name of free "choice." Debré offered a middle ground—the rapprochement of public and private educational spheres while preserving the "special character" of religious schools. He argued that private schools, the overwhelming majority of which were Catholic, were already part of the public educational system and had earned their "letters of Republican nobility" by accepting the (primarily Jewish) children that were banned from public schools during the Vichy period (ibid., 3596). The proposed law, he noted, would simply expand and codify the terms of this collaborative relationship.

To do so, the law abolished some of the structural and pedagogical boundaries between public and private institutions (Poucet 2005). Private secondary schools were given the option of remaining completely independent and receiving no state funds or entering into a *contrat d'association* with the state. Schools that chose this contractual relationship were henceforth to be staffed with state-appointed, state-salaried instructors who, once approved by the principal, were to teach the national curriculum. These schools were also to be granted per-student funds for regular operating expenses, like heat, electricity, and building maintenance (Bellengier 2004, 33). In return, contracted schools were expected to respect the basic principals of French national education and Republican laïcité, among them: enrollment of students regardless of "origins, beliefs or opinions"; respect for individual conscience and freedom from religious compulsion; faithful implementation of the Department of Education's standard national curriculum; and submission to the same pedagogical inspection regime as public institutions (Bellengier 2004, 52–53; Journal Officiel 1959, 3600).

Religious institutions were thus largely allowed to preserve their religious missions—what Debré called their special character—from state interference. But the maintenance of a schools' religious character depended (at least in theory) on the compatibility of that character with Republican understandings of privatized religion. In other words, religion was to be supplementary, one (potentially detachable) piece of a student's being. In keeping with this vision, the Debré government allowed religious schools to use *privately* raised funds—from student tuition, donations, or grants—for optional religion courses that would take place either before or after standard school hours. But special character was never legally defined, making it a subject of continuous contention (Poucet 2005). For decades, Catholic schools insisted that their special character involved the infusion of all instruction with Christian principals and Catholic theology, thereby abolishing any attempt to distinguish between a core Republican education and supplemental religious instruction (ibid., 6–10). Under the right wing governments that held power throughout the 1970s, this interpretation received significant legislative and judicial support, reinforcing private education's autonomy without curtailing its financial entitlements. For example, the 1971 Habib-Deloncle law required that private schools observe the "general rules" of public education, but not the exact form and content as had been stipulated by the Debré law. When the Left took control of the government in 1981 with the election of François Mitterrand, overturning these legislative changes took a backseat to more systemic attempts to retool the entire relationship between public and private schools. This preference for (failed) systemic change allowed the patently un-Republican legislation and precedents established in the

1970s to remain in force for an additional four years. After a 1984 government proposal to abolish most of the distinctions between private and public schools brought thousands of conservative demonstrators into the streets, the Left abandoned a holistic approach in favor of more immediate attempts to curtail the power of private education (Battut et al. 1995). But even then, special character continued to be a potent argument for otherwise unthinkable legal concessions, including leaving the effective power of hiring and firing state-salaried teachers in the hands of private school principals, rather than the state. As a result, through the 1970s and 1980s, the state's ability to ensure a commitment to Debré's Republican vision decreased dramatically.

The Debré law (and all successor legislation) primarily benefited Catholic schools, which still represent the overwhelming majority of government-contracted schools in France. But Jewish schools also ultimately flourished under the new liberalized legal regime. Over the 1980s and 1990s, fifty new Jewish schools were created, more than doubling the number of institutions extant at the end of the 1970s (Petit-Ohayon 2003). The number of students who were enrolled increased proportionally, rising from about 3,200 at the end of the 1970s to 16,000 in the late 1980s, and then doubling over the course of the 1990s to reach 30,000 in 2002 (Petit-Ohayon 2003; Haymann 1978).

But in contrast to Catholic schools, which have recently responded to a shrinking religious base and a burgeoning population disaffected with public schools becoming more diverse and ecumenical (for example, see Davidenkoff 2005), Jewish schools have gone in the other direction. Much of the explosive growth in Jewish schooling over the last twenty years has come from very observant institutions that embrace Judaism as a total way of life. Schools characterized as "Orthodox" or "*Haredi*" (from the Hebrew word for "fear" and translated as "one who trembles before God") account for thirty of the fifty new institutions created in France over the course of the 1980s and 1990s (Petit-Ohayon 2003). In 2002, almost two-thirds of elementary-aged children in French Jewish schools were enrolled in Orthodox or Haredi institutions; the same was true for 50 percent of middle school–aged students and 30 percent of high school students (ibid.). In Paris, five of the eight largest school networks were either Orthodox or Haredi, accounting for almost a third of the 21,300 young Parisians enrolled in Jewish institutions (ibid.). In addition, a number of schools considered "traditionalist," meaning not strictly observant of Jewish law (*halakhah*), were moving toward more pronounced forms of religious practice, including more stringent dress codes and the physical separation of the sexes in secular classes. Since almost half of the government contracts awarded to Jewish schools have been granted within the last twenty years, government funds probably disproportionately subsidize highly observant institutions (ibid.).

With few exceptions, in the mid-2000s, even the least religious Parisian Jewish day schools violated the Debré law. They did so by, among other things, requiring that students prove their Jewishness in accordance with Jewish religious law[2] and by making religious instruction mandatory for all students. Despite the growing concerns noted at the opening of this chapter about Republican norms and state law losing ground to the religious demands of minority populations, these violations have remained a public secret—well known, but studiously ignored. The Department of Education seemed to go to great lengths to avoid acknowledging what it already knew. One department official told me that only "retired" employees might talk to me about the issue of Jewish school laïcité compliance. Another noted: "We have a 'see no evil, hear no evil, speak no evil' policy with respect to Jewish institutions, including schools." In other words, they did not ask or tell.

Jewish Day Schooling and the Flight from Pluralism

Although not necessarily inherently problematic, these seemingly state-sanctioned legal violations helped produce an environment in which children found difference alienating and threatening. This was a result of the remarkable homogeneity within and across Jewish schools, homogeneity that state attitudes toward religious education inadvertently authorized. Allowing schools to demand that students prove their halahkic Jewishness unintentionally turned day schools into a vehicle not only for flight from religious (and even internal Jewish) difference, but also ethnic and economic diversity. How? The explosion of a demand for Jewish day schooling from the 1980s on did not necessarily come from religious families. It is true that in the mid-2000s a large number of Parisian day school students came from families that had "returned" to more intense religious practice over the last decade or two. Many of the students I interviewed described parents who did not observe *kashrut* (Judaism's elaborate dietary restrictions) or celebrate religious holidays before marrying or having children. Some had since introduced Shabbat observance (the

Jewish day of rest, during which a large variety of forms of "work" are prohibited) and stricter adherence to kashrut. Jewish schooling, in turn, contributed to this process as children brought home the more rigorous practices learned in school and refused their parents' compromises. In my interviews with day school students, few, however, described themselves or their families as "really" religious. The category most often used was "traditionalist," a term that suggests deep ethnic attachment to Jewishness rather than stringent observance of Jewish law. For most, being "traditionalist" meant doing distinctively "Jewish" things on a weekly, if not daily, basis—and this seemed to mean everything from attending synagogue on Friday nights to eating a McFish sandwich rather than a Big Mac at McDonald's.

Instead of religion, parental interest in Jewish schools seemed to be driven by attempts to negotiate Paris's class and race hierarchy and, more recently, to escape anti-Semitism. In 2004–2005, most of the students in Jewish day schools were the children of lower-middle to middle-class Jews who had either been born in France to Moroccan or Tunisian immigrant parents, or who had themselves left Morocco or Tunisia as children or very young adults. This demography did not reflect the ethnic diversity of the contemporary French Jewish population. According to a 2002 Jewish population study commissioned by the *Fonds Social Juif Unifié* (hereafter FSJU), the French equivalent of the American Joint Distribution Committee, 70 percent of the French Jewish population is *Sephardi*, a term that literally means "from Spain" but popularly refers to Jews who come from North Africa and the Middle East; 24 percent is *Ashkenazi*, or of European origin; and 6 percent is "both" (Cohen 2002, 12). Of the more than 50 percent of the Jewish population born outside the boundaries of metropolitan France, the largest plurality is Algerian (21 percent), followed by Moroccans (11.2 percent), and then Tunisians (10.6 percent) (ibid., 11). Jews with Algerian ancestry therefore most likely comprise the largest plurality in the French Sephardi population.

There was somewhat more socioeconomic range than ethnic diversity in contracted schools. Tuition rates were kept down by heavy state subsidies, which covered 50–60 percent of contracted schools' budgets. Parents were called on to pay for all other services, particularly cafeteria expenses, religious education, busing, up keep, and hall monitors. But each family's contribution was calculated on a sliding scale that factored in revenue, and school directors insisted that they had never turned away a family for financial reasons. A number of parents with whom I spoke were at least temporarily unemployed, and some students described their own economic conditions as straitened. But despite the theoretical accessibility of Jewish education to all socioeconomic strata, most students seemed to come from *petit bourgeois* homes with solidly middle-class incomes, but little social capital in Paris's steeply hierarchal social order (Bourdieu 1984). Teachers consistently described their students in precisely these terms, noting (often with derision) that students' families were well off but not cultured, more interested in material well-being than education (see further, Arkin 2014).

There are a number of related reasons for the overrepresentation of these particularly ethnicized and classed families in Jewish schools, many of which are too complex to enumerate here (see further, Arkin 2014). Suffice it to say that for historical reasons, Moroccan and Tunisian Jews have generally had a harder time with upward mobility in post–World War II France than have Algerian Jews or Ashkenazim. As a result, unlike many (although certainly not all) Ashkenazim and Algerians, many Moroccan and Tunisian families still lived in rough, lower-middle class, semi-urban neighborhoods: Aubervilliers, Bondy, Bobigny, Créteil, Sarcelles, and Saint-Germain-des-Prés (Strudel 1996). Those who lived in Paris itself often had homes on the literal and figurative margins of the city, in the 18th, 19th, and 20th arrondissements. These neighborhoods typically have large concentrations of recent immigrants, relatively high unemployment, and public schools that have suffered considerably from proportionally declining investments in education (Battut et al. 1995).

For these families, physical proximity with other immigrants, and most particularly Muslim immigrants, presented the related problems of ethnic and class distinction (Comaroff and Comaroff 1992). In these diverse neighborhoods, North African Jews' and Muslims' shared physical characteristics, family names, cultural practices, linguistic patterns, and even religious traditions made the maintenance of Jewish ethnic distinction both difficult and necessary (see further, Arkin 2014). Sephardi adults, whether implicitly or explicitly, recognized that it was far more problematic to be (mis)taken for "Arab" or "Muslim" than it was to be Jewish. During my fieldwork, I heard numerous stories about how Sephardi adults navigated such potential confusion—emphasizing, for example, the "French" first names that many thought were associated with Jews rather than Muslims. Sephardi adolescents and young adults had developed their own nonverbal, sartorial strategies for coping with the same kinds of situations (Arkin 2009). In addition to potential ethnic confusion, Jewish and Muslim proximity in these mixed socioeconomic neighborhoods created class anxieties. For many of my Sephardi interlocutors, only Jews were upwardly mobile. Having wealth and being able to show it, particularly in contexts of relative deprivation, helped underscore the distinctions between North African populations. As my teenage informants often explained: Jews were "classy," while "Arabs" were "cheap" (see further, Arkin 2009).

Jewish schooling, for many of these families, offered a way of shoring up the overlapping class and ethnoracial distinctions. For upwardly mobile but precariously positioned families, private schooling suggested a middle-class commitment to education and the resources to back up that commitment.[3] It also appeared to assure a child's future class status through the purchase of services imagined as better adapted for academic and, therefore, financial success than public schools, which were often seen as inflexible, as well as plagued with problems like drugs and violence (see further, Battut et al. 1995; Georgel and Thorel 1995). A twelfth grader's Tunisian-born mother, who had never completed her own high school education, described the tuition payments to an Orthodox school that she could barely afford as the structural equivalent of mortgage payments. She lived in subsidized, public housing and would never be able to buy her own home, but private schooling would allow her son to earn enough money to purchase one (or more) for her. "With what I paid for school I could have bought ten houses! It's that expensive... Everything that I put into education, I didn't put into the apartment for me. At least I'll have given you a good education," she said turning to her son. "We put everything on you."

In addition, Jewish students and parents openly admitted that Jewish schooling provided a means of escaping contact with other "immigrant" populations, which were sometimes in the majority at neighborhood public schools. Since 2001, which brought an increase in youth-on-youth anti-Semitic attacks, fear has further fueled the flight from mixed contexts. A Moroccan-born father of two boys enrolled in a Haredi institution told me that he had "to put them [his sons] in Jewish school and there are so few choices... I could not have put them in public schools with Arabs or blacks... They would have been hit and brutalized... That's the way it is with Arabs and blacks; they don't like Jews." An eleventh grader who had attended public school until high school described her decision to enroll in a Jewish institution as a reaction to her "extreme discomfort" at being "the only Jew in a school with 500 Muslims." Marion, a ninth grader at an Orthodox institution, told a similar story: "I was in public school through sixth grade, but as soon as I was supposed to go to middle school, my mother put me in [Jewish school]. The public schools in Bondy [a low-income suburb of Paris] are filled with Arabs and blacks. And my mother did not want me in school with Arabs and blacks." Students at an all-girls Haredi school also regularly claimed that they were enrolled in a Jewish school because public schools had "too many Arabs and blacks," so much so that the school director panicked when reporters came to film his school. He instructed the girls NOT to say that they were in day school because there were too many Arabs and blacks in public schools, but to explain that they were there for the religious education.

Given the way that day schools were structured, this separation from both non-Jews and otherly Jewish Jews was virtually complete. Many day school students traveled great distances from their local neighborhoods to attend school. To accommodate this, day schools tended to start and end later than neighborhood public schools, which meant that some day school students did not get home until well after dark. Day school vacations, which logically followed major Jewish holidays, almost never coincided with those of public schools. On top of this, by middle school and high school, day school students found maintaining extracurricular activities difficult because of the additional hours of religious education added to an already full national curriculum. And as we will see below, students also thought they were religiously discouraged from befriending non-Jews. As a result, not very many day schoolers had non-Jewish or even non–day school friends. One of the few students who admitted publicly to having such friends—whom she called "French"—found herself mercilessly mocked by her classmates.

The homogenization and segregation of Jewishness that occurred in government-funded Jewish day schools had two nefarious consequences. First, homogenization allowed students to mistake their forms of particularity for Jewish generality. By this, I mean that rather than see their classmates as particularly classed, ethnicized, and religiously positioned subjects—second and third generation, upwardly mobile, "traditionalist" Jews of Moroccan and Tunisian origin—day school students viewed them as tokens of universal "Jewishness." As a result, students had trouble recognizing the "Jewishness" of those who did not share their ethnic particularities. "Ashkenazi" Jewishness, for most students, had no clear referent; one student asked me whether Ashkenazim were from Morocco, Tunisia, or Algeria. If European Jewishness was a foreign concept, black

Jewishness was incomprehensible. Two eleventh graders—Jason and Joshua—told me about two black children—Salomé and Eric—who had been briefly enrolled in their Orthodox school. Jason explained that when he first met them: "I asked myself questions. They are here, but they are black, and this is a Jewish school. But Salomé, I think she was a real black, I don't know." What does it mean to be a "real black," I asked. "That means she is not Jewish," he explained. Joshua, who had previously insisted that Salomé was at least a "half-Jew" because her mother was Jewish and evidently white, clarified: "There were no signs of Jewishness." Again, I had to ask what that meant.

JASON: In France, there are no black Jews.
JOSHUA: Yes there are.
JASON: I've never seen any!
JOSHUA: We just do not notice them...It's rare. I know that in the synagogue I sometimes go to, I have an uncle who officiates at this synagogue. And when we go to his synagogue, sometimes there are blacks who come. And it's true, it seems really strange.
JASON: Saying Shabbat Shalom to a black, it's ummm...
JOSHUA: Yeah, when we see blacks we think non-Jews. We just do not have the experience.

In other words, to a large extent, being Jewish meant sharing Jason and Joshua's ethnic, historical, cultural, and even economic profile.

If homogenization encouraged the narrowing of Jewishness, Jewish segregation facilitated the misreading of student particularities as Jewishness when in fact the day-to-day routines of day school students were irreducibly French. In this sense, the Debré law had achieved its author's intentions. Jewish schooling, including religious instruction, was conducted almost exclusively in French. Day school students were required to take and pass national exams in order to receive their diplomas. The content of secular courses, which were taught by state-trained and salaried teachers, closely followed nationally established guidelines. And those guidelines still tended to be vaguely "nationalist," in the sense that Anglo-American politics and policies systematically appeared as foils for their French counterparts and "Europe" remained an administrative abstraction. Even institutional micropractices, the kinds of minute bodily regulations that Foucault (1977) described as the essence of subject formation, were similar across school contexts.

Modes of authority, the value placed on particular disciplines (math and science were for "smart" students, social sciences and literature for those who struggled), the desks students learned to sit in, and systems for evaluating student performance were more or less uniform across France.

Nonetheless, there was little recognition that these everyday banalities constituted a shared adolescent French universe that transcended the particularities of Jewish schooling. Although day schoolers' parents often had very complex understandings of the relationship between Jewishness and Frenchness—often insisting in different contexts on the centrality of each identity, their connections to one another, and their divergences (see further, Arkin 2014)—their children had much more dichotomous assessments. The students I interacted with routinely insisted on the mutual exclusivity of Jewishness and Frenchness, without any of the ambivalence evident in their parents' generation. An entire class of tenth graders in a Haredi school loudly insisted that they had no "French" friends, by which they actually meant no white, Christian friends. Similarly, students in Haredi and Orthodox schools told me time and time again that they were not "French," that "France was not [their] country," and that "the French" and the "the Jews" had nothing in common. Joshua, a senior, explained: "In fact, when we say French, we think of non-Jews and non-Muslims. We know that we are French. But that means, there is always this gap...."[4] Others expressed a similar sentiment with less subtlety. Levina, an eleventh grader in a Haredi school, explained: "I don't feel French...When there are reports of events on the news, none of us particularly care about what happens in France or in Europe...." Still, others told me that their Frenchness was reducible to a passport and did not correspond to any meaningful sense of self. Teachers at an Orthodox school even complained that confusion about national identity had seeped into uncertainty about citizenship. Apparently, many students did not know how to answer questions about nationality on government forms, writing in "Tunisian" or "Moroccan," depending on where their parents had been born.

Lost in Translation

So far we have seen the heady combination of two trends. First, the growth of increasingly stringent religious instruction, made possible by displacing public investment into private schools that are poorly regulated. This meant that Jewish families seeking non-Catholic private schooling were virtually forced to pick schools that excluded non-Jews—even those interested in a Jewish education—on religious grounds.[5] At the same time, homogenized Jewish schools allowed a socioeconomically marginalized population to partially escape the cultural, class, and ethnic proximities it shared with an even more marginal other. In other words, Jewish schools joined religiously inflected worries about intermixture with concerns about preserving classed and raced distinctions. This combination produced stunningly homogenous and remarkably isolated day school students who misrecognized their very narrow French Jewish particularities as Jewish generality.

With the addition of one more piece of the puzzle, this created conditions under which Jewishness became a racial and national identity incompatible with other modes of identification, endangered by pluralism. That additional puzzle piece was also a product of the vanishing state. Even as it made greater and greater room for religious control of otherwise state-funded establishments, the state did not introduce required pedagogical training for religious instructors. Recognizing the potential problem this created, private Jewish institutions tried to step into the breach. The FSJU, for example, established a training center and diploma program for religious educators, but many religion teachers objected to an ostensibly "secular" institution certifying religious teachers. Day schools were thus free to privilege embodied piety over any ability to understand/communicate with students. As one Haredi school director noted, when faced with the choice between someone who was pedagogically skilled and intellectually knowledgeable on the one hand, and someone who was visibly pious on the other, he would always choose the latter. Given this kind of logic—and the very poor benefits and pay associated with being a religious instructor—it is not surprising that most religion teachers had little training. They were overwhelmingly pious men and women looking for part-time work that would not compromise their religious convictions or practices. The men were often yeshiva scholars who had renounced secular pursuits and education for a life of Torah learning. The women, many of whom had spent a year or two in Jewish seminary, were predominantly Haredi housewives with large families and considerable domestic responsibilities.

In practice, this meant that few religion teachers in day schools were good teachers. Most shunned any real engagement with student questions; they also cut short any dialogue or debate about the material presented, preferring—in what some would say is un-Jewish fashion—to give students simple rules to follow in their daily lives. One religious instructor at a Haredi school taught his tenth graders about Shabbat as a series of pragmatic questions to which he immediately provided the answers: Can one open a bottle of wine on Shabbat? Yes, doing so does not create a new object. A soda bottle? No, unless you puncture the cap so that it can no longer be used. Otherwise, one has created a new object—a bottle cap. A packet of sugar? Yes, but you cannot tear it in any place with words; tearing words violates the injunction against erasing on Shabbat. Can you tear off a paper towel on Shabbat? No. What if there is a cake with writing on it, can it be cut and eaten? It can only be cut and eaten if the words are made of the same ingredients as the cake; otherwise, cutting into the letters also violates rules about erasing.

Some teachers articulated this avoidance of student questions and debate as part of a conscious agenda. Mme Grunspan, a very thoughtful religious instructor in an Orthodox school, explained that she was trying to teach children to defer to and respect (religious) authority. She claimed that day school children grew up thinking that nothing was sacred because ambient French popular culture taught them to challenge authority of all kinds loudly and impertinently:

> They all watch these television programs with the journalists who want to show off and look like know-it-alls. They interrupt the invited guests constantly... A student, copying what he's seen on TV, will tell a teacher that he's "totally wrong" or that he's in "total disagreement" with what the teacher just said. They have to learn that this is not an appropriate way to speak to someone like a teacher... Ten years ago, the journalist really just asked the questions and stayed in the background, but today kids have learned a really different model and need to be re-socialized at school.

So rather than teach them to argue, she encouraged "respect" and therefore silence. But most teachers did not have well-formulated pedagogical agendas; they simply could not understand or handle student puzzlement. Some were so uncomfortable with student questions that they chastised students for their curiosity. In what was actually an argument about action and intent in religious Judaism, Shoshanna, a tenth grader in a Haredi school, asked her teacher—Mme Benayoun—why someone ignorant of the *dinnim*, or rules, associated with Shabbat should be punished for turning on the lights. She also wanted to know whether turning them on accidentally (out of habit, for example) was a serious offense. For Shoshanna, these questions were motivated by secular concerns about individual intention and the distinction between exterior action and internal belief. She reasoned that if laws were broken without knowledge or intention, the perpetrator should not be punished, or at least not in the same way. But Mme Benayoun saw the questions themselves as frustrating and irrelevant, a distraction from the central point of a lesson focused on rule memorization. "Why are you asking these questions?" she demanded. "Do you typically transgress Shabbat? It's death if you do!" When Shoshanna tried to ask another series of questions about a (confusing) interpretation of a biblical passage, Mme Benayoun humiliated her for her trouble: she was accused of being "insubordinate" and acting inappropriately for a "Jewish girl."

Why do these poor pedagogical skills matter? What, if anything, does this have to do with day school students' sense that they were incommensurable and incompatible with non-Jews? Teaching religious Judaism to children who come primarily from secular families is difficult. As I argue elsewhere, Jewish tradition and secular modernity offer very different conceptions of community and personhood (see further, Arkin 2014, chapter 4). And when Jewish practices emphasizing separation and distinction are presented without their accompanying religious logics, they can easily be (mis)understood as implying that non-Jews are ontologically different and dangerous, and therefore can be ill accommodated under the same political regime.

For many religion teachers, as for observant Jews in general, Jewishness presupposed and entailed following the biblical command to be *kaddosh*, often glossed as holy or separate, in every aspect of daily life (i.e., Deuteronomy 7:6). Under the influence of post-Enlightenment ultra-orthodox interpretations of rabbinic Judaism, this has come to mean conscious and conspicuous separation from what are often Biblically termed "the nations," or non-Jews and surrounding non-Jewish society (Heilman 1994; Neusner 1996; Soloveitchik 1994). Those who strive to embody this distinctive form of Jewishness imagine themselves as not only guaranteeing a place in God's favor, but also as contributing to a larger Jewish eschatological project—the "return" to a theocratic Israel and the concomitant arrival of the Messiah. In a certain kind of context, this project is not about racial separation, but about ritual purity; in Mary Douglas' terms (2002), it is about managing structural dangers, not the physical or biological threat created by non-Jews. In fact, one could argue that the threat of social and cultural proximity between Jews and non-Jews fueled evermore rigorous attempts to establish boundaries in certain places (intimacy and marriage), while leaving others (commerce, daily interactions) rather open. This is very different than either presuming stable ontological difference (race) or attempting to create the presumption of that difference through absolute segregation (Jim Crow).

But when the rules governing Jewish separation are presented without their accompanying religious logic, they can appear to be about race contamination rather than ritual separation. A lesson at a Haredi school about *bishul akum*, or forbidden forms of cooking, illustrates the slippage between these two different understandings. Mlle Chitrit, a very imposing religion teacher, told seniors that wine touched or even looked at by a non-Jew was no longer kosher and therefore unfit for consumption. "If a *goy* [non-Jew] so much looks at my glass, I can't drink it; I throw it out. Others might [drink it], but I would rather be safe than sorry." The same teacher instructed students never to share a meal with non-Jews or eat even kosher foods cooked by a non-Jew because "the beginning of intermarriage is a meal together." A student, who was perhaps shocked by how this sounded, noted that this could not really apply to "a [female] Jew and a *goya* [female non-Jew]," who "logically would not marry one another." Mlle Chitrit shouted in response:

> God forbid, God forbid...The Torah that created us says that the table is a sacred space. We can be friends, [as in saying] good morning, good evening, but not at the table. I would never invite my neighbor, a goya, even if I've known her for twenty years. I would never even go to her apartment, because the day that she tells me to come in, I'll have to tell her to come in. And after that it's finished, it's hopeless. My children and her children will start playing together in the courtyard. And they can't do that; it's forbidden!

She also warned students about never feeling spiritually safe with non-Jews:

> I recently saw a guy I know. How's it going? [I ask] He tells me he has a problem. What? My son is twenty-six, and he has gotten involved with a non-Jewish girl. I'm sick [he says], and I don't know what to do. And I say: how did he meet her? At the university. It

starts with classes together and then it goes further. You think it's not true? Remember when we talked about hurting God. It's [hopeless] if we don't put ramparts and walls and everything up... Don't tell yourself that you're the son of a rabbi, [so you're safe]. Don't believe it... We have to take care of ourselves. We decide to keep them [non-Jews] at arms length. I say that for our ears only. How many times have the teachers, my colleagues, said to me, "come on, let's get a pizza amongst ourselves, a kosher one!" Never!...

Mlle Chitrit's discussion was a mixture of particularly stringent, Ashkenazi interpretations of Jewish law and intolerant personal embroidery. During the period of halakhic elaboration, now glossed as *tosafist* in medieval Northern Europe (a region commonly called *Ashkenaz*), it was indeed the case that wine touched by a Gentile after a certain point in its production was no longer considered kosher.[6] This (very onerous) legal stricture grew out of Talmudic concerns about *avodah zarah*, literally foreign work, which referred to idolatry and idolaters.[7] Rabbinic writers in the first centuries of the common era assumed that wine in non-Jewish hands was first and foremost used as a libation for idols, making it and anything with which it came in contact a source of apostasy and an affront to the one true God (Porton 1988, 252). The ban on libation wine was extended to any food that might contain wine or be used in heathen religious rituals. The restrictions on consuming kosher food cooked by non-Jews were also influenced by fears of aiding and abetting idolatry. The Talmudic term generally used for forbidden instances of such cooking, bishul akum, directly references idolaters, akum.

But early rabbis were simultaneously worried about the social implications of eating and, more particularly, drinking with the pagan nations. Such intimate social intercourse, it was argued, might lead to sexual intercourse and intermarriage. As the Talmud notes: "Their wine was forbidden on account of their daughters" (cited in Katz 1961a, 47). Indeed, well into the medieval period, when concerns about libation wine had virtually disappeared, many rabbinical scholars—but certainly not all[8]—continued to conflate Christians with idolaters, leaving the blanket Talmudic injunctions intact (Katz 1961a; Soloveitchik 1978). And even when halakhic thinkers reinterpreted those injunctions so as to disassociate Christians from idolaters, thus allowing for more Gentile contact with wine (particularly in its production phases) and Jewish contact with Gentile wine (for purposes of trade and debt repayment), the Ashkenazi prohibition against social (rather than simply economic) intercourse around wine and food remained (Soloveitchik 1978). Established social practice and medieval Ashkenazi revulsion at the perceived idolatry of Christians prevented this reclassification from vitiating the halakhic prohibitions on commensality (Berger 2002; Katz 1961a; Soloveitchik 1978). But this reclassification of Christians allowed for the loosening of a range of other social restrictions separating Jews and Gentiles, including, for example, the relatively intimate exchange of gifts. In non-Ashkenazi contexts, it had more direct consequences. There were several attempts by Sephardi halakhists to abolish the restrictions around wine entirely (Soloveitchik 1978, 178). And in places like Italy and Eastern Europe, widespread pragmatic dispensations made consumption of Gentile wine common (Katz 1961b).

Most crucially for the point I am trying to make, Mlle Chitrit presented a particularly stringent medieval halakhic interpretation without explaining its history or complexity. She dismissed a very reasonable student question as illogical and unthinkable. And she added her own very modern and perhaps irreligious disgust, disgust that seemed to reflect concerns about the fragility of racial distinction. The idea that wine merely *looked at* by a non-Jew would be dangerous and undrinkable is not part of any halakhic interpretation because it has nothing to do with the forms of interaction Jewish law strives to regulate. Her insistence that she refused to drink wine seen by a Gentile because she would rather be "safe than sorry" sounded suspiciously like contemporary racism with its theories of innate contagion. One has only to think of the widespread accusations in the southern United States against African Americans who were accused of violating white women with their eyes. The same extra-halakhic disgust applies to Mlle Chitrit's horror at the idea of socializing with business colleagues, allowing Jewish and non-Jewish children to play together or attend the same university classes, or inviting a non-Jewish neighbor into her house. Even in medieval Ashkenaz, maintaining cordial and even friendly relations with business partners was necessary and permitted; Jewish children were commonly apprenticed with other non-Jews to Gentile master tradesmen; and visiting non-Jewish households was regulated (in terms of ritual and food) but common (Katz 1961b). In fact, the importance of maintaining Christian good will for the sake of Jewish communal safety—what was called "preventing resentment" or "promoting peaceful relations"—*and* the glorification of God through exemplary Jewish conduct was a common halakhic justification for behaviors that allowed for the (temporary) crossing of Jewish-Gentile boundaries (ibid.).

Instead, Mlle Chitrit described a world in which even the most basic social contact between Jews and non-Jews appeared to open the door to ethnocide, turning non-Jewish neighbors into dangerous physical, as well as spiritual, enemies.

Did Mlle Chitrit intend for students to understand Judaism as an endangered racial identity? The answer to that question is unclear. But when she was confronted with the implications of such a student vision, she was religiously horrified. After Mlle Chitrit read a biblical passage in which the cries of young Ishmael—Abraham's son with his non-Jewish servant, Hagar—were heard and heeded by God, a shocked student asked: "God listens to the prayers of non-Jews?" Although Mlle Chitrit is hardly a conventional antiracist, she was disturbed by the question, which presumed that monotheism was impossible because religious differences reflected innate and unbridgeable differences between groups. In other words, the question presumed Jewishness as a race, and in the process, transformed the single God of Jewish monotheism into a tribal deity who jealously protected Jews and ignored everyone else. In fact, students frequently articulated visions of God that bordered on polytheism—often suggesting that there was a "Muslim" or "Christian" God who similarly took care of those who were "born" Muslim or Christian. Concerned about reinforcing the central message of monotheism, Mlle Chitrit shot back:

> Of course, and so what! There's a little bird that cries; he doesn't have anything to eat. What does HaShem [literally "the name," one of the most common ways religious Jews refer to God] do? He makes sure that the rain falls so that the worms come out of the earth so that the little bird can find something to eat. You need to know that. He does that for everyone. He's good, HaShem; he feeds everyone. And when I say everyone, that means everyone, even the little ant that you don't see but who sees you. HaShem feeds it.

But this reply may very well have reinforced the presumption that fueled the question in the first place. HaShem may feed everyone, but the only examples given were zoological ones.

With no pedagogical training and often little education in non-religious matters, religion teachers did not necessarily understand and certainly could not bridge the gap between the way they lived and understood Jewishness, on the one hand, and the assumptions and dispositions of their largely secular audience on the other. This forced students to poorly translate religious logics about collectivity and identity into terms that they understood—innate difference, inequality, and danger. Contrary to state intentions, the result was a very particular vision of Jewishness and a non-pluralist understanding of the foundation for livable political community.

We Are Jewish, Not French!

By funding—but not regulating—Jewish schools, the French state inadvertently created its own worst nightmare: a minority population that increasingly defined its religious differences not only in ontological terms, but also in opposition to "Frenchness." And in many ways, it has only itself to blame. The frenzied growth in Jewish schools over the last couple of decades would not have been possible without generous state financing that came, at least in part, at the expense of investment in public education in the difficult, multiethnic neighborhoods in which many Jewish day schoolers lived. In addition, the state's failure to enforce its own admission guidelines for publicly funded religious schools allowed Jewish schools to become havens from diversity of all kinds, whether that was internal Jewish difference or religious and ethnic pluralism. And finally, the state's decision not to create pedagogical requirements for religious instructors who teach in classrooms that it lights, heats, and maintains has helped a largely secular Jewish public understand their segregation as protection for a fragile form of racial difference *and* as a religious requirement.

This does not mean that the "assertive" secularists in France are right, that religious education in any form contributes to the growth of intolerance and the impossibility of pluralism. The example of Jewish day schools suggests something very different—that the context in which religious education is offered profoundly shapes the message. State funding that allows certain narrow communities (but not others) to opt out of sustained engagement with admittedly difficult forms of pluralism may be money poorly spent.[9] Ignoring the pedagogical qualifications of religious instructors whose work depends on facilities and captive audiences provided—at least in part—by the state may also be a mistake. As I have emphasized in this paper, the same religious content provided in a different social, physical, and pedagogical context might produce very different understandings of the meanings of Jewishness and Frenchness, as well as the contours of trust-based social and political community.

NOTES

1. The exception, as Ferrari notes, is in Alsace-Moselle, where the state still allows religious education in public schools.
2. This requirement was typically satisfied by the presentation of a *ketubah*, a contract certifying that the applicant's parents were married by a Consistorial or ultra-Orthodox rabbi, and therefore were both considered Jewish either by birth or conversion. In cases of intermarriage, children of Jewish mothers were eligible if the maternal grandmother's ketubah could be produced. Because Jewish law locates religious transmission in the maternal line, children with Jewish fathers and non-Jewish mothers were refused.
3. It is important to note that the Parisian bourgeoisie does not, in general, send their children to private schools. Public schools in well-heeled neighborhoods are still considered the most prestigious and promising educational route for those with the cultural capital to fully understand French educational hierarchies.
4. Some might say that this is a logical legacy of the Holocaust in France. There are a number of problems with this argument. Recall that Jewish schooling caters almost exclusively to a population that was spared most of the horrors of the Holocaust. In addition, students' parents and grandparents, who were generationally much closer to the horrors of World War II, did not necessarily share the dichotomous views of their children. And finally, as Maud Mandel (2003) has demonstrated, even Metropolitan Jews who lived through Vichy did not necessarily understand the experience as proof that Frenchness could not or would not accommodate Jewishness.
5. The director of a Haredi girls' school told me the story of a Moroccan Muslim family that was desperate to enroll their daughter so she could be in a protected, all-girls environment. Even when the director tried to dissuade them by emphasizing the amount of Hebrew and religious instruction offered, they remained interested.
6. For accounts of *yein nesekh*, or libation wine, see Katz (1961a) and Soloveitchik (1978; 2003).
7. By definition, idolaters do not conform to the seven noachide principles that make for "righteous" non-Jews.
8. Two major exceptions were, in the Spanish and then–North African context, Moses Maimonides (12th century), and in the halakhic tradition associated with *Ashkenaz*, what is now France and Germany, R. Menahem Ha-Me'iri (14th century) (Katz 1961a).
9. One can say the same thing for the other end of the class spectrum; state practices that allow the relatively wealthy to live in their own homogenous enclaves have their own nefarious consequences for pluralism.

BIBLIOGRAPHY

Agence France Presse. "Collège musulman d'Aubervilliers: 'Tout l'argent qui entre est tracé'." June 20, 2006.

Arkin, Kimberly. "Rhinestone Aesthetics and Religious Essence: Looking Jewish in Paris." *American Ethnologist* 36.4 (2009): 722–734.

——. *Rhinestones, Religion, and the Republic: Fashioning Jewishness in France*. Stanford, CA: Stanford University Press, 2014.

Battut, Jean, Christian Join-Lambert, and Edmond Vandermeersch. *1984: La guerre scolaire a bien eu lieu*. Paris: Desclée de Brouwer, 1995.

Baubérot, Jean. *Laïcité 1905–2005, entre passion et raison*. Paris: Éditions du Seuil, 2004.

Bellengier, Ferdinand. *Le chef d'établissement privé et l'Etat*. Paris: Berger-Levrault, 2004.

Berger, David. "Jacob Katz on Jews and Christians in the Middle Ages." In *The Pride of Jacob: Essays on Jacob Katz and His Work*. Edited by Jay Harris, 41–63. Cambridge, MA: Harvard University Press, 2002.

Bourdieu, Pierre. *Distinction: A Social Critique of the Judgment of Taste*. Translated by Richard Nice. Cambridge, MA: Harvard University Press, 1984.

Bowen, John. *Why the French Don't Like Headscarves: Islam, the State, and Public Space*. Princeton, NJ: Princeton University Press, 2007.

Brenner, Emmanuel, ed. *Les territoires perdus de la République: Antisémitisme, racisme et sexisme en milieu scolaire*. Paris: Mille et Une Nuits, 2002.

——. *France, prends garde de perdre ton âme: Fracture sociale et antisémitisme dans la République*. Paris: Mille et Une Nuits, 2004.

Cohen, Erik. *Les Juifs de France: Valeurs et identité*. Paris: Fonds Social Juif Unifié, 2002.

Comaroff, John, and Jean Comaroff. *Ethnography and the Historical Imagination*. Boulder, CO: Westview Press, 1992.

Davidenkoff, Emmanuel. "L'école catho veut un partage chrétien." *Libération*, September 21, 2005, p. 18.

Debray, Régis. "L'enseignement du fait religieux dans l'école laïque." Report for the National Education Minister, 2002. Available online, http://www.education.gouv.fr/cid2025/l-enseignement-du-fait-religieux-dans-l-ecole-laique.html. Accessed July 31, 2012.

Douglas, Mary. *Purity and Danger: An Analysis of the Concepts of Pollution and Taboo*. New York: Routledge, 2002 [1966].

Durkheim, Emile. *Moral Education: A Study in the Theory and Application of the Sociology of Education*. Translated by Everett Wilson. New York: Free Press of Glencoe, 2002 [1903].

Finkielkraut, Alain. *Au nom de l'autre: Réflexions sur l'antisémitisme qui vient*. Paris: Gallimard, 2003.

Foucault, Michel. *Discipline and Punish: The Birth of the Prison.* New York: Vintage Books, 1977.

Fourest, Caroline. *La tentation obscurantiste.* Paris: Grasset, 2005.

Georgel, Jacques, and Anne-Marie Thorel. *L'enseignement privé en France, du VIIIe au XXe siècle.* Paris: Dalloz, 1995.

Haymann, Emmanuel. Untitled. *Tribune Juive,* no. 541, November 10–16, 1978: 15.

Heilman, Samuel. "Quiescent and Active Fundamentalisms: The Jewish Cases." In *Accounting for Fundamentalisms.* Edited by Martin Marty and R. Scott Appleby, 173–196. Chicago: University of Chicago Press, 1994.

Hirsi Ali, Ayaan. *Infidel.* New York: New York Free Books, 2007.

Journal Officiel. "Compte rendu intégral des débats parlementaires, 1e séance," December 23 (Wednesday), 1959: 3595–3614.

Katz, Jacob. *Exclusiveness and Tolerance: Studies in Jewish-Gentile Relations in Medieval and Modern Times.* Westport, CT: Greenwood Press, 1961a.

———. *Tradition and Crisis: Jewish Society at the End of the Middle Ages.* Jerusalem: Hebrew University, 1961b.

Landrin, Sophie. "Une decision du rectorat de Lyon; Le college-lycée musulman de Décines ne sera pas autorisé à ouvrir." *Le Monde,* August 31, 2006: 12.

Mandel, Maud. *In the Aftermath of Genocide: Armenians and Jews in Twentieth-Century France.* Durham, NC: Duke University Press, 2003.

Neusner, Jacob. *Religion and Law: How through Halakhah Judaism Sets Forth Iits Theology and Philosophy.* Atlanta: Scholars Press, 1996.

Petit-Ohayon, Patrick, ed. *L'école juive en France 1945–2003; État des lieux.* Paris: Fonds Social Juif Unifié, Départment de l'Enseignement, 2003.

Porton, Gary. *Goyim: Gentiles and Israelites in Mishnah-Tosefta.* Atlanta: Scholars Press, 1988.

Poucet, Bruno. "L'application de la loi Debré." Paper presented at the conference Nouvelles approches de l'histoire de la laïcité au XXe siècle, held in Paris, November 18–19, 2005.

Soloveitchik, Haym. "Can Halakhic Texts Talk History?" *AJS Review* 3 (1978): 153–196.

———. "Rupture and Reconstruction: The Transformation of Contemporary Orthodoxy." *Tradition* 28.4 (1994): 64–130.

———. *Principles and Pressure: Jewish Trade in Gentile Wine in the Middle Ages.* Tel Aviv: Am Oved, 2003.

Stock-Morton, Phyllis. *Moral Education for a Secular Society: The Development of Morale Laïque in Nineteenth Century France.* Albany: State University of New York Press, 1988.

Strudel, Sylvie. *Votes juifs: itinéraires migratoires, religieux et politiques.* Paris: Presses de la foundation nationale des sciences politiques, 1996.

Taguieff, Pierre-André. *La République enlisée: Pluralisme, communautarisme et citoyenneté.* Paris: Editions Syrtes, 2005.

5

The Crises of Liberal Citizenship

RELIGION AND EDUCATION IN ISRAEL

Shlomo Fischer

Introduction

In this paper, I will discuss developments in citizenship education in Israel over the past fifteen years or so.[1] The basic movement that I will discuss is how the definitions of collective identity and the citizenship rules of the game, which had been implicit and taken for granted, became explicit and contested. As a result of this new contestation, state and educational elites mobilized religious citizenship discourses that were more group oriented and exclusionary. Yet, in dialectical fashion, due to the fact that religious citizenship discourse moved from a sectorial, or sectarian, context to being applied to general Israeli society—it also developed the potential to become more inclusive and open. I will now describe these processes in brief detail.

Israel was founded by the Jewish national movement, Zionism, as a Jewish nation-state. While the Jewish character of the state was mentioned explicitly in its Declaration of Independence on May 14, 1948, for the most part this crucial aspect of collective identity remained taken for granted and hence implicit in most citizen practices and discourses until the 1990s. In the 1990s—due to a host of factors including globalization, the successful integration of Israel into the world market economy, globalizing citizenship discourses that separated citizenship from ethnic-national identity (Soysal 1994), and the spread of a globalizing human rights regime—there arose in Israel a liberal citizenship discourse that began to challenge, at the edges, the collective definition of Israel as a Jewish nation-state (Shafir and Peled 2002). This development dovetailed with the increased assertiveness of Palestinian citizens of the state of Israel. Israeli-Palestinian intellectuals and leaders began to challenge the Jewish national definition of the state, and instead began to float alternative definitions such as a "Multi-cultural State," a Bi-National State, or a "State of all its Citizens" (together with the demand for a separate Palestinian state in the territories occupied by Israel since 1967 alongside the multicultural or binational state of Israel). These definitions entailed either denaturing the public sphere of its Jewish character or advocating collective group rights for the Palestinians. As we shall see, these developments had a noticeable effect on civics curricula and textbooks during this period.

In the first decade of the 21st century, certain sectors of the Jewish majority elites began to initiate academic, legal, educational, and Parliamentary reactions to these attempts to articulate a new citizenship discourse and new definitions of collective identity. The first reaction was academic and legal. Scholars such Amnon Rubenstein, Alexander Yakobson (Yakobson and Rubenstein 2009), and Ruth Gavsion (Gavison 1999) denied the claim that liberal citizenship conceptions excluded the possibility of maintaining a national state and necessarily implied "a state of all its citizens" or a "multi-cultural state." They stressed the fact that the Wilsonian right of self-determination is a liberal right and that the Jews along with other nationalities possessed this right. They argued that the State of Israel fulfilled this right, just as an independent Palestine would fulfill this right for the Palestinians.

Other reactions were Parliamentary and political. After "Operation Cast Lead" in Gaza during the winter of 2009–2010 and the Goldstone Report, a perception grew in certain circles that Israeli human rights organizations were involved in an effort to delegitimize and ultimately dismantle the State of Israel. This applied not only to the occupation of the West Bank and the interdiction of Gaza, but also to the Israeli state in general. Accordingly, right-wing parties in Israel initiated Parliamentary investigations of human rights groups and legislation demanding that they make their funding transparent. While some of these initiatives are blatantly illiberal and restrictive of free speech and freedom of information, there was a widespread feeling in the Israeli public that human rights NGO's needed more transparency and regulation. Despite this feeling, and because of their severely illiberal character, many of these initiatives have been frozen or rejected by the government, and only a few have been passed in revised or diluted forms. Nevertheless, this feeling persists and seems to be the basis for a new Jewish exclusivist basic law, "The State of Israel as the Nation-State of the Jewish People," which was initiated recently by right-wing parliamentarians in the current Knesset (elected in January 2013).

This paper will be specifically concerned with reactions to these events in the field of education. Starting in 2009, religious right-wing elements started to attack the Ministry of Education's textbooks and curricula in high school civics classes as placing too much emphasis upon individual rights, rather than stressing Jewish national identity, loyalty, and obligations. Furthermore, they claimed it served a post-Zionist or anti-Zionist agenda and advanced Palestinian claims. These attacks demanded that alongside the liberal conception of democracy that stressed individual rights, the civics curricula should also teach communitarian or republican versions of democracy, which place much more stress upon the group and upon group membership and obligations (Geiger 2009). With the advent of the right-wing Netanyahu government, these charges were taken up by the Pedagogical Secretariat of the Ministry of Education. The Ministry is now implementing new changes and guidelines in civic education. Toward that end, it is also enlisting religious conceptions of citizenship that are more communitarian and republican in nature. However, as I indicated above, these religious conceptions themselves are undergoing a transformation as they leave the arena of sectarian discourse and become part of the general Israeli public sphere.

In what follows, I shall give a detailed description and analysis of this process. To make my explication easier to follow, I shall start off with mapping the Israeli population and society in general, and follow with a mapping of the educational system. I shall conclude the first part of this paper with a description of the rise of the liberal citizenship discourse and its impact upon civics education.

The second part of this paper describes the discourses of democracy and citizenship among the religious Zionist community and in religious Zionist education. In this part, I will discuss how these discourses are rooted in religious Zionist theology and how this theology is applied to democracy and citizenship in Israel today. In the latter text of the second part, I will discuss the relationship of these discourses of democracy and citizenship to the new liberal citizenship discourse and the new civics education initiatives, undertaken under the inspiration of the new liberal discourse.

A Brief Mapping of Israeli Society

I shall begin with mapping out Israeli society, and then proceed to a mapping of its educational institutions. According to the latest Central Bureau of Statistics (CBS) surveys, over 75 percent of the population is Jewish, 20 percent is Arab, and about 5 percent do not fall into either category. These 5 percent consist of foreign workers (from China, Thailand, Ghana, and Latin America), refugees and migrants (from Sudan, Eritrea, and Somalia), and immigrants, mainly from the former Soviet Union, who are eligible for citizenship because of one Jewish parent or grandparent, but are not recognized by the Orthodox religious law or by the state as Jewish. Most in this latter category are sociologically Jewish.

The first and foremost classification categories in Israel are national. The most basic difference is between Jews and Palestinian Arabs. Both are citizens of the state, but Israel is a Jewish nation-state. In this manner it was defined in its Declaration of Independence, and thus it is defined in its Basic [constitutional] Laws ("Jewish and Democratic State"). The roots of the current shape of the Israeli-Palestinian community lie in the defeat of that community in the 1948 war. Of the 800,000 Arabs who lived within the borders of Israel before the war, only about 100,000 remained at the signing of the ceasefire in 1949. The rest either fled or were expelled. The Arab urban centers of Jaffa and Haifa had mostly been destroyed. (There are differing and highly contested narratives about the events of the 1948 war, and giving them adequate treatment would require its own book.) Of the Arabs that remained, most were illiterate fellahin. In the sixty-five years of Israeli sovereignty, universal male literacy in Arabic and Hebrew has been nearly achieved, and the population has become increasingly middle class (especially in the past ten years; Haider 2011). Israeli-Palestinian Arabs belong to the same ethnic-national group—Palestinians—that Israel has been in violent conflict with since its inception. From 1948 through 1965, as a defeated enemy, Palestinian Arabs were under military rule. In 1965, military rule was lifted, but Palestinians and Palestinian Arab municipalities continued to be discriminated against in various ways.

Over the decades, Israeli-Arabs have become increasingly politicized and autonomous in their political behavior. They are represented by about fifteen seats in the Knesset and organized into three political parties. Its leadership and intellectual classes have repeatedly stated that it does not identify with Israel as a Jewish state, and they have called for it to shed its Jewish identity and redefine itself either as "a state for all its citizens," "a multi-cultural state," or as a binational state entailing equal group rights for its Palestinian citizens alongside the creation of an exclusive Palestinian state (High Follow-Up Committee for the Arabs in Israel and National Committee for the Heads of the Arab Local Authorities in Israel 2006).

The common-sense understanding held by the majority of Jewish society in Israel is that it is divided into various sectors, according to degrees of adherence to the Jewish religion. Social science research reflects this understanding and attempts, through surveys and interviews, to establish the magnitude and the boundaries of the various sectors. The two measures commonly used in surveys are either self-definition or the degree of observance. According to these measures, the Observant—or Orthodox—population constitutes about 20 percent of the population, traditionist Jews (who selectively adhere to some of the religious observances and have an explicitly religious worldview) are another 39 percent, and non-Observant or "secular" Jews constitute about another 41 percent. Non-Observant Jews have an avowedly non-religious worldview, and the extent to which they participate in religious observances is mostly done for national, cultural, or traditional reasons (Central Bureau of Statistics 2011).

The Orthodox population itself is divided into two central "sectors." One sector, which constitutes about 8 percent of the Jewish population, is the non-Zionist Haredi, or ultra-Orthodox sector. This sector distinguishes itself not only by a strict observance of religious practice, but also by the fact that many of its adult males do not work, especially between the ages of twenty to forty, nor do the men and women of this sector participate in military service, which in Israel, in principle, is universal. Rather, these men devote themselves to studying the Torah within the framework of religious academies. Such study does not preclude marriage and most of them have large families (typically five or more children). This salient fact of Haredi existence is part of a larger pattern. The Haredi population constitutes an enclave with high barriers of dress, residence, and education (Sivan 2003). This population is non-Zionist insofar as it is indifferent or hostile to the modern Zionist nationalist project of establishing a Jewish national state. At the same time, it is highly ethnocentric and easily adopts xenophobic and extreme nationalist positions. Thus the Haredi political parties form part of the right-wing political bloc. According to a recent survey of democratic attitudes conducted by the Israel Democracy Institute, 72 percent of Haredi ultra-Orthodox Jews object to equal rights between Jewish and Arab citizens of Israel (Israel Democracy Institute 2010). The

Haredim have about sixteen members of the Parliament and are also part of the governing coalition.

The other Orthodox sector, which constituted about 12 percent of the Jewish population in 2009 (Central Bureau of Statistics 2011), is the religious Zionist sector. This population is well integrated into the general Israeli-Jewish population. Its adult men and women work in the general economy, and a substantial portion of it is middle class. Its young men and some of its young women perform military service. Indeed, a substantial percentage of elite combat and commando units are composed of young religious Zionist males, and religious Zionist make up about 30 percent of the junior officer corps (B. 2010), while they represent only about 12 percent of the Jewish population. Religious Zionist young men and women also attend higher education and are well represented in the academy, in the o learned professions of law and medicine as well as in high-tech economic sectors. Thus, while to a certain extent the religious Zionist sector has its own residential quarters and educational institutions, it is much less oriented toward an "enclave" mentality. It does seriously observe the religious ordinances; however, it has a somewhat more relaxed attitude, especially with regards to mixing the sexes.

Over the previous generation or two, it was considered that Jewish religious observance was orthogonal to national and political commitments, and that observant Jews could be found across the political spectrum; since the late 1960s and 1970s, this has no longer been the case. After the 1967 and 1973 wars, the religious Zionist community has led the settlement effort in the West Bank and Gaza and has adopted an orientation of integral nationalism. This orientation has gotten sharper or more extreme over the years. Thus in the 1970s and 1980s, leading rabbis affiliated with the Jewish Orthodox religious Zionist community affirmed equal rights for Arab citizens of the State of Israel, if they recognized the Jewish character of the state and that the state "belongs" to the Jewish people (Fischer 2007). Moreover, while *Gush Emunim*—the settlement movement of the religious Zionist Orthodox Jews—called for the annexation of the West Bank and Gaza to the Israeli state, it explicitly stated that the Palestinan residents of these territories would receive full citizen rights—again, if they recognized the Jewish character of the state (Gush Emunim).

In contrast to this, since the Oslo accords of the early 1990s, the religious Zionist community has developed an active discourse denying full citizenship rights, particularly active political rights, to the Arab citizens of Israel, and in particular with regard to major questions of war, peace, and national identity (Fischer 2007). In the past five years, this trend has exacerbated itself with religious Zionist rabbinic pronouncements prohibiting the renting of apartments and the hiring of Arab citizens of the State of Israel (Tesslar 2010; Valmer 2011b). According to an Israel Democracy Institute (IDI) survey, 65 percent of the "religious" population objects to equal rights for Arabs (Israel Democracy Institute 2010).

The IDI survey in general claimed that objecting to equal rights for Arabs highly correlated with a level of religiosity. Only 33 percent of the "secular" population had such objections, as opposed to 51 percent of the traditionist population. Nevertheless, it should be born in mind that 86 percent of the total Jewish population believe that critical decisions for the state should be taken by a Jewish majority. A total of 53 percent also maintain that the state is entitled to encourage Arabs to emigrate from Israel.

The Israeli state privileges one form of religion: Jewish Orthodoxy. The Chief Rabbinate is an Israeli state institution, and the state funds and sponsors Jewish Orthodox synagogues, cemeteries, and educational institutions as well as Kashruth (Jewish Orthodox dietary laws) regulations. It also funds and sponsors Muslim and Christian houses of worship, cemeteries, and schools. The Knesset (Parliament) in 1953 awarded control over marriage, divorce, and personal status to the respective religious communities: to the Chief Rabbinate above all, but also to the Muslim and various Christian communities (Greek Orthodox, Catholic, Maronite, etc.). Non-Orthodox Jewish denominations are not accorded official recognition and are, for the most part, not funded by the state.

The Educational System in Israel

The educational system mirrors the divisions of society. There are four state educational systems in Israel.[2] The first is the State General Educational system (State Education Law—1953). This system is designed for Israeli-Jewish non-Orthodox children. The language of instruction is Hebrew, and the cultural content is roughly nationalist Israeli-Jewish. In recent years, there has been more emphasis on instrumental disciplines (Math and English) than on traditional identity-building disciplines (the Bible and Jewish history).[3] The vast majority of students are either secular or come from traditionist backgrounds. However, there is a small minority of Arab and Bedouin students in some schools.

The second state school system is that of the Arab sector (Abu-Asbeh 2007). Here, the language of instruction is Arabic and Hebrew and is taught as a second language from second grade on. Palestinian or Arab identity-building subjects, such as history, are discouraged. This sector is under the overall supervision of the Ministry of Education and to varying degrees, the security services.

The third state school system is the State Religious system. According to the State Education Law—1953, the state religious school system is to provide autonomous curricula and supervision for those subjects that are relevant to "the [Jewish Orthodox] religious way of life." From a statutory point of view, the supervision of this system is in the hands of an autonomous Council on State Religious System, which is appointed by the government (generally at the behest of the National Religious Party). The vast majority of students come from the religious Zionist sector or from traditionist home backgrounds.

The fourth school system is the Haredi, or ultra-Orthodox, networks (Vargan 2007). These have varying legal statuses. One—the Shas system—is a bona fide state system funded entirely by the Ministry of Education. Some are non-state systems recognized by the government, which contributes considerably to their funding. Others are not recognized and do not receive substantial government funds. The state does not supervise their curricula. For the most part, these networks only offer religious studies. These networks resist the introduction of what are called the core curricula—math, English, Hebrew language, and civics. (They generally cover Hebrew language in their own internal curricula.)

Israeli Civic Culture until the 1980s

From the early part of the 20th century (and especially from 1932) until May 1977, the major factor in Zionist immigration, settlement, and state building in Mandatory Palestine and in the State of Israel was the Labor Zionist movement. This carried a collectivist, republican social democratic vision of nationalist construction and state building (Eisenstadt 1967; Shafir and Peled 2002). At the heart of its vision of citizenship was the republican virtue of contribution to the national Jewish collective. It constructed a corporatist-state economy built upon cooperative ventures (the kibbutz and moshav), industries owned by the nationalist labor federation (the Histadrut), and the state. It privileged unobservant male Jews of European origin (*Ashkenazim*) who were active in the Labor Zionist economic, political, and military frameworks. It considered these to be a nationalist vanguard contributing to the national Jewish collective. It excluded—to one degree or another—Arabs, women, Jews from North Africa and the Middle East (*Sepharadim* or *Mizrachim*), and Orthodox and traditionist Jews.

The Labor Zionist movement led the State of Israel from its founding in 1948 to 1977, and very much resembled similar collectivist, "secular," state-building elites in Turkey, India, Russia, and Mexico. Though the State of Israel formally extended citizenship privileges to the Arabs in its territory without regard to religion, nationality, etc., Israel was avowedly a nationalizing nation- state and worked to advance (a certain version of) the interests of the Israeli-Jewish population. Only Israeli-Jews were truly awarded full membership (especially if they were male and Ashkenazi). The regime consisted of Parliamentary democracy. Even though the Supreme Court guaranteed basic freedoms (Agranat 1953), there was no written constitution guaranteeing civil rights as well as no explicit doctrine of judicial review. The central values conveyed in this period in the school system were that of Zionist nationalism (Adar and Adler 1965). Society maintained a somewhat totalist character, and the state controlled most of the avenues of communication. The civics curriculum consisted of one hour a week in twelfth grade, which equaled one unit of matriculation credit, and focused upon the technical procedures of government.

The Introduction of Liberal Citizenship Discourse

Starting in the mid-1980s, Israel started to slowly dismantle its statist-corporatist economic regime (Shalev 1992), introducing neoliberal economic policies as well as integration into the world market economy. In order to facilitate and accommodate this change—and to bring its culture, economy, and politics into closer alignment—its leading elites started to introduce a liberal citizenship discourse (Shafir and Peled 2002). As I have indicated above, other related factors that brought about this change included globalization and labor force population flows, globalizing citizenship discourses that separated citizenship from ethnic-national identity (Soysal 1994), and the spread of a globalizing human rights regime (Shafir and Peled 2002). The institutional expressions of this change were constitutional legislation that guaranteed human and civil rights (Basic Law: Human Dignity and Freedoms—1993), the formulation of an explicit doctrine of judicial review (Barak 2002, 2006, 1998), and the strengthening of the Bank of Israel as an autonomous arm of policy making. In connection with this new orientation, the Supreme Court gave favorable rulings in regard to gay and women's rights.

The introduction of liberal citizenship discourse also opened up the issue of the place and status of the non-Jewish citizens of the state, particularly the Palestinian Arabs. One very important issue in connection with this is land policy. About 14 percent of the land in Israel belongs to "the Jewish People," that is, the Jewish National Fund. Kibbutzim, moshavim, and individuals lease such land for forty-nine or ninety-nine years. Such land is generally not permitted to Arab leasers. An Arab family (Ka'adan) disputed this by claiming that such discrimination challenged their civil rights and sued in the Supreme Court (sitting as the High Court of Equity). The Supreme Court ducked the issue by deciding the case on a technicality (Schmidt 2001; Barak 1999).

The desire to integrate into the world market economy was also a major factor in the initiation of the Oslo peace process as well as attempts to resolve the Israel-Arab and Israel-Palestinian conflicts. In connection with this, the new discourse of human rights was adopted by NGO's opposed to Israel's occupation of the West Bank and Gaza, especially B'Tzelem and the Association for Civil Rights in Israel, as well as Amnesty. Israeli-Arab and general human rights organizations started to sue both the Israeli government and the IDF for human rights violations of Palestinians (Galchinsky 2008). Both of these processes—the advent of liberal citizenship discourse and the peace process—empowered the Israeli-Palestinian Arab community first to utilize this discourse to challenge the discrimination against the Israeli-Arab community, and second, to challenge the definition of the state claiming that the very definition of the state as Jewish violated basic liberal tenets of equality and the neutrality of the public sphere. As we have seen, in its stead they posited "a state of all its citizens," a "multi-cultural" state, or a binational state (Rouhana 1997). The general "post-Zionist" ambience also found expression in the work of the "New Historians" (Benny Morris, Avi Shlaim, and Ilan Pappe), which challenged prevalent Israeli national myths and narratives and the work of critical sociologists.

Effects upon the Civics Curricula

These changes also had a noticeable effect upon the teaching of civics. In the 1990s and the first decade of the 21st century, educational and academic elites attempted to align civics with the new liberal citizenship discourse. The assassination of Prime Minister Rabin in November 1995 by a Jewish Orthodox activist who was opposed to the peace process provided additional impetus for revising the civics curricula. The first stage in this attempt was the Kremnitzer Committee (headed by Prof. Mordechai Kremnitzer of the Hebrew University Law School) and the interim report that it produced. The committee was appointed in May 1995 and issued its interim report in February 1996 (Civics Education Steering Committee 1996).

The Kremnitzer Committee interim report stressed that civics education in Israel must emphasize liberal and democratic values instead of mere technical procedures, and especially laid great emphasis on individual human and civil rights. It also recommended that civics education be expanded from one year of instruction in the twelfth grade to other grades in elementary, junior high and high schools. It envisioned that shared Israeli citizenship would cease to be merely a technical category and would become a meaningful category of collective identity.

The Kremnitzer Commission's report was adopted by the Ministry of Education, which began to take various concrete steps to implement it. The first was a new textbook written by a staff headed by Prof. Benny Neuberger of the Open University (Ministry of Education 2001). This textbook devoted a long and well-written section to democratic and liberal values, especially those concerned with individual rights. The title of the book is *To be Citizens in Israel: A Jewish and Democratic State* (Jerusalem: Ministry of Education, 2001). Thus, it mentioned the Jewish character of Israel in its title and it devoted its opening section to Israel as a Jewish nation-state. That section, however, seems to be poorly conceived; it is convoluted and difficult to teach. The book also included a large section on "Divisions in the State of Israel." The section on Arab society was written by Dr. Assad Ghannem, one of the authors of *The Future Vision of the Palestinian Arabs in Israel* (Nazareth, Israel: National Committee for the Heads of Arab Local Authorities in Israel, 2006), which called for ending the Jewish definition of the state. *To be Citizens in Israel* was published simultaneously in Hebrew and Arabic and became the prime textbook in all the state educational systems (general, state religious, and Arab). Its publication coincided with a decision to unify civics teaching across all the sectors. The rationale for this is that citizenship is what the various sectors have in common and it should form the basis of a common civic identity.

Together with the creation of a new textbook, the Ministry of Education also set up new teacher training programs in the universities and teachers' colleges. The purpose of these programs was to give a new disciplinary grounding to the subject of civics (in Political Science) and to increase the training and professionalism of civics teachers. During the tenure of Prof. Yulie Tamir as Minster of Education, civics education was expanded to include two matriculation units, in addition to being taught in ninth- and eleventh-grade classrooms as well as in the twelfth grade.

Democracy and Civics among the Religious Zionist Community and in the State Religious School System

All of these changes affected the state religious school system as well. As we shall see, it elicited a complex response that also impinged upon the general state school system. In order to understand this response, it is now necessary to briefly explicate the major discourse of democracy and citizenship that the religious Zionist sector created, and that which was derived from its own religiously based understanding of Jewish nationalism. This discourse is theologically based and has strong republican and communitarian orientations with a noticeable exclusivist strain.

Theology and Politics

Radical religious Zionism is a resurgent religious movement.[4] It is also part of the Jewish Zionist national movement. This link between religion and nationalism has resulted in a new, transformed Jewish theology. At the center of this theology is granting religious meaning to the material, secular, mundane world and bringing this world under religious regulation. Initially, this meant especially the granting of religious meaning to the secular mundane realms of nation building—politics, settlement, and economic and cultural production.

In order to achieve this, the major stream of radical religious Zionist theology employed an intellectual structure (taken from early-19th-century Idealism and Romanticism) that the philosopher Charles Taylor has called "expressivist" (Taylor 1977, 1–13). According to this structure, spiritual phenomena such as Divine ideals and perfection find their most complete realization when expressed in the material, mundane world. Conversely, phenomena of the material world reach their most adequate self-realization when expressing their spiritual "inner form." According to the expressivist conception of the radical religious Zionist community—within all finite-created material creatures, there is an inner will to become reunited with its source in God.[5]

These central theological ideas are connected, respectively, to equally central political-theological ideas that also have an expressivist character (Fischer 2007, 215–269). The first such idea is connected to the notion just discussed—that the inner authentic will of each finite, material creature is to return to one's source in God. One very major way that the individual recovers and realizes his authentic self and will is by identifying with the "universal generalness," or the *general will*, of the collective-cosmic entities outside of him. In a manner reminiscent of Rousseau, one crucially important method of recovering this inner authentic will is by identifying with the general (or universal) collectivities of the Jewish people, humankind, and the cosmos.

In this path, one concentrates upon the inner will of the cosmic entities that are outside the individual. The aim of this effort is for every particular being to recognize and experience itself as belonging to the all-embracing, all-inclusive *All*, and to recognize the connection of the All with God. As every particular being overcomes its own particularity and partialness and identifies with the universal, it reveals its own inner will, which is to identify with the universal and with God (Cohen 1963b, 17–38).

The will of each particular being to experience itself as part of the divinely rooted All is itself rooted in the fact that the inner will of each particular being is a "spark" or a part of the cosmic general will (הרצון הכללי) (Kook 1963b, vol. 3, p. 39; Cohen 1963b, 29–30). For much of the history of the world, this inner will animating the world is "blind" and not conscious of itself and its origins (Strassberg-Dayan 1995, 136; Kook 1984,[6] 29–31, 234–236). As the individual identifies with the generality, with the divine All of existence, he realizes and makes conscious his own inner will and the inner will of the cosmos as a whole.

The realization of the inner will of the finite elements is accomplished by action in the world. This is true on both the universal and on the national levels. On the universal level, as the world develops in law, mores, social institutions, literature, philosophy, and art—progressing toward the Good, the Moral and Beautiful—it realizes its inner unity and rootedness in God and becomes increasingly conscious of it (Strassberg-Dayan 1995, 137–138; Kook 1984, 243–245). Similarly on the national level, the universal Whole of Israel achieves realization through the concrete activity of the national renaissance—nation building and territorial repatriation to the

Land of Israel. The general/universal is realized in public-national activities relative to the nation as a whole, and not to any particular individual or sector.

The second central political-theological notion is that of the *divine state*. This idea derives from the notion that God fulfills himself by clothing and embodying his divine ideals in the mundane material world. In a manner very similar to Hegel's political thought, R. Kook (the spiritual leader of the radical religious Zionist movement) and his followers considered the (modern) state to be the most appropriate vehicle for the embodiment of divine ideals because it is the most all-inclusive, all-embracing human framework. Thus, it reflects the universal all-embracing nature of the Divine. The Jewish state in particular (because of the intimate relations of Israel and God in Jewish theology) is considered to be an emanation of God. R. Kook and his followers considered that the frameworks of the Jewish state that organize the public collective life of the entire Jewish people represent the Divine ideals embodying themselves in the material world. Thus, R. Kook considered this Jewish state to be the Foundation of God's Throne in the World (Kook 1963a, 160).

According to the notion of the Divine state, it is the *state itself* that has to embody the Divine ideals of peace, righteousness, and justice. In his writing, R. Kook contrasts the embodiment of these ideals in the existence of the collective national body and the state that it organizes with the morality of mere individuals, no matter how saintly. The collective national-political entity has a life and is a being in its own right. In R. Kook's ideal political community, "righteousness and justice" are embodied in the norms and mores of the community and constitute its animating spirit that the individuals partake of and participate in (as in Hegel's conception, the individuals participate in the life of the community and its norms and mores). The individual righteousness of "the wise, the pious and the holy ascetics" are viewed by R. Kook as not sufficient; the collective public life of the community must embody "righteousness and justice" (Kook 1963a, 104).

As in the thought of Hegel, the creation of a public-statist organization of the collective life of the Jewish people that realizes Divine ideals is the result of a complex dialectical historical process. Also, as in Hegel's philosophy, human beings are actors in a drama that is not fully theirs, but belongs to God who fulfills himself by expressing and embodying his Ideals in the material and mundane world. Thus, human beings are not fully conscious of the meanings and ends of their own actions. With the exception of a few saintly mystics who can apprehend synoptically the entire historical process, humans will only understand the meaning of their history at its end, with the "fullness of time." Thus, they will understand that they were the means by which God embodied his Ideals in the mundane world and achieved self-realization.

The Application of Political Theological Ideas to Israeli Political Reality

R. Kook expressed these ideas on the abstract metaphysical plane. His disciples, especially his son R. Tzvi Yehuda, translated them to concrete Israeli political reality. R. Tzvi Yehuda designated the concrete, mundane, secular State of Israel to be the *divine state*, embodying the realization of the Divine Ideals in the Kingdom of God. Thus, he and his followers accorded the Israeli state and its institutions great loyalty, honor, and obedience. In the 1960s and 1970s, after the Six Day War (1967) and the 1973 war between Israel and its neighboring Arab countries—under R. Tzvi Yehuda's leadership, R. Kook's followers embarked upon the campaign to settle the Greater Land of Israel (including the West Bank and Gaza) and incorporate it into the Israeli state, claiming that such a policy—like the Zionist movement itself—was the *general will* of the Jewish people. According to R. Tzvi Yehuda, Jews from all walks of life and ideological orientations, religious and secular, rightists and leftists, participated in this historical movement (Fischer 2007, 235–269).

Both of these leading political theological ideas brought about an orientation of endorsing democracy—in the sense of a government that expresses the will of the people, and is based upon its consent. The major theme of the discourse of radical religious Zionism concerning political theory is that the Torah supports the realization of the (Jewish) people's will and their consent in regard to government, hence the Torah supports democracy in the sense of rule of the people (*demos-cratia* [demos = people] + [cratia = rule]). This argument is found with greater frequency and centrality among Kookist writers on the subject of democracy than any other argument. While various expressivist religious Zionist writers will respectively tend to adduce differing arguments for or against democracy, they, very frequently—possibly in the majority of cases—will return to this argument and give it saliency. Furthermore, Kookist educational materials that specifically address the issue of Torah and democracy all prominently display and discuss this claim.

I suggest that this emphasis upon the people's will and consent is due to the expressivist infrastructure of Kookist thought and culture as well as its two central religio-political ideas—the general will and the divine state. As we have seen, the inner, general will of the Jewish people is a central theological and political notion for Kookists. This general will carries the inner purpose of God and the cosmos as a whole—which is that the cosmos manifest and realize its true Godly nature. Thus, the will of the Jewish people is a central religious value and its realization is the central means for realizing the ultimate eschatological redemption. As we have seen, according to Kookist ideology, this general will receives concrete expression in the exercise of the people's will in the politics of the Jewish state. At the same time, the State of Israel is the divine state that organizes the public-collective life of the entire people of Israel in its general state frameworks. This public-collective life, it will be recalled, is the embodiment of God's emanating and clothing himself in the material word. Its will is hence the divine will progressing toward the realization of divine ideals in the material world. The will, then, of the people of Israel—expressed empirically in the concrete Jewish state—has divine sanction. Thus, the expressivist "will of the people" argument draws support for political democracy (in the restricted sense of the rule of the people) from the deepest layers of Kookist religious conceptions and sentiment: the will of the people is both the inner will of the Jewish people striving toward union with God and the will of God striving to realize itself in the material world (Fischer 2007).

Within the Jewish Orthodox context, the radical religious Zionist approach to democracy is not a trivial one. For many of its adherents, especially its non-Zionist ultra-Orthodox ones, Orthodox Judaism is considered to be at odds with democracy for at least two reasons. The first is its heteronymous character. Orthodox Judaism is considered to be a religion of commandments deriving from divine fiat: God issued commandments and Jews are expected to obey. There seems to be no place for the autonomous will of the people. Secondly, the political form associated with Orthodox Judaism is commonly regarded as monarchy, as it is written in the book of Deuteronomy: "then thou mayest appoint a king over thee, whom the Lord thy God shall choose," (Deut. 17:15).[1]

---

1. The Holy Scriptures, Koren Publishers Jerusalem, 1977, "The English text revised and edited by Harold Fisch.

Expressivist religious Zionist writers dealt with both of these objections in terms of a common strategy—the will of the people is the will of God. Thus, they are at pains to demonstrate that a king is never, according to Jewish religious law, imposed upon the people, rather he is chosen by the people in a manner that reflects the expression of their will (for example, see Bin-Nun 2001; Zoldan 2001; Ministry of Education, 2001). Furthermore, the moment his rule ceases to rest upon the people's consent, it loses its legitimacy—and in legal terms, the king becomes a commoner. Expressivist religious Zionist writers state explicitly that the importance of the consent of the people—in legitimating political rule—is grounded theologically in the notion that the will of the people—expressed in the political process—reflects the will of God. This they claim (citing noted medieval authorities) is the plain sense of the verse in Deutronomy, cited above. Furthermore, they explicate this ideal by additionally stating that, in fact, the king acts only on the basis of power delegated to him by the people, and that the fount of all political power and legitimacy is the inherent right of the people to govern themselves (Bin-Nun 2001; Zoldan 2001). In support of this, they refer to the famous statement by R. Kook: "Since the laws of kings extend to the general affairs of the nation, it would seem in the absence of a king the prerogatives of these laws revert to the nation as a whole" (Kook 1966, sec. 144, p. 15) They revert back to the nation as whole, because they derived from the nation in the first place.

This understanding forms the basis of the legitimacy that expressivist religious Zionist writers extend to the contemporary democratic government of Israel. Just as the people can delegate power to a monarch, they can delegate power to a democratically elected Parliament, Prime Minister, and cabinet. Thus, expressivist religious Zionist writers hold that it is a religious duty to respect and obey the duly elected officials of the State of Israel.

This expressivist outlook regarding the political legitimacy of the people's will and democracy also reached a broad audience through education materials. Such materials were produced for informal educational frameworks (Zoldan n.d.) and formal school frameworks (Bramson 1985; Aviner 1996). Being formal educational materials, these curricula attempt to combine and balance an expressivist commitment to the political centrality of the people's will, with a haredi-halachic commitment to the heteronymous dictations of the Torah. While the realization of "the holy"—or the realization of religious ideals in and through the political, social, and cultural life of the state—is the ultimate aim of Kookist ideology, its first aim in educational frameworks is to inscribe in the outlooks, norms, and habits of its adherents, the moment of "the religious"—or rather, to instill an absolute, overriding commitment to the total, punctilious observance of the Halacha (Jewish religious law).

As a result, educational curricula (e.g., Bramson 1985; Aviner 1996) are often more conservative than theological or halachic writing on this subject. They do insist that the people's will is the font of all political legitimacy, and they recognize the democratic—and hence religious—legitimacy of the contemporary government of Israel. At the same time, they emphasize that the government must at all times follow Jewish religious norms, and they adduce Maimonides' ruling that if the government (the king) arbitrarily orders one to violate a religious norm, the order must be disobeyed. Furthermore, they cite a Talmudic tradition that all communal regulations must be approved by an "important [rabbinical] personage" (b. Bava Batra 9a).

Expressivist Religious Zionist Republicanism and Ethno-Nationalism

The religious Zionist conception has a decided republican cast. Religious Zionist writers explains that the term עם—which I have rendered as "people"—in the concept of שלטון העם—rule of the people—"relates to a national entity, that is, the People of Israel, in its historical and cultural totality" (Aviner 1996, 56); and not to a collection of contracting individuals.[7] In other words, the people who is sovereign and whose "will" legitimates democratic government is a corporate, collective, even holistic entity.

What are the implications for citizenship of this ethno-republican conception of democracy? What in fact will be the place and rights of non-Jews who do not belong to the national *demos* of the Jewish people? To this question we find several answers, some of which are more inclusive than others. One approach—which is perhaps more characteristic of earlier decades in the history of the state—is to extend to the non-Jewish and especially Arab population of the state full formal political and citizenship rights on the conditions that such an extension does not harm the Jewish character of the state, nor negates the understanding that the state "belongs" to the Jewish people.

An alternative approach involves curtailing the political rights of non-Jewish citizens. This latter approach has gained adherents in recent years with the advent of individualist liberal democracy in Israel and the various attempts at a peace process. We can speak of a "hardening of the line" in the 1990s and in the current century: a feeling that if equal political rights physically and politically endangers the Jewish State of Israel, then they must be sacrificed for the higher good of the Jewish nation-state (Ben Artzi 2002).

Curricula published in the 1990s that hold to this ethno-republican conception make an attempt to respond to the new "liberal citizenship discourse" that had taken hold in Israel since the 1980s and had intensified in the 1990s. One very important and mainstream curriculum whose author is very close to the leadership of the West Bank settlers movement (Aviner 1996) includes a chapter entitled "A Democratic Regime vs. the Culture of Democracy" (בין משטר דמוקרטי לתרבות הדמוקרטיה). This discusses the theme of liberal democracy and its non-compatibility with the Torah and normative traditional Judaism. R. Elisha Aviner, the author of the curriculum, does not use the term "liberal democracy" or "liberal citizenship"; rather, he marks the phenomenon that he talks of as "the culture of democracy," which he distinguishes from a "democratic regime." In his reading, "democratic culture" represents a system of ultimate values that is designed to *replace* Judaism as a central component of Israeli identity. These values include an extreme individualism that talks exclusively in a language of "rights" and not of duties, and endorses atomizing economic competition and "self-realization." Secondly, they include an extreme universalism, or cosmopolitism. The new democratic culture does not recognize the essential importance of national groupings, nor of national history or culture. The world is made up of a cosmopolitan "humanity" that is composed entirely of individuals. Aviner condemns this democratic culture totally as being against the fundamental values of Judaism. In contrast, Aviner writes (in a Kookist fashion) the national collective is central in Judaism and the individual does not have "rights," but rather duties toward his religion, his fellows, the national collective; he is committed to the national collective, its well-being, and the realization of its historical destiny (ibid., 55–56). It is very important to point out that R. Aviner's objection to liberal individualism is not rooted in Halacha, nor in the religious-halachic orientation. Rather, it is rooted in the expressivist nationalism of the Kookist philosophy that views the individual as an organic part of the corporate whole of the nation.

It must be mentioned that alongside this mainstream republican ethno-nationalist approach to democracy and citizenship there has been a persistent minor current (that is, minor since the late 1960s), which has advocated a more pluralistic and inclusivist approach. To a certain extent, this current has tried to give a Jewish theological interpretation and endorsement of liberal values and to ground tolerance and acceptance of the "other" in the Jewish tradition itself. For example, it grounds the notion of human rights not in the Kantian idea of human dignity, but in the Biblical idea of *Imago Dei*, that all human beings are created in the image of God. It also argues that the Torah commands one to learn from Jewish history, and that if the Jews were a persecuted minority throughout most of their history, they ought not persecute others, but instead extend to minorities, which exist in Israel, recognition and tolerance. In the educational field, this trend has been represented by *Yesodot—Center for Torah and Democracy*, which was founded in 1996 in the wake of the assassination of the prime minister. Since its founding, Yesodot has engaged in teacher education and programming for students, which demonstrates the compatibility of open, inclusive, and tolerant civic orientations with Orthodox Judaism. (This writer is one of the founders of Yesodot, and has served as its Executive Director until 2007. His current title is Founding Director.)[8]

Despite these objections to the liberal citizenship discourse held by the republican mainstream of radical religious Zionism, some of the changes advanced by the Ministry of Education in civics education in the wake of the Kremnitzer Commission report were accepted and even welcomed by the religious Zionist community and the state religious educational system. They accepted the expansion of civics education to the ninth and eleventh grades and its expansion to two matriculation units. They also welcomed the initiative to deepen teacher training in civics as well as make it more professional. In the wake of the expanded Ministry funding for teacher education in civics, two Orthodox Jewish teachers colleges and Bar-Ilan University, which is under Orthodox auspices, opened up special programs for training teachers in civics. The program in one of these colleges in Elkana, a settlement on the West Bank, has a unequivocal republican orientation; the orientations in the other programs are more balanced (Cohen 2011).

The Attack on the New Civics Program by Religious Zionist and Nationalist Elements

Toward the end of the first decade of the 21st century, religious Zionist elements began to formulate their dissatisfaction with the new liberal civics curricula. A veteran civics teacher and a former member of the Ministry of Education civics curriculum committee, Dr. Yitzchak Geiger formulated a long attack upon both the Kremnitzer Commission report and the new textbook *To be Citizens in Israel*. His major argument against both of these documents is that they present a one-sided version of democracy, that is, they present liberal democracy as the only legitimate version of democracy, and that they downplay Israel's character as a Jewish nation-state, presenting Israel as a democratic state without any definite national character. The Kremnitzer Commission report, the textbook, and the matriculation exam, which is largely based upon the textbook, practically do not require the students to have studied the Declaration of Independence as declaring a Jewish state, nor do they discuss loyalty to the nation-state and patriotism. Geiger charged that while the textbook does mention Israel as a Jewish nation-state, it presents this fact in a negative light—as encouraging conflicts between the ethno-national majority and the other minorities. Geiger further charged that the one-sidedness of the textbook, and of the foci for the matriculation, discouraged critical thinking and encouraged intellectual conformism.

Geiger raised further objections concerning the treatment of the Arab sector. He claimed that it was full of inaccuracies, and that it advanced the Palestinian agenda of redefining Israel not as a Jewish state, but as "a state of all its citizens"—or as a multi-cultural state. In sum, Geiger charged that the civics curricula had been "hijacked" so as to serve the liberal and post-Zionist interests of an ideological group in the educational establishment and in the academy (Geiger 2009).[9]

It took a few years before Geiger's critique received public recognition. However, in the fall of 2009, he was able to bring it to the attention of the religious Zionist chairman of the Knesset Education committee. The committee chairman held special hearings and subpoened leading officials of the Ministry of Education, such as the Director General and the Superintendent of Civics (Zemer 2009). In the wake of this meeting, the Council of Religious Education also held hearings.

In February 2009, elections were held, and the right-of-center Likud Party became the leading party in the coalition, with Benyamin Netanyahu as Prime Minister. The Likud Party took over the Ministry of Education, and Gideon Saar was appointed the new Minister. He appointed a new chair of the Pedagogical Secretariat, Dr. Zvi Zameret, over the body in the Ministry of Education charged with all curricula and instruction. Dr. Zameret agreed with Geiger's critique and added several criticisms of his own. He gave immediate instructions for the revision of the civics curricula (Kashti 2008). Dr. Zameret is not Orthodox and hence not religious Zionist. However, he does adhere to an old Labor Zionist, collectivist Jewish national republican vision of Israeli citizenship. He had repeatedly stated his position that the civics curricula ought to include a substantial portion of the history of the pre-state Zionist settlement of Mandatory Palestine (*Palestine/Eretz Yisrael*) and of the State of Israel (about 50 percent). This history should detail Israel's achievements in growing a successful democracy, economy, and society.[10]

It must be understood that much of the passion—on both sides of the debate—concerning the civics curricula derives from the connection between the civics curricula and the definition of Israeli collective identity, and between both of these and the Israeli-Arab conflict. The liberal textbooks—in the name of "pluralism," or "multi-culturalism"—tend to grant space to the Israeli-Arab proposals for Israeli collective identity, such as "a state for all its citizens" or a "multi-cultural state," which deny the national Jewish character of the state. Furthermore, they also tend to present (alongside the Israeli-Jewish narratives) the Palestinian narratives concerning the 1948 war, which present the Jewish military forces as engaging in expulsion or massacre of the Palestinian population. The Israeli-Jewish narratives stress the Arab aggression against Jewish population centers (starting in December 1947) and the invasion by regular national Arab armies (May 1948). According to the standard Israeli narrative, most of the Arab population was encouraged to flee by their leaders. The nationalist critiques of the liberal textbooks and curricula claim that these provide false and malicious information as well as undermine Israeli patriotism and the moral legitimacy of the Israeli state.

In 2010–2011, due to the connection between the civics curricula and the issues of collective identity and the political-military struggle over Israel's existence as a Jewish nation-state, the debate over the nature of the curricula has assumed sharp personal and political dimensions. In May 2011, Dr. Zameret clashed with the curriculum committee over the introduction of Israeli history into a substantial portion of the civics curricula. The committee argued that this would change, in unacceptable ways, the very nature and aims of civics education. They also argued that since the alternative definitions of the State of Israel (as a binational or multicultural state) were in the Israeli public sphere, civics classes should discuss them, even though civics teachers should stress the constitutional definition of Israel as "a Jewish and democratic state." The outcome of that clash was that Dr. Zameret did not renew the tenure of two of the committee's most senior academic members (Kashti 2011). Among these is Prof. Yedidyah Stern, the chairmen of the committee and former Dean of Bar-Ilan Law School. Prof. Stern is a liberal religious Zionist and a firm believer in finding common ground between Orthodox Judaism and liberal democracy. He was replaced by another religious Zionist on the curriculum committee, Prof. Asher Cohen, who was believed to have a more nationalist orientation, though he could be more accurately described as a centrist.

Pursuing his objections to the existing materials, Dr. Zameret commissioned an alternative textbook from Prof. Avraham Diskin of the Political Science Department of Hebrew University who, like Zameret holds a collectivist Jewish national republican vision of Israeli citizenship (and is also a Fellow of the right-wing Institute for Zionist Strategies) (Nesher 2011). Here too, there were struggles between the curriculum committee and Prof. Diskin over specific formulations that appeared in the book (Adar Cohen 2011). In addition, Tel Aviv University published a new "left-wing" textbook, which would be a response to Prof. Diskin's "right-wing" version.

These struggles culminated, for the time being, in a malicious attack upon Adar Cohen, the Superintendent for Civics Studies, published in a right-wing newspaper, in December 2011 (Bringer 2011). Based upon anonymous sources, the article alleged that Cohen was a post-Zionist and lacked patriotism, and also that he forged protocols of meetings and was guilty of other bureaucratic misconduct. Cohen responded to each of the charges and initiated legal proceedings against the newspaper (Adar Cohen 2011). Following the newspaper article, the chairman of the governing coalition in the Israeli Parliament,[11] M. K. Zeev Elkin of the Likud Party, called for immediate hearings concerning "irregularities in the supervision of Civics education"(Valmer 2011b). In the meantime, the hearings have been deferred. The Minister of Education—Gideon Saar, also from the Likud Party—thought it was inappropriate that a mid-level bureaucrat should be the target of a Parliamentary investigation.[12]

In the midst of all this, on the last day of the midwinter vacation (December 28, 2011), both Superintendents of Civics Education—the General Superintendent, Adar Cohen, and the Civics Superintendent of Religious Education, Bilha Glicksberg—together with the curriculum committee sponsored a conference of civics teachers from all the streams: General, Arab, and Jewish-Religious.[13] About 200 teachers came from all the streams. At that conference, the Director General of the

Ministry of Education publicly supported Adar Cohen against anonymous attacks, as did other functionaries and colleagues. The main issue that the conference discussed was the different narratives (mainly Israeli-Jewish and Palestinian) of Israeli history and collective identity. While the teachers did express a diversity of opinion (some teachers thought that history ought to be avoided altogether because it only causes divisiveness and civic discord); the prevailing opinion seemed to be (as expressed in both the plenary and breakout sessions) that all narratives ought to presented to all students—that Jewish students ought to be made familiar with the Palestinian narratives, and that the Palestinian-Israeli students ought to learn the Jewish-Israeli narrative, and that all students must learn that this is the constitutional narrative and definition of the state.

A New Role for Religious Zionist Citizenship Discourse?

Dr. Zamret thought that, given the new neoliberal, individualist, and post-Zionist discourses that had sprung up in the civics curricula in the general state school system, the religious Zionist community—with its republican, collectivist Jewish ethno-nationalist vision of Israeli citizenship—ought to be given a leading role in shaping the national curricula in civics.

Certainly, the religious Zionist community had its share of difficulty with the expanded and intensified liberal citizenship civics curricula. Yet, on the other hand, it felt that this was a challenge that it ought to rise up to. As we have seen, it welcomed the expansion in hours of instruction in civics and the new resources devoted to teacher training in that subject. It opened new teacher training courses in its teacher training colleges and in Bar Ilan University. Furthermore, for the first time, it appointed a Superintendent of Civics education who was able to devote significant time and resources to civics instruction. In previous years, the superintendent split his or her time between history and civics (with priority given to history). This too shows that they attribute new importance to this subject.

The criticism of the new curricula, plus difficulties in the field, brought about one change in the curricula. Whereas until 2010 all the sectors of society had studied one unified curriculum, due to complaints both from the Arab sector and from the Orthodox Jewish sector, this was modified. From 2011, only two thirds of the curriculum is joint, while in one third of the hours, each sector is to deal with issues and problems that are specific only to it. Both the Arab and the Jewish religious sector claimed that they have special issues to deal with. The Arabs stated that loyalty to Israel is a special issue that they must deal with, while the religious Zionists must deal with issues of conflict between religious and civil authority and the equality of all citizens, even non-Jews.

It must be stressed that despite these difficulties and the difficulties that religious Zionists have with the liberal citizenship discourse, the state Orthodox school system has not insisted upon *only* an ethno-nationalist republican discourse, which excludes categorically all "others." Both in its teacher training courses and in its programming, it has included—alongside communitarian and exclusivist components,—elements that are inclusive and open to "others." One index of this is the way that the Administration of Religious Education and its superintendent of civics have structured the "practical task" for religious schools. As part of the matriculation requirements, each student must participate in a "practical task." She must form a team with other students, identify a genuine civic or social problem, do research upon that problem, and propose practical ways of dealing with it. Each student's participation is evaluated. The Administration of Religious Education has issued a directive, authored by the Head of the Administration and the superintendent, strongly recommending that religious schools partner with schools of a different stream—whether a general Jewish "secular" school, or even a school from the Arab stream (an event that is much less likely). The directive explicitly encouraged the formation of student teams composed of religious Jewish students along with "others," mainly non-observant Jewish students but also possibly Palestinian-Israelis.[14] Furthermore, the Administration of Religious Education has made Yesodot—with its inclusive, tolerant, and even liberal approach—a full partner in teacher training and Internet programming.

At the conference, I spent considerable time speaking with Prof. Asher Cohen, the recently appointed Chairman of the Curriculum Committee in civics (with whom I have been acquainted for several years). I asked him explicitly about the place of non-Jewish citizens in his vision of civics programming. He replied that "Israel is the state of 100 percent of its citizens, but is the *nation-state* of only 80 percent of its citizens [the Jewish population]." His remarks echoed the remarks, from fifteen years ago, of another Israeli scholar who is well known as a liberal constitutional expert. Speaking at a Yesodot symposium in 1997, Prof. Mordechai Kremnitzer asserted that Arab citizens must have full individual rights, but they cannot have "group rights."[15] Prof. Cohen was, of course, speaking in his capacity as Chairman of the Curriculum Committee of the entire school system, and he is a respected political scientist. Nevertheless, he is very much identified as a religious Zionist, both personally and politically, and as we have seen, he had been appointed as such. Thus, it is also as a religious Zionist that Prof. Cohen made no bones about his commitment to Israel as a Jewish nation-state, but also evinced his commitment to individual rights and civic equality for all citizens. Orthodox teachers at the conference also displayed awareness that citizenship requires equal individual rights as well as non-discrimination against any class of citizens.

During the High Holiday season in October 2011, the Religious Civics Superintendent held a conference for religious civics teachers. About 250 came. During the breakout sessions, the individual teachers were asked to speak about their work, their professional and religious identities, and their dilemmas and conflicts. Many of the teachers who spoke indicated that though even they may have misgivings about democracy—and especially about its more liberal variety—they understood that in their role as civics teachers, they represented Israeli democratic civil culture in the schools. Thus, while they had some role conflicts between their religious identities and their roles as civics teachers, they seemed determined to fulfill the expectations of civics teachers, and came to the conference seeking resources and guidance. Many teachers feel that they are "marked" in their schools as representatives of "leftist" values and orientations; nevertheless, they understand this to be their role. In accordance with this, Bilha Glicksberg, the Religious Superintendent of Civics, speaks of "civics educators," not "civics teachers." The teachers under her supervision, she says, are not mere technicians; they educate toward values and worthy citizenship (which bear a relation to other values and identities), not merely knowledge and passing the matriculation exam.

Conclusion

I believe that we must understand that the religious Zionist community is in dialogue with its environment. In a certain sense, it is starting to respond to the challenge posed to it by Dr. Tzvi Zameret. Can it formulate a citizenship discourse that could apply to the entire Israeli public? While it certainly wishes to be loyal to its nationalist, republican vision, it wishes to do so while taking into consideration the larger Israeli public as well as its needs and orientations.

The religious Zionist community is starting to understand the place of civics and citizenship within the new Israeli public discourse, and it wishes to be part of that discourse. It understands too, that it can make its own unique communitarian or republican contribution to that discourse, but it understands two further things as well: it understands that if it entirely disregards the liberal citizenship discourse of individual human and civil rights, of tolerance and of pluralism, it will lose its ability to communicate with the larger Israeli public. Much to its chagrin, it has all ready experienced such a break in communication during the Disengagement from Gaza in 2005. It discovered then that it had no allies in the Israeli public sphere to help it prevent the evacuation of seventeen settlements in the Gaza strip. It wishes very much to reestablish lines of communication in order to prevent a reoccurrence of that event. Secondly, it understands that it cannot seriously offer a citizenship discourse for the entire country if it offers no modicum of inclusion, of membership, and of tolerance to the non-Jewish minorities of the country. Alongside its communitarian and republican orientation, and alongside its integral nationalist demands that Israel remain a Jewish country, it must find room for the other non-Jews, even the Palestinians. Hence, it seeks from within the Jewish tradition resources of tolerance and inclusion. Only time will tell whether it actually achieves a new synthesis of nationalism and democracy, and of republicanism and inclusiveness.

NOTES

1. This paper describes developments up to 2012. In January 2013 new elections were held in Israel and a new minister, Rabbi Shai Peron from the centrist Yesh Atid Party was appointed to the Ministry of Education. The new elections also resulted in a slight growth in ultra-Orthodox (Haredi) representation, from eighteen to nineteen members of Knesset. However the Haredi parties are not part of the current governing coalition. The Arab parties, declined in their parliamentary representation and have only 11 seats in the current Knesset.
2. See Wikipedia, "Education in Israel," https://en.wikipedia.org/wiki/Education_in_Israel.
3. See for example, http://www.ifeel.co.il/page/12803.
4. This section is largely taken from my doctoral dissertation, Fischer 2007.
5. Shlomo Fischer, *Self-Expression and Democracy*, 75–126.
6. *Essays of R. Kook* (see bibliography).

7. A similar ambiguity seems to attend to the term "nation" within the context of the French Revolution. It was used both in the sense of the sum of individuals who agreed to form a body politic and work for the common good (as in Sieyès' famous pamplet, *Qu'est-ce que le Tiers État?*) and in the sense of the historical, linguistic, and cultural French collectivity.
8. See www.yesodot.org.il.
9. Before its publication in 2009, Geiger's paper circulated privately among civics teachers, academics and educational officials.
10. Personal communication to the writer. See also, Valmer (2011a). Dr. Zameret wrote an important history of education in Israel in the first decade of the state.
11. This position is equivalent to the House Majority Leader.
12. Dr. Zameret himself was relieved of his duties in December 2011. It is possible that the controversies surrounding civics education were partially responsible for this.
13. The description of this conference and the religious teachers' conference is based upon my participation and field notes.
14. Lecture by Bilha Glicksberg at the 'teacher's conference held on December 28, 2011 and discussed above.
15. This approach, of course, echoes the famous lines of Count Stanislas Clermont-Tonnere in the debate over the emancipation of the Jews in the French National Assembly in 1791: "To the Jews as individuals everything. To the Jews as a group (corporate entity) nothing." Prof. Kremnitzer was the Chairman of the Kremnitzer Committee (the Committee on Civic Education), which in 1995 called for the revamping of civics education along liberal democratic lines.

BIBLIOGRAPHY

Abu-Asbeh, Khaled. *The Arab Education in Israel: Dilemmas of a Minority.* Jerusalem: Florsheimer Institute for Policy Research, 2007.

Adar, Leah, and Chaim Adler. *Values Education in Schools for Immigrant Children.* Jerusalem: School of Education, Hebrew University, 1965.

Aviner, Elisha. *Introductory Chapters in Jewish Democracy.* Jerusalem, 1996.

B. "The Place of Orthodox Men in the Tactical Command of the IDF." *Maarachot* 432 (August 2010): 51.

Bava Batra, Babylonian Talmud.

Barak, Aharon. "The Civil Code Interpretation in Israel." In *Israel among the Nations.* Edited by Alfred E. Kellermann, Kurt Siehr, and Talia Einhorn, 1–34. The Hague, The Netherlands: Kluwer Law International, 1998.

———. "Israeli Legal History." In *The History of Law in a Multicultural Society: Israel 1917–1967.* Edited by Ron Harris. Aldershot: Ashgate Pub Ltd., 2002.

———. *The Judge in a Democracy.* Princeton: Princeton U. Press, 2006.

Ben Artzi, Hagi. "A Covenant in a Sheep Skin," *Nekudah*, 2002.

Bin-Nun, Yoel. "A Democratic Regime According to the Torah: The Desirable Regime and Its Limitations." In *Human Mores, Religion and State: A Collection of Essays and Lectures on Religion, Governance and Democracy*. Edited by Amichai Berholtz, 297–350. Jerusalem: Ministry of Education and Yesodot, 2001.

Bramson, Joseph. *History of the Jews: Torah and Democracy*. Jerusalem, Published by the author, 1985.

Bringer, Gil. "Civic Revolution," *Makor Rishon*, December 9, 2011. Justice Section, 1.

Central Bureau of Statistics. Statistical Abstract of Israel 2011. Available online, http://www.cbs.gov.il/reader/shnaton/templ_shnaton.html?num_tab=st07_04x&CYear=2011.

Civics Education Steering Committee. *Being Citizens: Citizenship Education for All of the Students of Israel, Interim Report*. Jerusalem: Ministry of Education and Culture, 1996.

Cohen, Adar, letter to the editor, *Makor Rishon*, December 16, 2011. Justice Section, 2.

Cohen, David. " Introduction to Lights of Holiness." In *Orot Hakodesh*. Edited by Abraham Isaac Kook, vol. l, 17–38. 1963b.

Cohen, Shimon. "Problematic Values in the Teaching of Civics." *Arutz 7*, October 4, 2011. Available online, http://www.inn.co.il/News/News.aspx/218146.

Eisenstadt, S. N. *Israeli Society*. London: Weidenfeld and Nicholson, 1967.

Fischer, Shlomo. "Self-Expression and Democracy in Radical Religious Zionist Ideology." PhD diss., Hebrew University of Jerusalem, 2007.

Galchinsky, Michael. *Jews and Human Rights: Dancing at Three Weddings*. Lanham, MD: Rowman & Littlefield, 2008.

Gavison, Ruth. "Jewish and Democratic: A Rejoinder to the Ethnic Democracy Debate." *Israel Studies* 4.1 (1999): 44–72.

Geiger, Yitzchak. "The Study of Civcs: Education or One-Sided Indoctrinatiion?" Position Paper, Institute for Zionist Strategies, Jerusalem, 2009.

Emunim, Gush. *Movement for the Renewed Fulfillment of the Zionist Ideal*. Jerusalem, n.d.

Haider, Aziz. *Arab Society in Israel: Population, Society, Economy*. Jerusalem: Kibbutz HaMeuchad and the Van Leer Institute, 2011.

H.C. 73/53. Kol Ha'am vs. Minister of Interior. Majority Opinion of the Supreme Court Sitting as the High Court of Equity, Jerusalem, 1953.

H.C. 8060/03-T. The Kaadan-Katzir case, Majority Opinion of the Supreme Court Sitting as the High Court of Equity, Jerusalem, 1999.

High Follow-Up Committee for the Arabs in Israel and National Committee for the Heads of the Arab Local Authorities in Israel. *The Future Vision of the Palestinian Arabs in Israel*. Nazareth, Israel: National Committee for the Heads of Arab Local Authorities in Israel, 2006.

Israel Democracy Institute. *The Democracy Index 2010*. Jerusalem: Israel Democracy Institute, 2010.

Kashti, Or. "Ministry of Education Re-Writes Civics Text Book because too Critical of State," Haaretz, October 29, 2008. Available online, http://www.haaretz.co.il/news/education/1.1218779.

———. "Director-General of Ministry of Education Fires Chairman of Civics Curriculum Committee," *Haaretz*, May 26, 2011. Available online, http://www.haaretz.co.il/news/education/1.1175241.

Kook, Abraham Isaac. *Orot* [Lights]. Jerusalem: Mossad HaRav Kook, 1963a.

———. *Orot Hakodesh* Jerusalem: Mosad HaRav Kook, 1963b.

———. *Mishpat Kohen*. Jerusalem: Mossad HaRav Kook, 1966.

———. *Essays of R. Kook*. Edited by Shlomo Aviner. Jerusalem: Mossad HaRav Kook, 1984.

Ministry of Education. *To be Citizens in Israel: A Jewish and Democratic State*. Jerusalem: Ministry of Education, 2001.

Nesher, Telilah. "New in the Curriculum: A Civics Textbook Written by a Member of the Institute for Zionist Strategies," *Haaretz*, August 19, 2011: A11.

"Rabbi David Drukman Investigated over His Rabbinical Opinion against Hiring Arabs," *YNET*, November 13, 2011. Available online, http://www.ynet.co.il/articles/0,7340,L-4147608,00.html.

Rouhana, Nadim. *Palestinian Citizens in an Ethnic Jewish State: Identities in Conflict*. New Haven, CT: Yale University Press, 1997.

Schmidt, Yvonne, "Foundations of Civil and Political Rights in Israel and the Occupied Territories," PhD diss., Faculty of Law, University of Vienna Norderstedt, Germany, 2001.

Shafir, Gershon, and Yoav Peled. *Being Israeli: The Dynamics of Multiple Citizenship*. Cambridge, UK: Cambridge Universtiy Press, 2002.

Shalev, Michael. *Labour and the Political Economy in Israel*. Oxford: Oxford University Press, 1992.

Sivan, Emmanuel. "The Enclave Culture." In *Strong Religion: The Rise of Fundamentalisms around the World*. Edited by G. Almond, R. S. Appleby, and E. Sivan, 23–89. Chicago: University of Chicago Press, 2003.

Soysal, Yasemine. *Limits of Citizenship: Migrants and Post-National Membership in Europe*. Chicago: University of Chicago Press, 1994.

State Education Law—1953. Available online, http://cms.education.gov.il/EducationCMS/Units/Zchuyot/ChukimVeamanot/Chukim/ChokChinuchMamlachti1953.htm.

Strassberg-Dayan, Sarah. *Individual, Nation, Humanity: The Concept of Man in the Philosophy of A.D. Gordon and Rabbi Kook*. Tel Aviv: HaKibbutz HaMuechad, 1995.

Taylor, Charles. *Hegel*. Cambridge, UK: Cambridge University Press, 1977.

Tesslar, Yitzchak. "Fifty Municipal Rabbis: Don't Sell Apartments to Arabs," December 7, 2010. Available online, http://www.nrg.co.il/online/1/ART2/186/505.html.

Valmer, Tomer. "Revolution in Education? To Study Together History and Civics," *YNET*, May 4, 2011a. Available online, http://www.ynet.co.il/articles/0,7340,L-4064089,00.html.

———. "The Civics Storm: 'The Likud Dictates Political Contents,'" *YNET*, December 28, 2011b. Available online, http://www.ynet.co.il/articles/0,7340,L-4167949,00.html.

Vargan, Yuval. The Educational System in the Haredi Sector: A Picture of the Situation. Jerusalem: Knesset Research and Information Center, 2007.

Yakobson, Alex, and Amnon Rubenstein. Israel and the Family of Nations: The Jewish Nation-State and Human Rights. Milton Park, Routledge, 2009.

Zemer, Efrat. "Education Committee: Change the Study of Civics," *NRG Ma'ariv*, November 25, 2009. Available online, http://www.nrg.co.il/online/1/ART1/971/311.html.

Zoldan, Yehuda. "The Will of the People and the Principles of Democratic Rule." In *Human Mores, Religion and State: A Collection of Essays and Lectures on Religion, Governance and Democracy*. Edited by Amichai Berholz, 351–364. Jerusalem: Ministry of Education and Yesodot, 2001.

Zoldan, Yehuda. "The Military, The People and the State," Work Book I, Gush Katif, n.d.

6

Secularism(s), Islam, and Education in Turkey

IS *E PLURIBUS UNUM* POSSIBLE?

Ahmet T. Kuru

WHAT KIND OF relationship between religion and secularism, particularly in education, can play a bridging role in society? It is difficult to answer this question because, rather than being solutions for socio-political controversies, religious and secular education are themselves highly polarizing issues in several countries. Education has a pivotal position in public debates on state-religion relations, due to its importance in shaping identities, mindsets, and behaviors of new generations. Ideologically motivated politicians may turn public education into an instrument to impose a particular reading of a nation's history, indoctrinate a particular ideology, and engineer certain modes of behavior. On the other hand, public education can also be employed for positive goals, such as bridging social divisions, transforming historical antagonisms, and promoting equal opportunities.

In analyzing the divisive or unifying impacts of its schooling, Turkey presents an intriguing case where the relationships between Islam, secularism, and education are at the heart of sociopolitical polarization. In 2008, Turkey's Constitutional Court decided that the ruling Justice and Development (AK) Party was a center for anti-secular activities. The indictment against the party was mostly about its attempts to lift restrictions related to Islam and education, such as the headscarf ban for university students, discrimination against the graduates of public Islamic

(Imam-Hatip) schools in the university enrollment system, and the legal and bureaucratic prohibitions over Qur'an courses. By 2012, these illiberal restrictions were abolished. Nevertheless, this did not mean that Turkey reached a balanced approach on Islam and education. Prime Minister Tayyip Erdoğan became extremely powerful and began implementing a discretely Islamist agenda. Recently, he declared that his government would train "a pious generation." He has tried to put the Imam-Hatip schools at the center of this project. He has perceived the Gülen movement as a rival and tried to close down the movement's preparatory schools, which prepare hundreds of thousands of students to take the nation-wide university entrance exam.

The triangular relationship between politics, religion, and education is obviously not unique to Turkey. It is, for example, at the core of the "culture wars" in the United States as well. During the early 20th century, there was a deep controversy between American public schools, which taught the Protestant King James Version of the Bible, and Catholics who opposed the practice and sought to open alternative private schools (Hamburger 2004, 220; Ravitch 1999, 5–6). The secularization of American public education has been a long process, marked by Supreme Court decisions prohibiting Bible reading and organized prayer in public schools, starting in the 1960s. The debates about religion and education still continue in America on such issues as the pledge of allegiance (its reference to God) and school vouchers that provide public money to parents for religious and other private school tuitions.

Education has similarly had a central position in state-religion controversies in France. In the early Third Republic, secularization policies primarily targeted Catholic schools. Pope Leo XIII (b. 1810–d. 1903) was very concerned about this, stating that "the school is the battlefield where it will be decided if the society will remain Christian or not" (Haarscher 2004, 25). In 1876–1877, there were 19,890 religious primary schools in France, with 46,684 teachers and 1,841,527 students. As a result of the state's secularization policies, by 1906–1907 the number of religious primary schools declined to 1,851, with 7,387 teachers and 227,213 students (Ozouf 1982, 233–234). French state policies toward religion moderated in favor of Catholic schools by the Debré Law of 1959, which provided public funding for Catholic schools. The debates on such funding triggered mass rallies in 1984 and 1994. Recently, Islam has replaced Catholicism in discussions on religion and education in France, as seen in the headscarf debate that took place from 1989 to 2004.

The United States, France, and Turkey are secular states that share two criteria: (1) they do not have official religions and (2) their legal systems are not under institutional religious control. During recent debates on education, neither religion nor secularism has been monolithic in these three cases. Instead, each of the three has experienced struggles between competing understandings of secularism. "Passive secularism" requires the state to play a passive role by allowing public visibility of religion. "Assertive secularism," however, demands that the state play an assertive role in excluding religion from the public sphere. Passive secularism is dominant in the United States, yet this country has faced a struggle between two interpretations of passive secularism: accommodationism and separationism. In France, supporters of assertive secularism (*laïcité de combat*) are dominant, while those of passive secularism (*laïcité plurielle*) are in opposition. Similarly, in Turkey, there is a conflict among the historically dominant assertive secularists (Kemalists) and the recently prevailing passive secularists (conservatives and liberals) and Islamists (Kuru 2009, esp. 11–14).[1]

The case of Turkey provides crucial lessons in the ways that the relationship between assertive secularism, passive secularism, and Islam shapes public education. Turkey is the first secular state in a Muslim-majority country, but it is no longer the only one. Out of forty-nine Muslim-majority states, twenty-three are secular, as (a) they do not declare Islam as their official religion, and (b) their legislative and judicial processes are not constitutionally based on Islamic law (see Kuru 2013). The next section will provide a brief historical background on the Turkish case.

Ottoman Diversity, Republican Uniformity, and Education

The framers of the Turkish Republic (1923) were deeply affected by the traumatic collapse of the Ottoman Empire. After four centuries of victory and magnificence, the empire faced international and domestic challenges in the 18th century. The Ottoman rulers tried to reform the empire's institutions in the 19th century by imitating European models, but they could not prevent the collapse. For the founders of the Republic, the multi-ethnic and multi-religious regime was a reason for the empire's demise; therefore, they designed a new republic as the opposite of the Ottoman *ancien régime* by making Turkish nationalism and assertive secularism the new republic's two main ideological pillars. In this regard, the Turkish framers differed from American founding fathers who used *e pluribus unum* (out of many, one) as the official motto.[2]

Education was crucial for the Turkish framers' project of creating a nation homogenized by the Turkish identity and the secular public sphere. The pledge, which was recited daily by students in all primary schools from 1933 to 2013, reflected this project. The following is the last version of the pledge, which was shorter before the revision in 1972, and was once again slightly revised in 1997.

> I am a Turk, I am trustworthy, I am hard working. My principle: it is to defend my minors and to respect my elders, and to love my homeland and nation more than my self. My goal: it is to rise and progress. O Atatürk the great! I swear that I will enduringly walk through the path you opened and to the target you showed. May my personal being be sacrificed to the being of the Turkish nation. How happy is the one who says: "I am a Turk!"

This essay focuses on issues related to assertive secularism and its impact on restrictions over Islamic instruction. An analysis of Turkish nationalism and its influence on the ban on Kurdish instruction would require an independent study.[3] I use the term "Islamic instruction" instead of "Islamic education" because the former refers to the content of instruction, while the latter implies institutional characteristics of education. Ali Fuat Başgil, a professor of law and a politician, argued in the 1950s that Higher Institutions of Islam should be opened in Turkey to provide Islamic education in an atmosphere where professors and students shared and reflected Islamic piety. He claimed that a department of theology at a secular university could train "a critic of Islam" at worst, and "a philosopher of theology or a sociologist of religion" at best, "but not a pious Islamic scholar, never an alim" (Başgil 1977, 194–195, 276). Currently, there are no such higher institutions in Turkey; there only exist departments of theology at universities, which provide Islamic instructions within secular academic frameworks (for an alternative term—"Muslim education"—which means education systems and practices produced by Muslims, without necessarily being fully based on Islamic principles; see Hefner and Zaman 2007).

For the framers of the Turkish Republic, the Ottoman reform projects—starting with the Tanzimat Edict (1839)—remained unsuccessful because they tolerated the bifurcation of political, legal, and educational institutions through the coexistence of traditional Islamic and modern Western institutions. The new republic was supposed to end this duality by unifying institutions, as well as people's ways of life, even including their dress codes and musical tastes (Ward and Rustow 1964, 446–447; Berkes 1998, 409, 468; Özbudun 2012; Hanioğlu 2012).

Ziya Gökalp was a leading Young Turk philosopher of the late Ottoman era who also influenced the framers of the republic, including Mustafa Kemal (Atatürk). According to Gökalp, the coexistence of European-type schools with traditional madrasas was a major problem of the Ottoman educational system (Gökalp 2007, 210).[4] Sharing this view, Turkish Parliament passed a law on March 3, 1924, named "Tevhid-i Tedrisat" (Unification of Education, Law no. 430; T.B.M.M. 1942, 242). Based on this law, all of the 479 madrasas were closed; to partially replace them, the minister of education opened twenty-nine Imam-Hatip schools and a department of theology at Darülfünun (the only Turkish university) in Istanbul.

The republican rulers' policies against Islamic instruction became more exclusionary over time. They entirely abolished Islamic instruction in public schools in 1927, and removed Arabic- and Persian-language classes from school curricula in 1929 (Kaplan 1999, 159–160; Özdalga 1999, 418). They closed all Imam-Hatip schools by 1930 and the department of theology in 1933. Until 1949, except for a few Qur'an courses, there was no legal institution for Islamic learning in Turkey. According to Frederick Frey, in 1932, there remained only nine Qur'an courses with 232 students. By 1942, these numbers increased to thirty-seven courses and 938 students (Frey 1964, 222–223).

Did the Turkish state's policies, which marginalized Islamic instruction in the 1920s and eliminated it in the 1930s and 1940s, successfully create a unified society? The answer would definitely be no; these policies made Turkish society even more divided. Throughout the republican period, the relationship between assertive secularism and Islamic instruction became a major reason for sociopolitical polarization, as explained below.

The Assertive Secularist State, Pious Society, and Islamic Instruction

Following 1949, the Turkish state became more accommodationist toward Islamic instruction, while also maintaining certain restrictions. Its policies on this issue have been inconsistent and even contradictory. From

1982 to 1996, the Turkish state supported Islamic instruction by constitutionally mandating courses in public and private schools, and running public Islamic (Imam-Hatip) schools. Yet from 1997 to 2011, it discriminated against graduates of the Imam-Hatip schools in nation-wide university entrance exams and forbade the teaching of the Qur'an to children under twelve.

Beyond the issue of Islamic instruction, the Turkish state has been bifurcated in terms of its general policies toward Islam. For example, it has paid the salaries of over 80,000 imams in mosques, who are all civil servants of the state's Directorate of Religious Affairs (Diyanet). Yet, until very recently, the state banned wearing headscarves in all public and private educational institutions, including K–12 schools and universities; the ban also covered all civil servants and, in certain cases, was extended to citizens who wanted to visit public institutions, such as universities and military buildings.

There are three main reasons for these contradictory policies. First, although ideologies refer to consistent utopias in the minds of the state elite, public policies often deviate from these utopias, given the need to adapt to social conditions. Thus, while assertive secularist rulers in Turkey aimed to confine religion to an individual's conscience (*vicdan*)—in practice, it was impossible to entirely exclude Islam from the public sphere, given the high level of individual religiosity in Turkish society. The weekly religious participation ratio is around 70 percent in Turkey (Friday prayer for men, and daily prayer for women, who rarely attend mosques on Friday for various reasons) ("Survey of Milliyet & AG," *Milliyet*, May 31, 2003). Moreover, there has been substantial social demand for Islamic instruction or other types of public religious expression in Turkey. The tension between assertive secularist ideology and social reality has caused policy exceptions in other cases, too. In France, for example, despite persistent restrictions, state policies toward the Catholic majority have been moderated since the 1940s; this is why some scholars define it as a *"catho-laïque"* country (Laborde 2008, 66–79).

Second, the Turkish state's ambition to control Islam is also a reason for policy contradictions. For the sake of keeping Islam under control, it prohibited private Islamic education, but provided Islamic instruction in its own ways: state-designed obligatory religious classes in schools, public Imam-Hatip schools, and Qur'an courses supervised by the Diyanet. These institutions helped the state to turn religious leaders and scholars into civil servants who are paid and regulated by the state. Moreover, through them, the state tried to promote a particular understanding of Islam that emphasized personal piety over any public religious claims.[5]

This fund-and-control relation has a fairly long history in Turkey. During the founding period, the state confiscated the properties of the Islamic foundations that had funded the imams; thus, the state has paid salaries of the imams in exchange (non-governmental associations and mass donations, not the Diyanet, have funded the construction of mosque buildings). The Diyanet has played the central role in this control mechanism because it centrally organizes the sermons in the mosques. That is why the Law of Political Parties prevents any political party from aiming to abolish the Diyanet (Law no. 2820, Article 89).

Nonetheless, assertive secularists have regarded Diyanet and related institutions as temporary instruments, which were supposed to be marginalized when society became secularized. That is why they closed the only department of theology, all Imam-Hatip schools, and a majority of the Qur'an courses, in addition to trivializing the Diyanet from 1933 to 1949. However, since societal secularization—in terms of the decreasing ratio of religious participation and the declining public role of Islam—did not happen in Turkey, the state had to reopen and even multiply these institutions. This has been the assertive secularists' dilemma in Turkey: they needed certain institutions to keep Islam under state control, but they also sought to minimize these institutions' social impacts.

In short, the tension between assertive secularist ideology and social religiosity, and the state's aim to control Islam, are two causes of the Turkish state's contradictory policies toward Islam. The third cause is that these policies are products of two struggling groups—assertive secularists and passive secularists. The analysis of these complex struggles requires a specific section.

Assertive and Passive Secularists

Assertive secularism was dominant in Turkey for decades, but it was also challenged by passive secularists and Islamists since the first democratic elections in 1950. The assertive secularists included the Kemalist parties (especially the Republican People's Party [CHP]), military generals, high court members, influential media corporations (e.g., the Doğan group), and the main business association (TÜSİAD). They claimed to represent the legacy of Atatürk and declared that Islam should be an affair of conscience. Passive secularists and Islamists, on the other hand, included conservative parties (e.g., the AK Party), business associations (e.g., MÜSİAD and TUSKON), and movements (the Gülen movement).

From the late 1990s to recently, Islamists became marginal in Turkey. Necmettin Erbakan's moderate Islamist Felicity Party (SP) received around 2 percent of the votes in the 2002, 2007, and 2011 parliamentary elections, while the pro-Islamic conservative AK Party got 34 percent, 47 percent, and 50 percent, respectively. The main allies of conservatives in supporting passive secularism were liberal intellectuals. Conservatives opposed assertive secularism primarily due to the restrictions over their freedoms of religion, association, and education. Liberals, on the other hand, criticized assertive secularism because of their liberal understanding of state-religion relations. Therefore, the two groups had disagreements, despite their common disapproval of assertive secularism. The difference between conservatives and liberals in Turkey resembles the distinction between accommodationists (who tolerate close interactions between the state and religions) and separationists (who seek a wall of separation between the state and religions) in the United States. Following his 2011 electoral victory, Erdoğan has gradually leaned toward Islamism in terms of not only his approach to education, but also his foreign policy perspective. He has deviated from passive secularism and received substantial criticisms from liberals, and even conservatives who were once his former allies.

The main disagreements between passive and assertive secularists focus on issues related to Islam and education. One controversial issue is the obligatory religious instruction in public schools. This was put into the current constitution by the generals who had staged a coup in 1980. The courses on religious instruction are officially entitled "Knowledge of Religions and Ethics." Although they briefly cover all religions, these courses primarily teach Islam. Passive secularists have various views on this issue. The liberals have clearly opposed obligatory religious instruction, while conservatives are divided. Many conservatives have regarded these courses as a compensation for the lack of private institutions to provide Islamic instruction. Yet, some conservatives have criticized the content of these courses as contradictory to their understanding of Islam. Although some assertive secularists have preferred that the state draft courses on Islam, instead of permitting private institutions to design them, several others have opposed all such courses.

Alevis are particularly critical of these courses, perceiving them as promoting a Sunni understanding of Islam. According to the survey by

Milliyet and Konda, the ratio of Sunnis is 91 percent, Alevis is 5 percent, other Muslims is 2 percent, Shias is 1 percent, and followers of other religions is 1 percent in Turkey ("Türkiye'de Alevi Sayısı 4.5 Milyon," *Milliyet*, 21 Mart 2007). In another survey, the ratio of self-defined Alevis appears to be 6 percent; when the ratio of those who hold pictures of Ali or twelve Imams is added, the total ratio becomes 11 percent (Çarkoğlu and Toprak 2006, 38). The democratization process in Turkey should address Alevis's concerns about religious instruction in public schools.

A similar discussion has taken place on the status of the Diyanet. In 2011, the liberal *Taraf* newspaper started a discussion by revealing that, since 1982, imams and other Diyanet personnel have taken the civil servants' oath, which includes being loyal to "Atatürk's Reforms and Principles," "Turkish nationalism," and "the Turkish Republic," which is a national, democratic, and secular state" ("Bu Yemin İmamı İmandan Çıkartır," *Taraf*, April 11, 2011). The liberals have asked that the Diyanet be separated from the state. Some conservatives have supported the Diyanet as a partial satisfaction of public religious demands, while others have criticized it as serving a state-engineered Islam. Assertive secularists have also been divided regarding the Diyanet's position within the state bureaucracy. Although some assertive secularists have regarded Diyanet as a necessary instrument to keep Islam under state control, others have opposed its status as contradictory to secularism. Alevis have especially criticized the Diyanet's public funding as the state promotion of Sunni Islam.

Some inside and outside the Diyanet rightly stress that a feasible solution to these debates would be to separate the Diyanet from the state hierarchy and governmental budget by making it an autonomous institution. If the Diyanet is ruled by a board of trustees and funded by pious foundations, it will become separated from the state bureaucracy and political control over it. This solution will require the end of the state control over, and confiscation of, the pious foundations too.

Another controversial issue is state funding of private schools. Because private Islamic schools have not been allowed in Turkey, Islamic movements have opened private secular schools. Although they have used the same curricula as secular schools, assertive secularists have still criticized these schools because they are run by conservative Muslims. In 2003, the minister of education of the AK Party government issued a circular to publicly fund the private school tuitions of ten thousand students from poor families, chosen by a nation-wide exam. Assertive secularists pursued a media campaign against the project by arguing that it would support schools run by conservative Muslims, especially the Gülen movement.[6] They claimed that 89 out of 415 private schools in the project belonged to Islamic movements, and these schools would receive 2,218 out of 10,000 students ("En Özel Okullar," *Sabah*, July 26, 2003). The Council of State cancelled the circular. The AK Party group in Parliament then passed a legislative bill as a legal framework for the project. President Necdet Sezer, a leading assertive secularist, vetoed the bill. The AK Party did not insist, and cancelled the project.

The debates on religious instruction in public schools and the state funding of private schools have been less important than much deeper controversies on the restrictions over the graduates of the Imam-Hatip schools, the age limits on the Qur'an courses, and the headscarf ban.

Imam-Hatip Schools, Qur'an Courses, and Headscarves

Although only a minority of Turkish society supported assertive secularism, it remained as the dominant ideology shaping state policies for decades. The reason was that assertive secularists dominated the military and judiciary, and mobilized these institutions to impose restrictive policies toward religious expression. My depiction of assertive secularists as a minority in Turkey depends on two sets of data. The first one is the vote-shares of assertive secularist parties in the parliamentary elections. The total vote-share of the CHP and the other Kemalist party (Democratic Left Party) was only 21 percent in both the 2002 and 2007 elections; it increased to 27 percent in 2011. The second data source is public surveys that revealed how unpopular assertive secularist policies were. According to polls, those who supported the ban on headscarves were only 22 percent, whereas the opponents constituted 78 percent (the Survey of *Milliyet* and Konda, *Milliyet,* December 4, 2007; Çarkoğlu and Toprak 2006, 71).[7] Another unpopular policy was the restrictions on Imam-Hatip graduates in the university entrance exams; 85 percent of the people opposed this assertive secularist policy (Çarkoğlu and Toprak 2006, 55).

Therefore, assertive secularists regularly needed military and judiciary interventions to prevent democratically elected parliaments and governments from changing assertive secularist policies. The most important recent intervention was the "soft coup" on February 28, 1997. During this coup process, generals imposed certain policies on politicians to fight against "Islamic reactionism." Assertive secularists from varied backgrounds—judiciary, media, politics, and academia—supported the military in these policies. The generals and their civilian allies directly targeted the Imam-Hatip schools and the Qur'an courses.

The number of Imam-Hatip schools had increased from 382 in 1990 to 604 in 1997, and by then, the ratio of students they had taught reached 10 percent of all secondary and high school students (Çakır et al. 2004, 67–68). The generals and their supporters regarded the increasing number of students attending Imam-Hatip schools and Qur'an courses as a voter reserve for the Islamists. Following the 1997 intervention, they closed the secondary Imam-Hatip schools, changed the university entrance exam system to one with an extremely low coefficient for calculating the scores of Imam-Hatip graduates, and forbade the teaching of the Qur'an to children under fifteen years of age, only allowing those between twelve and fifteen to attend summer Qur'an courses. As a result of these policies, the number of students attending the Imam-Hatip schools decreased from about half a million in 1996 to 64,000 in 2002 (Soğukdere 2004), and the number of students in Qur'an courses decreased from 158,000 in 1996 to 85,000 in 2000 (Çakır and Bozan 2005, 87). Another policy of the semi-military rule from 1997 to 2002 was to strictly impose the headscarf ban in all educational institutions.

The AK Party won the elections in 2002 by receiving about two-thirds of the parliamentary seats. Yet it could not lift the prohibitions over headscarves, Imam-Hatip schools, and Qur'an courses due to assertive secularist dominance in the military, judiciary, and media. The president has a key position in the Turkish political system, having the final signature in the process of appointing all generals, many high court members, and all university presidents. Until 2007, assertive secularist President Sezer played a central role in blocking the AK Party's attempts to abolish restrictions on Islamic instruction. The balance of power between assertive secularists and passive secularists changed in 2007.

Transformation from Assertive to Passive Secularism

President Sezer's term ended in 2007. Assertive secularists launched a campaign, including rallies and media propaganda, to prevent the AK Party from electing one of its members as the new president. Since this was not sufficient, the military stepped in by putting a warning on its website on April 27, 2007, which was then called the "e-coup" attempt. This memorandum depicted attempts to reinterpret secularism and some religious activities as threats to secularism, against which the military declared it would be ready to react. Following the military warning, the Constitutional Court upheld the CHP's appeal and cancelled the presidential election by inventing a technical justification. Failing to elect a president, Parliament had to immediately call for an election. The AK Party won the elections and new Parliament elected Abdullah Gül from the AK Party as the president.

Parliament also acted to lift the headscarf ban at universities. In the late 1980s and early 1990s, Parliament, led by passive secularist Turgut Özal's Motherland Party, passed three bills to lift the ban. Yet, these initiatives were blocked by a presidential veto and two decisions by the Constitutional Court. In 2008, AK Party parliamentarians allied with the National Action Party, and they passed constitutional amendments to lift the ban by a vote of 411 to 103. President Gül signed the amendments into law. The CHP and DSP applied to the Constitutional Court to strike these amendments down, while assertive secularist professors protested them and insisted on keeping the headscarf ban. Although Article 142 of the Constitution explicitly prevented the Constitutional Court from intervening in the contents of amendments, the court cancelled these amendments, referring to the principle of secularism and arguing that those who wore headscarves might exert a pressure over those who did not (decision no. 2008/116).[8] Moreover, the chief public prosecutor opened a closure case against the AK Party, which was then called the "judicial coup" attempt. The party was saved from closure by only one vote.

The failures of the "e-coup" and "judicial coup" attempts, as well as the AK Party's electoral success and the election of Gül as president, meant the decline of assertive secularist dominance in Turkish politics. Some court cases and constitutional amendments caused further weakening of military and judiciary tutelage over Turkish democracy. The Ergenekon case opened in 2007 and resulted in the prosecution of military officers accused of organizing assassinations of political figures, judges, and religious minorities in Turkey, in order to frame the AK Party government and the Gülen movement and in order to make conditions ready for a military coup d'état. This and other related cases, such as "Sledgehammer," resulted in the detainment and/or prosecution of more than seventy on-duty generals and admirals, and about three hundred other military officers. These cases sharply limited the military's influence over Turkish politics. Assertive secularist dominance was also weakened by the changing nature of high courts. In the 2010 referendum, a constitutional amendment package was passed by 58 percent. The package included a redesign of the Constitutional Court, as well as the High Council of Judges and Prosecutors, which decides on the promotion, appointment, and disciplinary issues of judges and prosecutors. These changes substantially weakened the assertive secularist domination in the judiciary.

Passive secularist appointments by President Gül and the AK Party government have recently become dominant in the Council of Higher Education (YÖK). The YÖK redesigned the national university entrance exam by providing equal coefficient to regular and vocational (including Imam-Hatip) schools in calculating the scores of their graduates. Again in 2010, the YÖK issued a circular stating that professors could not kick students out of classrooms because of their headscarves; they could only report them for a disciplinary process. This ended the headscarf ban de facto at most of the universities. In 2011, a governmental decree abolished the age limit for the Qur'an courses. A year later, Parliament allowed the reopening of the secondary branches of the Imam-Hatip schools.

These policy changes meant a transformation from assertive to passive secularism in state policies toward religion; this transformation was sealed by a recent decision (no. 2012/128) of the newly designed Constitutional Court. On September 20, 2012 the court upheld the new law that made "The Qur'an" and "The Life of Our Prophet" optional courses in secondary and high schools. In this decision, the court stresses that there are two types of secularism—rigid vs. liberal (this can also be read as assertive vs. passive). By defending the liberal/passive secularism, the court rejected its earlier precedents that had endorsed rigid/assertive secularism. This historical decision was made by a 15 vs. 2 majority.

Transformation from assertive to passive secularism in Turkey has been a result of the democratization that shrunk the gap between the state policies and the majority of people's demand for religious freedom. This transformation is also promising to the contribution of rights and freedoms of Christians and Jews in Turkey. In 2008, Parliament—led by AK Party deputies— passed a bill to recognize the legal status and property rights of Christian and Jewish foundations, and Gül signed it into law (Kılınç 2008, 243–312). More recently, Erdoğan signed a governmental decree to return or compensate the properties of 162 Christian and Jewish foundations, which had been confiscated by previous governments ("Azınlıklara Jest," *Hürriyet*, August 28, 2011).

Nevertheless, there are still important reforms that Turkey needs to achieve, in terms of truly transforming from assertive to passive secularism. Although the headscarf ban has been de facto lifted in most universities, legal and judicial changes are still necessary to prevent a future reemergence of the ban. Another major issue is the Alevis' cemevis. Erdoğan and some courts have insisted on rejecting the definition of cemevis as places of worship, arguing that mosques are the only appropriate places of worship for Sunni and Alevi Muslims. The cemevi-mosque dichotomy is misleading, giving the fact that Muslims have had various places of worship, e.g. tekkes and zaviyes, for centuries. Moreover, in a secular democracy, it is up to the people, not the state, to define what a place of worship is. Alevis have the right to define the cemevis. Passive secularism also requires that the Halki Seminary—the only theological school of the Greek Orthodox Church in Turkey—be reopened. It was closed in 1972 as a result of the tension between Turkey and Greece; but today it means a violation of religious freedom, regardless of its symbolic meaning in international politics. Last but not least, the increasingly authoritarian tendencies and the discreetly Islamist agenda of Erdoğan have worried many in Turkey and abroad. Turkey needs a genuinely pluralistic system of state-religion relations. If Turkey achieves to consolidate a passive secularist regime, particularly on issues related to religion and education, it can become a model to other Middle Eastern countries.

Conclusion

Secularism has been regarded as a way of creating state neutrality toward various religious and non-religious doctrines. Yet, it may itself become a doctrine that provides particular understandings of the good life to compete with religious views. Thus, secularization of a public education system may result in the state's imposition of secularism at the expense of religions, instead of promoting state neutrality (Monsma and Soper 1997). From a more philosophical point of view, scholars have discussed how secularism itself can become an alternative to religions, rather than providing a neutral public sphere (Asad 2003; Casanova 2009; Taylor 2009; Stepan 2011). This essay specifically stresses how assertive secularism in Turkey has been a "comprehensive doctrine" à la Rawls (1996). Therefore, assertive secularist public education has not played a bridging role in Turkey; on the contrary, it has created its own "believers" and motivated them to monopolize the public discussion by excluding conservative Muslims as well as other voices.

Turkey has recently been in a transformation period, in terms of replacing dominant assertive secularism with passive secularism. The major challenge for the passive secularists will be to produce a liberal democratic discourse that can bridge different ideological and religious groups in Turkey. Given the fact that conservative Muslims (such as the AK Party and the Gülen movement) are increasingly influential in Turkish public life, an Islamic discourse that supports pluralism and liberal democracy will be more effective now than ever.

To persuade and motivate religious people toward pluralistic sociopolitical relations can become easier if a principled, not simply pragmatic, discourse on toleration is produced by referring to authentic sources of a religious tradition (Seligman 1999; 2004, esp. pp. x, 10). In the traditional Sufi understanding, there is a crucial phrase similar to *e pluribus unum*—*kesrette vahdet* (unity within diversity). It implies understanding oneness of God through the diversity of its creatures, which as being mirrors, reflect His numerous names and attributes. For decades, assertive secularist domination in Turkish public discourse was so influential that it did not allow the development of alternative Islamic discourses; it even eliminated the rich Ottoman legacy of Islamic thought. Because of this amnesia, when the Turkish Islamists became visible again in the 1970s and 1980s, they mostly used translations of Egyptian and Pakistani Islamist works. The future will show whether conservative Muslims in Turkey (from politicians to academics, from civic associations to religious leaders) will succeed in responding to the dual challenge of returning to their religio-cultural roots and producing a modern pluralistic perspective in various domains, from education to politics. Such a synthesis will be a big step forward in bridging the gap between conservative Muslims and assertive secularists in Turkey, and may as well provide an inspiring experience for the rest of the Muslim world.

NOTES

1. Some portions of this essay were adapted from my book (Kuru 2009); they are reprinted with permission.
2. In 1782, Congress adopted *e pluribus unum* as a dictum in the Seal of the United States. In 1956, Congress passed a law to replace it with "In God We Trust" as the national motto (31 U.S.C. 5112 [d] [1]). *E pluribus unum* is still written on

several US coins and currencies. Initially, it primarily meant the federal unity among the states; but later on, it began to refer to the American "melting pot," which combines people with various identities.

3. Recently, several restrictions over the use of the Kurdish language in Turkey were lifted. A public television broadcaster, TRT, launched a new channel to broadcast exclusively in Kurdish, several public universities opened new departments of Kurdish Language and Literature, and Kurdish language became an optional course in secondary schools.

4. Some of these European-style schools were opened by the Ottoman government, while others were run by American, French, or British missionaries (see Doğan and Sharkey 2011). Although it is very difficult to know the exact total number of these schools, some publications note that in 1905 the British missionaries had 120 schools and about 10,000 students; while in 1914, American missionaries had 473 primary schools, 54 secondary schools, 4 seminaries, and 11 high schools, with 32,252 students in the Ottoman lands. French Catholic missionaries focused on, is today, Syria and Lebanon; and in these regions, again in 1914, they had 150 schools and a university (Doğan 2009, 385–388).

5. A major assertive secularist justification for state control over Islam in Turkey is that Islam, unlike Christianity, has particular characteristics that require a rigid secularism. Turkish Constitutional Court used this argument in its decision on March 7, 1989 (no. 1989/12), which became an important precedent for its subsequent decisions on secularism. For a critique of the court on this issue, see Kuru 2009, 17–20, 174–176, 242–246.

6. For the Gülen (or Hizmet) movement and its schools, see Kuru 2003; Kuru 2010; Sabrina Tavernise, "Turkish Schools Offer Pakistan a Gentler Vision of Islam," *New York Times*, May 4, 2008.

7. About two-thirds of women in Turkey wear some sorts of headscarves. According to the survey of *Milliyet* and Konda, women who wear headscarves do so for: their religious beliefs (73 percent), customs and habits (18 percent), demands of parents or husbands (6 percent), adaptation to social environment (3 percent) (*Milliyet*, 3–4; Aralık 2007). For an anthropological analysis of the headscarf ban's impact on Muslim women's subjectivity and their productions of new Islamic discourses in Turkey, see Akbulut 2011.

8. The Turkish court's decision was inspired by the European Court of Human Rights's (ECtHR) *Leyla Şahin vs. Turkey* decision on November 10, 2005. The ECtHR justified the Turkish state's ban on individuals' wearing of headscarves. In *Lautsi vs. Italy* (March 18, 2011), however, the ECtHR held that crosses in Italian public school classrooms did not violate freedom of religion. Although the court argued that students wearing headscarves might constitute pressure over their adult peers at Turkish universities, it claimed that crosses would not constitute a pressure over teenager students in Italian schools.

BIBLIOGRAPHY

Akbulut, Zeynep. "Banning Headscarves and Women's Subjectivity in Turkey," PhD diss., University of Washington, Seattle, 2011.
Asad, Talal. *Formations of the Secular: Christianity, Islam, Modernity.* Stanford, CA: Stanford University Press, 2003.
Başgil, Ali Fuat. *Din ve Laiklik.* Istanbul: Yağmur, 1977 [1954].
Berkes, Niyazi. *The Development of Secularism in Turkey.* New York: Routledge, 1998 [1964].
Çakır, Ruşen, and İrfan Bozan. *Sivil, Şeffafve Demokratik Bir Diyanet İşleri Başkanlığı Mümkünmü?* Istanbul: TESEV, 2005.
Çakır, Ruşen, İrfan Bozan, and Balkan Talu. *İmam Hatip Liseleri: Efsanelerve Gerçekler.* Istanbul: TESEV, 2004.
Çarkoğlu, Ali, and Binnaz Toprak. *Değişen Türkiye'de Din, Toplumve Siyaset.* Istanbul: TESEV, 2006.
Casanova, Jose. "The Secular and Secularisms." *Social Research* 76 (2009): 1049–1066.
Doğan, Mehmet Ali. "Missionary Schools." In *Encyclopedia of the Ottoman Empire.* Edited by Gábor Ágoston and Bruce Masters, 385–388. New York: Facts on File, 2009.
Doğan, Mehmet Ali, and Heather J. Sharkey, eds. *American Missionaries and the Middle East: Foundational Encounters.* Salt Lake City: University of Utah Press, 2011.
Frey, Frederick W. "Education: Turkey." In *Political Modernization in Japan and Turkey.* Edited by Robert E. Ward and Dankwart A. Rustow, 205–235. Princeton, NJ: Princeton University Press, 1964.
Gökalp, Ziya. *Kitaplar 1: Türkçülüğün Esasları.* Istanbul: Yapı Kredi, 2007 [1923].
Haarscher, Guy. *La laïcité.* Paris: PUF: Que Sais-Je? 2004.
Hamburger, Philip. *Separation of Church and State.* Cambridge, MA: Harvard University Press, 2004.
Hanioğlu, Şükrü. "The Historical Roots of Kemalism." In *Democracy, Islam, and Secularism in Turkey.* Edited by Ahmet T. Kuru and Alfred Stepan, 32–60. New York: Columbia University Press, 2012.
Hefner, Robert W., and Muhammad Qasim Zaman, eds. *Schooling Islam: The Culture and Politics of Modern Muslim Education.* Princeton, NJ: Princeton University Press, 2007.
Kaplan, İsmail. *Türkiye'de Milli Eğitim İdeolojisi.* Istanbul: İletişim, 1999.
Kılınç, Ramazan. "History, International Norms, and Domestic Institutional Change: State-Religion Relations in France and Turkey," PhD diss., Arizona State University, 2008.
Kuru, Ahmet T. "Fethullah Gülen's Search for a Middle Way between Modernity and Muslim Tradition." In *Turkish Islam and the Secular State: The Gülen Movement.* Edited by M. Hakan Yavuz and John L. Esposito, 115–130. Syracuse, NY: Syracuse University Press, 2003.

———. *Secularism and State Policies toward Religion: The United States, France, and Turkey*. New York: Cambridge University Press, 2009.

———. "Afterword: Education, Islam, and the Secular State in Turkey." In *Citizenship, Identity, and Education in Muslim Communities: Essays on Attachment and Obligation*. Edited by Michael Merry and Jeff Milligan, 189–193. New York: Palgrave Macmillan, 2010.

———. "Assertive Secularism, Islam, and Democracy in Turkey." In *Islam in the Modern World*. Edited by Jeffrey T. Kenny and Ebrahim Moosa. New York: Routledge, 2013.

Laborde, Cécile. *Critical Republicanism: The Hijab Controversy and Political Philosophy*. New York: Oxford University Press, 2008.

Monsma, Stephen V., and J. Christopher Soper. *The Challenge of Pluralism: Church and State in Five Democracies*. Lanham, MD: Rowman and Littlefield, 1997.

Özbudun, Ergun. "Turkey—Plural Society and Monolithic State." In *Democracy, Islam, and Secularism in Turkey*. Edited by Ahmet T. Kuru and Alfred Stepan, 61–94. New York: Columbia University Press, 2012.

Özbudun, Ergun. "Turkey—Plural Society and Monolithic State." In *Democracy, Islam, and Secularism in Turkey*. Edited by Ahmet T. Kuru and Alfred Stepan. New York: Columbia University Press, 2012.

Özdalga, Elisabeth. "Education in the Name of 'Order and Progress': Reflections on the Recent Eight Year Obligatory School Reform in Turkey." *Muslim World* 89 (1999): 414–438.

Ozouf, Mona. *L'Ecole, l'Eglise et la République: 1871–1914*. Paris: Éditions Cana, 1982.

Ravitch, Frank S. *School Prayer and Discrimination: The Civil Rights of Religious Minorities and Dissenters*. Boston: Northeastern University Press, 1999.

Rawls, John. *Political Liberalism*. New York: Columbia University Press, 1996.

Seligman, Adam B. "Toleration and Religious Tradition." *Society* 36 (1999): 47–53.

———. *Modest Claims: Dialogues and Essays on Tolerance and Tradition*. Notre Dame, IN: University of Notre Dame Press, 2004.

Soğukdere, Özlem. "İmam Hatip Liseleri," *CNN Turk Online*, May 28, 2004. Available online, http://www.cypriot.org.uk/Documents/Haber1/Imam-Hatip-Liseleri.htm.

Stepan, Alfred. "The Multiple Secularisms of Modern Democracies and Autocracies." In *Rethinking Secularism*. Edited by Craig Calhoun, Mark Juergensmeyer, and Jonathan van Antwerpen. New York: Oxford University Press, 2011.

Taylor, Charles. "Foreword: What is Secularism." In *Secularism, Religion, and Multicultural Citizenship*. Edited by Geoffrey Brahm Levey and Tariq Modood. New York: Cambridge University Press, 2009.

T.B.M.M. 1942 [1924]. *T.B.M.M. Kavanin Mecmuası, Vol. 2, Devre II, İçtima 1*. Ankara: T.B.M.M. Matbaası.

Ward, Robert E., and Dankwart A. Rustow. "Conclusion." In *Political Modernization in Japan and Turkey*. Edited by Robert E. Ward and Dankwart A. Rustow, 434–468. Princeton, NJ: Princeton University Press, 1964.

7

Walking the Tightrope

PROSPECTS FOR CIVIL EDUCATION AND
MULTICULTURALISM IN "*KETUANON MELAYU*" MALAYSIA

Joseph Chinyong Liow

Schools are where the seeds for national unity and national integration are sown.
—ABDULLAH AHMAD BADAWI,
NINTH MALAYSIA PLAN, 2006

IN 2003, JUST prior to his retirement as Malaysia's longest serving Prime Minister, Mahathir Mohammad pushed through his controversial PPSMI (*Pengajaran dan Pembelajaran Sain dan Matematik dalam Bahasa Inggris* [The teaching of science and mathematics in the English language]) policy in national and private vernacular schools. According to its architects, the policy was intended to arrest an alarming decline in the standard of English in Malaysian schools, and to enhance the competitiveness of the Malaysian labor force. What would seem an innocuous and sensible decision in most other contexts elicited a maelstrom of protest in Malaysia. A wide spectrum of Malaysian society—including Malay politicians, Chinese civil society groups, and Tamil educators—spoke out in favor of the continuation of a vernacular model of education, with some Malay-language groups even challenging the constitutionality of the policy.[1] Under pressure from Malay-language groups in particular, and with the political stakes increased after the March 2008 elections, the Malaysian government decided to reverse the policy in 2009.[2]

Meanwhile, a controversy erupted concerning ethnic stereotypes portrayed in a Malaysian novel, used widely as a classroom text. In the novel *Interlok*, authored by Abdullah Hussain, references were made to ethnic Indians as "pariah," and allusions also to Chinese as foreigners. The novel kicked up a storm in Malaysian politics, with the Malaysian Indian Congress, a component party of the ruling National Front, demanding that the novel be removed from the Form Five literature syllabus. Lost in the debate and politicking was the fact that the novel talks of how the fates of three Malaysian youths—a Malay, an Indian, and a Chinese—were ultimately intimately intertwined, or the fact that the novel itself has been around for forty years, and during that time, barely caused a fraction of the discontent.

The controversy surrounding the PPSMI policy and the *Interlok* issue gets to the heart of one of the most fundamental challenges for civic education in Malaysia today—how to frame and institutionalize multiculturalism in the classroom and, more broadly, across the Malaysian education system. Indeed, the road to multiculturalism in Malaysia has proven to be a perilous one, wrought with challenges and obstacles. Since the days of the British colonial administration, the institutionalization, compartmentalization, and segregation of ethnic groups have been main features of state policy in almost all aspects of life. For the most part a consequence of this legacy, ethnic elites in post-colonial Malaysia have taken on the mantle of defenders of the "rights" and "privileges" of their respective communities; and in so doing, have perpetuated not only differences, but more importantly, stereotypes and hierarchy. Against this backdrop, one of the biggest policy and intellectual challenges for education in Malaysia is the matter of fostering multiculturalism as well as a sense of unity among its various ethnic and religious groups.

The purpose of this chapter is to examine whether the education system in Malaysia has served as a vehicle for the promotion of values of pluralism, equality, inclusivity, and unity, or if it has in fact been an impediment. By exploring debates and discourses surrounding education policy, the school system, and academic curriculum in Malaysia—it is through these three reference points that two issues dictate the conceptualization and formulation of education policy—language and religion; this chapter argues that racial discourses, narratives, and politics continue to frame educational policy making in the country, and hence have been major impediments to the advancements of pluralism, integration, and democratization in Malaysia. This state of affairs is attributable to the polarization of communal narratives, which have come to be reflected in the discourses and debates surrounding the realm of education. While the National Front–controlled Malaysian government is cognizant of the importance of education reform for purposes of enhancing the competitiveness of the Malaysian labor force, as well as improving relations between ethnic groups toward the ends of fulfilling Prime Minister Najib's vision of "1 Malaysia"—it has, at the same time, also used its control of education to perpetuate the politically driven narrative of Malay supremacy. As such, education policy has become an extension of identity and power, but it is precisely because of local conflicts that an inclusive political society—which typically requires social organizations and ethical discourses for bridging religious and ethical divides—remains elusive; conflicts of a religious and public-ethical sort are in fact profoundly local and "embedded." In other words, political expediency has held the noble and lofty goals of education hostage, and inasmuch as the narrative of Malay supremacy continues to define the parameters of social, political, and cultural discourse, it is likely to do so for the foreseeable future.

Mapping the Education Terrain

According to Malaysia's Department of Statistics, the population of the country in 2000 was 28.25 million, comprising 50.4 percent indigenous Malays, 23.7 percent Chinese, 11 percent other indigenous groups, 7.7 percent Indian, and a further 7.2 percent other non-indigenous ethnic groups and non-Malay citizens. Islam is the religion of 62 percent of the population, including practically all Malays and segments of other ethnic groups. Of the other religions, 19.2 percent of the population professes to be Buddhists, 9.1 percent Christians, 6.3 percent Hindus, 2.6 percent Confucian, and 0.8 percent "animist" (Kraince 2009, 115). *Bumiputera*—literally meaning "son of the soil," and includes ethnic Malays and a host of indigenous communities, mostly residing in Eastern Malaysia—account for 65.1 percent of Malaysia's overall population (Ibrahim 2007, 158).

From these census figures, it has been estimated that approximately 27.5 percent are youths of the age fifteen and below, whereas 68.1 percent fall within the fifteen to sixty-four year bracket (Ibrahim 2007, 158). As far as Malaysia's teenage population is concerned, the estimated figure is 7.8 million. Of this figure, 5,289,209 are registered in national/ national-type primary and secondary schools; 105,143 are enrolled in private, state, and independent Islamic schools; 50,280 in private Chinese secondary schools; and 27,209 in other secular private institutions (Kraince 2009, 121–124). The status of an additional 2,510,791 is, presumably, unknown.

Formal education in Malaysia starts at the age of seven and stretches to age twelve for compulsory primary schooling (Standard One to Six), thirteen to fifteen years old for lower secondary schooling (Form One to Three), sixteen and seventeen years old for upper secondary and college education (Form Four to Six), and from nineteen years old onward for tertiary education. By replacing the *Sijil Rendah Pelajaran* (SPR) examination with the *Penilaian Menengah Rendah* (PMR) public examinations taken at the end of the lower secondary school (Form Three), the government has paved the way for students to proceed to the upper secondary level and complete five years of secondary education instead of three years, thereby enhancing opportunities for higher levels of attainment of educational qualifications (Lee 2004, 438). The national education system will gradually be restructured from eleven to twelve years, including six years of compulsory education in line with the practice in many developed nations (Ministry of Education 2008, 19). The Malaysia government also intends to implement universal secondary education for its citizens in order to enhance human resource development and capacity building.

The foundations of modern education in Malaya can be traced to the colonial era of British administration (c. 1824–1957). Under the British colonial administration, ethnic communities were allowed to form their own vernacular schools to cater to the educational needs of their respective communities. This was very much in line with a broader colonial policy of ethnic segregation. The result of this was the proliferation of Malay, Chinese, and Tamil schools across the peninsula. At the same time, the colonial administration and Christian missionaries established their own English schools, which quickly became recognized as elite establishments that catered to the educational needs of the children of British colonial officials and the members of the Malay aristocratic elite. These schools also played an important role in educating and producing officers for the colonial administrative machinery.

The Education Ordinance Act of 1952, however, marked a significant (if short-lived) shift in education policy. In it, Malay vernacular schools were required to introduce the teaching of English, while Chinese and Tamil vernacular schools had to provide education in both the English and Malay languages. This policy would later be superseded by the Razak

Report in 1956 (to be discussed later), which mapped out the education policy in Malaya, in preparation for independence. For a short while during the interim of the Japanese occupation of 1942–1945, Japanese schools proliferated in Malaya, but they served mostly as instruments of Japanese propaganda—instructing students in the virtues of Japanese culture, values, and language, and propagating the concept of the Greater East Asia Co-Prosperity Sphere.

Education in Malaysia would change drastically with decolonization and independence. A key feature to the negotiations between the British colonial government and the Malay elite that culminated in the Malayan independence of 1957 was the issue of the centrality of Malay identity and interests in the configuration of post-colonial Malayan society.[3] To that end, the state apparatus bequeathed by the British to the Malay elite was used to reinforce, and to certain extents—to amplify, the notion of Malay supremacy. Nowhere was this more clearly evident than in the matter of education policy.

Representing the newly minted Malay-dominated post-colonial state on educational matters, and also empowered by constitutional provisions that defended the primacy of the Malay language in the country, the Ministry of Education (which would eventually become one of the most important ministries in Malaysia) oversaw the proliferation of Malay language schools at both primary and secondary levels. At the same time, in order to placate minority groups, the government allowed for the formation of vernacular primary schools (using the Chinese and Tamil languages). In terms of nomenclature, while the Malay language primary schools are known as national schools, or *Sekolah Kebangsaan*, the vernacular primary schools are known as national-type schools, or *Sekolah Jenis Kebangsaan* (elsewhere, these schools are also known as standard and standard-type schools).

The diversity in Malaysia's system is further complicated by the existence of public and private Islamic schools. Recent studies have identified five types of Islamic schools—People's Religious Schools (*Sekolah Agama Rakyat*, or SAR) that are maintained by private individuals, communities, foundations, and organizations; State Islamic Schools (*Sekolah Agama Negeri*, or SAN), which are managed by state governments; Private Islamic Schools (*Sekolah Agama Swasta*, or SAS), which follow the national curriculum, but are operated by private groups; National Islamic Schools (*Sekolah Agama Kebangsaan*, or SAK); and National Schools (*Sekolah Kebangsaan*, or SK). The Malaysian government administers the last two categories. These privately, state-, and federally run schools provide primary and secondary stream education using Malay and Arabic languages, and have Islamic, vocational, and secular subjects in their curriculum (Kraince 2009).

Student progression from the primary to secondary level is governed by a similar framework that provides for state and private schools. There are, however, two discernible policy differences. First, Tamil language schools ceased to operate at the secondary level. Hence, students who chose the Tamil medium in primary school have to switch either to national (Malay language) schools, Chinese medium private schools, or Arabic medium private religious schools. Second, while Chinese language secondary schools were permitted, they lost their "national-type" status and became purely private schools. The system also allows for voluntary migration from one stream to another, with the only condition being that language requirements are fulfilled. In other words, students from Malay or Chinese medium primary schools have the option of switching to a secondary school of the other medium. To do that however, the student would need to achieve a minimum of sixty marks in both languages taught in their primary school leaving examination.[4] In addition, students from national and national-type primary schools can also enroll in private secondary schools (e.g., Chinese students who wish to undertake secondary education in the Chinese language). For students from religious schools (whether private or public) who wish to enter secular secondary schools, they will have to demonstrate proficiency in the medium of the school of choice.

To some extent then, the system provides for the flexibility to transfer across streams and mediums fairly easily. Underlying this is the need to negotiate assertions of cultural identity against the backdrop of multiculturalism and integration. This is especially true for students from national, national-type, and religious primary schools run by the federal and state governments, as well as students from the SARs or People's Religious Schools that are often associated with the Islamist opposition party, PAS (*Parti Islam Se-Malaysia*, or the Pan-Malaysian Islamic Party). Students from SAS private Islamic schools managed by private organizations such as *Angkatan Belia Islam Malaysia* (ABIM), however, enjoy no such liberty, and upon graduation from primacy school, have to transfer to either national, secular, or religious schools. Unlike SAR schools that are mostly independent in terms of funding and control, SAS schools are dependent on the Malaysian government for funding and subscribe to the national curriculum with the incorporation of religious studies. Because SAS primary schools combine national, secular, and religious curriculum and are government funded, they effectively serve as instruments for the perpetuation of the government's Islamization program targeted at both counteracting the opposition party, PAS, and balancing against the existence of private Chinese secondary schools—by funneling their students to national schools.

Notwithstanding the general flexibility built into the system, a cursory glance at post-secondary education reveals the underlying opportunities and constraints confronting students as they look further into the horizon beyond secondary education. In effect, students who graduate from national schools, from either Malay language-based or Islamic language-based schools, proceed fairly seamlessly on to public polytechnics, vocational institutes, and matriculation colleges, and subsequently to public universities. For graduates of private Chinese schools, on the other hand, the only educational route available for them is the private university educational path, since their secondary qualifications are not recognized.

To sum up, national schools are fully funded by the government, while the national-type (vernacular) schools are either partially funded or fully sponsored by private organizations. Private schools comprise not only Chinese vernacular primary and secondary schools (and also Tamil medium primary schools), but also Islamic religious schools, such as the SAR- and SAS-type schools. These private schools practice their own system of administration and follow, either in part or entirely, an independent curriculum, albeit under some general supervision by the Ministry of Education (Ibrahim 2007, 160). In other words, their education curriculum and administration practices have to abide by broad guidelines established by the Ministry, with allowances for variations unique to the circumstances of these private schools, mostly due to the vernacular and religious nature of their syllabus.

What is striking about the diversity mapped out above is the entrenched nature of ethnic, religious, and class referents that have been, and remain, inherent in Malaysian society. Clearly too, given the nature of the government's education policies, the point can be made that, while these polarizing forces in Malaysian education are very much a product of colonial history, today they also carry the imprimatur of the post-colonial state. Yet they also bedevil the state at the same time, establishing restrictive parameters for its formulation of education policy. It is to this enduring paradox that the chapter now turns.

The Foundations of Malaysia's Educational Policies: Ketuanan Melayu

Clearly, as would be the case elsewhere, the education system in Malaysia socializes younger generations of citizens into the norms and organizing principles of Malaysian society. In this respect, deep religious and cultural divisions built into the education system and perpetuated by the state have posed significant obstacles for multilateralism and inclusive and democratic interaction. At the heart of this is the freighted notion of *Ketuanan Melayu*, or "Malay Supremacy." This paper contends that a full appreciation of the impact of discourses and narratives of *Ketuanan Melayu*, as it is represented through its place and role in education, is critical to understanding the prospects and limitations of civic education in Malaysia. This is because to understand the place of *Ketuanan Melayu* in national and civic education is to "forecast what political claims it (the Malay community) makes, what idiom it speaks in, what issues divide it from others, what counter-claims the others make, and generally how each will behave in and out of power" (Horowitz 1985, 228).

According to the *Kamus Dewan* produced by the influential *Dewan Bahasa dan Pustaka* (Institute for Language and Literature), *Ketuanan* refers to "the right to rule or control a country (*Negara*), state (*Negeri*), or a district (*Daerah*), or sovereignty (*Kedaulatan*)." Its root word, *Tuan*, in this context means "master" (in relation to a slave), or "owner." Hence, literally, *Ketuanan Melayu* means Malay sovereignty or the ownership claim of the Malay on the *Tanah Melayu*, or the land belonging to the Malays and everything in/on it. The concept is further romanticized in the following manner in a Form Three textbook:

> The love for whatever that is related to the Malay race such as political right, language, culture, heritage, customs and homeland. The Malay Peninsula (*Semenanjung Tanah Melayu*) is regarded as the ancestral land of the Malays (Ting 2009, 3).

It is important to register the fact that the notion of *Ketuanan Melayu* is constitutionally sanctioned. According to the Federal Constitution of 1957, while non-Malays were granted citizenship rights, Article 153 of the Constitution decrees that it is the responsibility of the king (*Yang di Pertuan Agong*) to safeguard the special position of the Malays and

Bumiputra (literally, Sons of the Soil), as well as the "legitimate interests" of other communities.[5] In this way, the "special position" of the Malays and *Bumiputra* are codified. Many Malay politicians, educationists, religious leaders, civil society activists, and culturalists have come to define this as Malay *"ketuanan"* over other ethnic groups. Moreover, given the intimate relationship between Malay ethnic identity and the religion of Islam—also constitutionally enshrined, *"Ketuanan Melayu"* can in Malay minds immediately translate to the concept of *"Ketuanan Agama"* as well—the supremacy of religion, in this case, Islam (Liow 2009, 43–68). For current purposes, the point to be made is that the realm of education has become one of the more controversial arenas where the concept of *Ketuanan Melayu* has been expressed and contested.

The foundations for post-colonial education policy in Malaysia were laid out in the Report of the Education Committee of 1956—otherwise known as the Razak Report—crafted by a committee led by then-Minister for Education Abdul Razak Hussein. Central to the Razak Report was the policy recommendation to reinstate the primacy of the Malay language, which had been eroded somewhat in the context of the 1952 Education Act formulated during the twilight of British colonial administration, while retaining non-Malay vernacular schools. In so doing, the Razak Report effectively gave institutional form and substance to the principal of *Ketuanan Melayu* by recognizing the primacy of the Malay language in the education system and defining the terms through which minority communities were to integrate into Malaysian society.

In 1960, the Rahman Talib Educational Review Committee Report not only further institutionalized the suggestions of the Razak Report regarding the primacy of Malay-language education, but also called for Malay to be recognized as *Bahasa Malaysia*, or the national language, in the education system. Further to that, under the pretext of national unity, the Rahman Talib Report also proposed the elimination of communal schools from the national system, and for all national schools to focus only on Malay and English.

Following the publication of the Rahman Talib Report, which formed the basis of the 1961 Education Act, a seven-year period began (1961–1968), during which English medium national-type schools were converted to Malay language national schools, with English as a compulsory second language. Other timelines for conversion to the Malay medium articulated in the Rahman Talib Report included: primary schools (1975), secondary schools (1982), and universities (1983).

In addition to the changes to language instruction, the Rahman Talib Report also went further than the Razak Report by incorporating Islamic religious instruction in all assisted primary and secondary schools for all Muslims students.

Purportedly, the main motivation behind the Rahman Talib Report, as alluded to earlier, was the need for unity and to create a sense of national consciousness. This could be done, the authors of the report envisaged, through the introduction of a single language that all ethnic communities would be compelled to accept and master. Thus, by stressing the centrality of the Malay language, it was assumed that ethnic and linguistic differences could be reduced, and national unity augmented (Jamil and Razak 2010, 81). What materialized, nevertheless, has been the exact opposite. The language policy has buttressed Malay views of their dominant position, amplified the hegemony of Malay norms and views in Malaysian society, and further sensitizes non-Malays to their minority status in Malaysia. Indeed, the only benefit that accrued to ethnic minorities from the Razak Report and Rahman Talib Report was the minor victory of the reports' acknowledgement that non-Malay vernacular schools could be retained, albeit in private capacity, so long as they accepted the subordinate role of their ethnic languages to the Malay language in primary schools.

Following the race riots in May 1969, discussions within the government about the elusive balance between Malay supremacy and multiculturalism resurfaced quickly. In response, the administration of Tun Abdul Razak developed the five governing principles of the Rukunegara (which bear a striking similarity to Indonesia's Pancasila): belief in God, loyalty to King and Country, upholding the Constitution, rule of Law, and good behavior and morality. Following this, a National Cultural Policy was formulated in 1971 that again stressed the centrality of Malay language and culture, and the peripheral role of minority languages and cultures, even as they were accepted as part of the national culture. In addition to the highly controversial National Cultural Policy, the educational system was viewed as critical to the promotion of the idea of national unity. Concomitantly, one of the main vehicles envisaged to promote this conception of national unity was the teaching of civics and moral education.

Civic education was taught as a separate subject through the 1970s, until it was phased out and replaced by moral education as a compulsory subject in the 1980s. Implemented in the 1980s, moral education was to be taught to non-Muslims, while Muslims studied Islamic education. The Moral education syllabus for the secondary schools contains values based on religious considerations, and traditions and values of the multiracial society as well as the Rukunegara. The last value added to the Moral Education syllabus is citizenship, which was included in the mid-1990s (Barone 2002). In line with the emphasis on Rukunegara and citizenship, a major facet to civic education in Malaysia has been the teaching of history as a means to inform how students think about issues of race, religion, and belonging.

The construction of history in the Malaysian education system is instructive of prevailing views on issues of culture, identity, and place, and how these influence the interpretation of civic education. Indeed, the introduction to the Form One history textbook declares as much, that history can show students how to be "good citizens." In this regard, what is important to note is the persistence of debates among interest groups that continue to question the special rights of Malay supremacy—in what have been deemed "sensitive" subjects in the national narrative of Malaysian history—as well as the roles and contributions of particular ethnic groups to the development of modern Malaysia and how this is portrayed in historical texts used in the school curriculum. The latter issue is particular controversial, for, as Helen Ting has argued, "the homeland/immigrant discourse is not only the central theme of the ideology of *Ketuanan Melayu*, it also sets the framework of the historical representation of the various races as well as the appreciation of the citizenship issue" (Ting 2009, 39).

Citing the following examples found in the Form Three and Form five history textbooks, Ting points out how contradictory attitudes toward the presence of non-Malays can be discerned. Non-Malays are described as *orang dagang, golongan pendatang,* or *imigran*, which Ting explicated to mean foreigner or immigrant, as opposed to *penduduk tempatan*, or local inhabitants. This is done to implicitly delegitimize their position in relation to Malay rights whenever the issue of citizenship rights is discussed. Moreover, the terms *orang dagang* and *golongan pendatang* are used in pejorative fashion to describe non-Malays in the context of Malay opposition to the Malayan Union and advocacy of *Ketuanan Melayu*, thereby obliquely implying that these texts convey the impression that the granting of equal rights to non-Malays was essentially a threat to the position of the Malays. The polarization is compounded, Sandra Manickam further suggests, by referencing British colonialism and how non-Malays (namely, Chinese and Indians) were allied to the British, and hence were beneficiaries of colonial rule, not to mention that unlike the Malays, the Chinese and

Indians had not, as it were, resided in the Malay Peninsula since the dawn of time (Manickam 2004).

There is however, slippage and inconsistency in the application of these terminologies—particularly in the most recent versions of these textbooks—that speak to the subjective and controversial nature of questions of citizenship. Chief of these inconsistencies is the usage of the terms like "*Rakyat*" (citizens or subjects) and "*Bangsa*" (nation). It has been observed that both terms have been used in contradictory fashion within the same textbook: they have been used in exclusive fashion to refer only to the Malays during the period of the *Melaka Sultanate*, but have also been used in inclusive fashion when referring to the Malaysia of today, which encompasses a multiethnic society. In other words, as R. Santhiram notes:

> An inconsistency thus arises by the usage of the same term, *Rakyat*, to refer to separate groupings in the past and present. In reference to Melaka, the *Rakyat* are presented racially as Malays, *Orang Laut*, and *Orang Asli*, and are not the other racial groups presented as traders. Yet in the present, the textbook tries to reach out to a *Rakyat* who just pages ago were referred to as outsiders. *Rakyat* takes on the tones of referring specifically to Malays, making it an unviable option in which to build unity. (Santhiram 1999, 127)

Rolling Back Ketuanan Melayu?

Having encouraged racial and ethnic polarization by virtue of its foundational education policies, the Malaysian government attempted to reverse the trend by launching the Vision School Project in 1995. This followed concerns that the vernacular education system was polarizing Malaysian society and creating barriers to the realization of what Mahathir Mohammad, then-prime minister, envisaged as a *Bangsa Malaysia*, a Malaysian nation that celebrated its diversity. The Vision School Project essentially entailed locating two or three vernacular primary schools in the same compound, such that students had to share common facilities as the school canteen, field, and courtyard. The idea behind it was to encourage interaction among students of vernacular schools in a way that ostensibly did not require cultural compromise and extensive negotiation of identity markers. Currently, there are six such vision schools operating—in Selangor, Kedah, Penang, and Negeri Sembilan, and two in Perak.

Though the aims and objectives of these vision schools are laudable—in practice, they merely gloss over fundamental differences, for core problems of segregation and polarization remain, and in addition, the Vision School Project has gained little currency among non-Malay communities. In point of fact, the vision school idea continues to be vehemently opposed by Chinese educationists and educational organizations on the grounds that national schools (i.e., Malay-language schools) were "first among equals" in the vision for a school formula, since they were often the largest component, and, moreover, that the "working language" of extracurricular activities and communications outside the classroom remains Malay in the vision schools. Hence, suspicions continue to abound that what the Vision Schools Project endeavored to do was to undermine Chinese and Indian schools using a common multiethnic platform that actually emphasized Malay first, at the expense of other ethnic schools interests and objectives (Lee 2010, 186–187).

There are further practical, functional problems associated with the Vision Schools Project. One such problem is the lack of cultural understanding among teachers employed in vernacular schools. This lack of understanding is likely to be due to pedagogical and curriculum deficits stemming from the absence of teacher exposure to multicultural training. It was discovered, for instance, that teachers very seldom went beyond technical explanations of the cultural practices and social mores of other religions and ethnic groups. As a result, students may know what not to do or say, but have little appreciation of why they had to do or say certain things (Malakolunthu et al. 2010). Because of this, teachers were oblivious of the need to promote and facilitate multicultural exchange on the grounds of the "common spaces" of the vision schools; what resulted was basically the formation of cliques, creation of invisible barriers, and emergence of silos on the playground and in the canteens. In other instances, principals involved in the Vision School Project were not given instructions as to how to actually implement the initiative in their schools. As a result, they were often left to their own devices, and the creation of vision schools was left to their interpretation (Malakolunthu et al. 2009, 127–129).

If the Vision School Project was one policy conundrum carried over from the Mahathir administration that continues to bedevil the Malaysian government, then the PPSMI (introduced at the beginning of the paper) must surely be another. In order to reverse what he saw to be an alarming decline of English in national schools, in 1996 Mahathir floated the idea of changing the medium of instruction from Malay to English in the national school curriculum subjects of mathematics and sciences, so as to keep up with global trends.

Mahathir's suggestion of the change sparked a nationwide debate that pitted reformists who supported Mahathir's idea against the defenders of vernacular education. Stiff opposition came not only from the Malay educationists, but also from Chinese and Tamil teachers who felt that students from vernacular schools would be heavily disadvantaged by the implementation of a compulsory English medium education in the school curriculum, given their lack of competence in even the basics of the language. All three groups shared a further concern—the loss of cultural identity. On the other hand, proponents of the shift argued that such a measure was necessary—indeed long overdue—in order to enhance the competitiveness of the Malaysian labor force and prepare the country for the economic challenges of globalization. Some elites and Mahathir allies from the ruling UMNO party also supported the policy, on the grounds that such a move would actually further strengthen the growing Malay middle class, and in so doing, enhance the party's power, and, consequently, *Ketuanan Melayu* as well (Lee 2010, 443).

Despite widespread opposition, the policy was forced through during the twilight of the Mahathir administration. Nevertheless, opposition remained—and indeed, intensified. Under persistent pressure from vernacular school educationists and heading a ruling coalition that had lost significant ground at the last general election, Prime Minister Najib Razak,(himself an eloquent and articulate member of the traditional Malay elite and a product of Britain's elite schools), was forced to overturn the policy and return to the use of the Malay language in the teaching of mathematics and science. So categorical was the response to this pressure that the Najib administration could not even countenance a middle ground as suggested by some lobby groups, namely, that students and parents be allowed to choose either the English or Malay mediums for these subjects.

Islamic Education

A corollary to the debate on *Ketuanan Melayu* in the education system has been the role of religious education, and in particular, Islamic education, in Malaysian schools. The matter of the Malaysian government's "Islamization" program—which has permeated every branch of the civil service, including education policy—has already received extensive treatment elsewhere and need not occupy us here. What is important to note for current purposes is the effort to enhance the imprint of Islam on the education system as part of the broader concept of *Ketuanan Melayu* by virtue of Islam's role as a key identity marker of "Malayness," the nature and manifestations of this process, its impact on how civic education is conceptualized and understood in Malaysia today (against what scholars have termed the rising tide of "Islamization"), and the reactions it has elicited from the non-Muslim community.

For champions of the Islamization of Malaysia's education system, the introduction of religious values (specifically, Islamic values) plays an important role in addressing the need for civic and moral education toward the ends of character building. To them, this is premised on the belief that Islam is a life-long process of preparing an individual for his role as a vice-regent (*Khalifah*) of Allah on earth, and in that manner, contributing to the development of society in preparation for the hereafter by viewing one's education as *ibadah* (an act of worship) (Hashim and Langgulung 2008, 1). To that effect, the Education Act of 1996—designed to revise the Education Act of 1961—called for morality, integrity, God-consciousness, and the holistic development of individuals for the benefit of society (Hashim and Langgulung 2008, 1). Yet while the adoption of overtly Islamic values and principles as core tenets of civic education—in order to motivate a sense of purpose and direction—is laudable, insofar as many of these values are, after all, universal and shared with other faiths and creeds—there are nevertheless two issues that have given rise to disputes between Muslims and non-Muslims: the nature of the Islamic elements to the curriculum, and the impression that has been created (whether real or perceived) in the minds of non-Muslims that Islam has assumed a hegemonic position in the education system, and that Islamic values and principles were being imposed on them.

Illustrative of the predominance of the Islamic narrative in discussions of religion and religious values in civic education is the nature and extent of coverage that Islam has gradually been accorded in history and civics textbooks in Malaysia. For instance, while secondary level history textbooks contain chapters on "World Civilizations," the syllabus is very much oriented toward discussions of Islamic civilization. Moreover, scholars have noticed that whereas Islamic history was described as a central feature of world history and a key influence on other civilizational traditions, in the most recent texts, discussions of Islamic civilization apparently occupy up to half the content of the books (Barr and Govindasamy

2010, 301). The Malaysian government has also invested RM150 million to equip national primary schools across the country with 1666 special teaching laboratories that will be used for training in the Jawi script and Quranic recitation (Barr and Govindasamy 2010, 301). Meanwhile, Islamic education is now compulsory for all Muslim students enrolled in national schools (with a minimum of five Muslim students).

The increasing visibility of Islamic influences in the curriculum of general education is not the only matter of concern for non-Muslims. Equally evident—and all too regular—has been the imposition of Islamic norms on everyday school life in many Malaysian schools. For instance, students in some schools in Penang have had to endure changes in their Physical Education curriculum because the attire hitherto permitted by the schools are deemed inappropriate because they reveal too much "flesh." In another instance, the Chinese New Year celebrations in a national school in Penang had been curtailed by the principal who banned the beating of drums during the lion dance segment on the grounds that it was "unIslamic" and "too noisy."[6]

Religious education is also highly politicized in Malaysia. Hence, the amplification of Islamic content in national schools has also served the politically expedient purposes of undercutting the influence that PAS enjoys among the Malay-Muslim population through its extensive network of SARs that have proven particularly popular with Muslim constituents in northern Malaysia. In fact, the Malaysian government took the extreme step in 2001 of cutting funding to SARs on the grounds that these schools were being "politicized" by members of PAS. The move was a measured success insofar as managing to move a significant number of students and teachers from the SAR system to national schools where there were better facilities as well as education and work-related prospects (Hashim and Langgulung 2008, 15).

More important than the mobilization and instrumentalization of Islamic educational institutions, though, is the "type" of Islam and the manner in which it is "taught" in government schools and institutions. To that end, it is notable that the Islamic studies curriculum in national schools stresses a strict adherence to interpretations of Islamic norms and mores that are just as, if not more, exclusivist and insular than the SARs that come under the orbit of PAS (Kraince 2009). Moreover, many of these government programs have abandoned the tradition of the modernist *madrasah* schools that once emphasized critical readings of Islamic texts and the expansion of the curriculum to cover the sciences for the "rigidification" of Islamic knowledge. The exclusivist nature of Islamic education is brought home with the fact that non-Muslim students of national schools are not permitted to attend classes on Islam, which are only conducted for Muslim students, as it was deemed *"haram"* (forbidden) for them to do otherwise. Further compounding the problem was the lack of a strong command of Arabic, even among students who had taken the subject for six years in primary school. The result of this was a discernible weakness in Quranic exegesis, lending further to the uncritical nature of Islamic studies in Malaysia.

While there are drawbacks to the manner in which Islamic education is integrated and conducted in the Malaysian schooling system, it is notable that the establishment of the International Islamic University Malaysia (IIUM) provides a curious exception to general trends. Specifically what is striking about IIUM is the fact that its primary language of instruction is English, and not Malay as in the case of other Malaysian tertiary institutions. Even more striking was the silence of Malay nationalists and educationists when this practice was instituted at the university's inception. This perhaps signifies a willingness to concede some ground when the matter of Islamic ideals is concerned. Be that as it may, Islamization trends of a rigid and exclusivist nature, and the absence of pluralist approaches to the teaching of Islam (even among Muslims) such as those identified above will pose grave problems for prospects of advancing multiculturalism in Malaysia, for these problems reinforce racial and religious identities and prejudices.

Responding to Ketuanan Melayu

Malay political leaders have often singled out the existence of vernacular schools as a factor that has aggravated ethnic polarization in Malaysia. However, this is vocally refuted by non-Malays, in particular the Chinese educationists, who have defended their rights to uphold the use of their language in the schooling of children from their community. To these guardians of the interests of the Chinese community, Chinese language schools were a crucial vehicle for the defense of Chinese culture and identity.

As observed earlier, for reasons of political expediency, a compromise was reached during the drafting of the 1961 Education Act, where the state agreed to retain vernacular primary but not secondary schools. In order to be eligible for government funding, secondary schools had to drop Chinese as the medium of instruction. Needless to say, this drew the ire of the Chinese education lobby. While a large number of Chinese secondary schools gradually fell in line with official policy for pragmatic reasons, changing their medium of instruction first to English, and then to Malay when the English medium was phased out in the 1970s, many secondary schools also opted not to comply with the Act and became independent schools funded by the Chinese community and managed by Chinese educationists affiliated to the United Chinese School Teachers' Association (UCSTA, or *Jiao Zong*) and the United Chinese School Committees' Association (UCSCA, or *Dong Zong*)—collectively known as *Dong Jiao Zong* or DJZ (Santhiram and Tan 2010, 117–331). Since the 1970s, the Chinese educationists have made concerted efforts to strengthen the independent Chinese secondary schools. More importantly, these schools are seen as an alternative form of secondary education for Chinese children outside the government public school system.

Organizations such as the DJZ have acted as pressure groups, employing a range of strategies in dealing with the Malay-led government and safeguarding the interests of the Chinese community. These strategies range from cooperation with the government to outright opposition (and working with opposition parties). In fact, Chinese lobby groups have had to traverse a fine line in their activism. In safeguarding Chinese interests, they have had to be careful not to tread on Malay sensitivities. As some have rightly noted, there should be little doubt that Malay nationalists perceive the DJZ as a threat to the dominant position of the Malay community in the education system (Collins 2006, 298–318). This is evident from the criticisms, often emanating from Malay nationalist quarters in politics and civil society, that groups such as the DJZ place the parochial interests of the Chinese community above the larger national interest.

The persistence of the *Ketuanan Melayu* narrative and the limitations of the traditional non-Malay educationist movements, such as DJZ, have given rise to alternative expressions of minority identity, especially in tertiary education institutions. One such movement that has emerged in recent years is the *Saya Anak Bangsa Malaysia* (SABM, or "I'm a Malaysian") movement that has gradually expanded its presence among Malaysian tertiary student communities.

The SABM movement is actively engaged in promoting awareness beyond racial boundaries. It is particularly active in civic education through the organization of public lectures and forums to foster an understanding of constitutional and civil rights among Malaysians, both Malays and non-Malays. The movement also engages in acts of resistance against prejudicial racial narratives. For instance, leaders of the group have encouraged Malaysian students—both Malay and non-Malay—to refrain from penning their race in official forms. Instead, SABM followers pen "*Saya Anak Bangsa Malaysia.*"

A second movement that has emerged is the "One School For All" (*Satu Sekolah Untuk Semua*, or SSS) movement. Started by urban ethnic Malays, the SSS movement seeks to transform the school system by taking away vernacular schools, the existence of which they argue has undermined pluralism in the country as they polarize students based on race, language, and religion. Proponents of this movement have declared the following on its website as its raison d'être:

> Every single one of us, of all origin and ethnicity, must speak in one tongue and undergo the same educational journey as Warganegaras of this land. No single Anak Bangsa Malaysia should be allowed to fall into the communal trap laid by selfish groups and denied the same opportunity as Mainstream Malaysians.[7]

While the SSS movement claims fostering true unity to be its central objective, several aspects of its proposal have predictably caused alarm in non-Malay quarters. For instance, the movement has proposed the elimination of vernacular schools and the creation of a single schooling system that would conceivably break down the ethnic silos inherent in the current practice of having a range of different types of schools—vernacular, religious, and national. Not surprisingly, this proposal has been met with resistance from Chinese and Tamil educationists (such as the DJZ), who have staunchly defended the existence of vernacular schools as a "right" of the respective minority communities. Similar reactions have come in response to the movement's promotion of the Malay language as the "*Satu Bahasa*" (One Language) of the new education system that they envisage, while relegating the status of vernacular languages to that of "electives." Nevertheless, the reactions of the Chinese and Tamil educationists speak to an equally insular perspective on their part. Underlying these reactions from the non-Malay quarters is an acute concern that such initiatives, even if they arise from civil society rather than the UMNO-led government, are designed to encroach further into their sacrosanct cultural and religious space.

Partisan Politics and Racial Discourse

Up to this point, a central theme in this paper has been the intense politicization of civic education in Malaysia, where school curricula have become vehicles for ethnic mobilization by political actors and interests. Elements of this can be found in how history and civics is conceptualized and taught in schools. Given the recent ascendance of a purportedly multi-ethnic opposition coalition, the question remains as to whether there would be a sharp contrast between the opposition's conceptualization of citizenship and the hitherto dominant model whose contours have been mapped out above.

In March 2008, a coalition of the Islamist PAS, the Chinese-dominated socialist DAP, and the PKR (*Parti Keadilian Rakyat*, or People's Justice Party, led by charismatic former deputy prime minister Anwar Ibrahim) managed to gain substantial ground on the UMNO-led incumbent BN (*Barisan Nasional*, or National Front) coalition. It was not merely the make up of the opposition coalition—the *Pakatan Rakyat*, or the Peoples' Alliance—but also the fact that one of the cornerstones of its electoral campaign was the push for a more democratic, egalitarian, and pluralist model of Malaysian society. To that end, de factor opposition leader Anwar Ibrahim has assailed the notion of racial primacy, remarking that: "notions of social dominance and racial superiority find no resonance among the people except for those diehards still bigoted over ancient and archaic forms of political ideology" (Anwar 2008).

Notwithstanding the optimism, there are reasons to be cautious that a marked shift in the discourse is seriously in the cards.

First, while the opposition is keen to project its successes at the 2008 elections as a ringing endorsement of its agenda, the picture is in truth far more complex. What was notable was the swing of non-Malay support *en masse* to the opposition (including PAS), ostensibly on the grounds that the Chinese component parties in the BN had failed to adequately assert non-Malay interests and fend off increasing encroachment into their cultural and religious space by Malay political leaders' intent on playing the race card. In comparison, Malay's support remained for the most part with UMNO and the BN. In other words, insofar as the discourse on race is concerned, rather than the demonstrative of the invigoration of multi-culturalism, the election results could well be indicative of just how polarized contemporary Malaysian society is.

Second, one cannot dismiss the element of opportunism that brought these three parties together. Euphoria of the 2008 elections aside, it is important to keep in mind that as remarkably resilient as unity in the opposition has proven to be, the ideological underpinnings of the two anchor parties in the opposition coalition—PAS and DAP—remain diametrically opposed. Moreover, while PAS leaders have, in recent years, strained to demonstrate their pluralist credentials by opposing racial discrimination (*assabiyah*, or tribalism) as unIslamic, there has been disquiet within the rank and file about the evident swing away from supporting the Malay cause in a number of issues, including the exclusive rights of Malay-Muslims to the term "Allah" (Liow 2011).

Finally, while education policy has been subject of occasional debate in the Malaysian parliament, politics has for the most part been preoccupied with other more visible and opportunistic issues, such as cases of corruption, political intrigue (as in the case of the change of hands with the state legislature in Perak state), and other more prominent cases of heavily racialized public discourse. Education matters, on the other hand, have been elided. For instance, the Malaysian parliament rejected outright a motion to debate *Interlok*, the controversial book referred to earlier. At the time it was raised (in May 2011), the speaker of the lower house, Pandikar Amin Mulia, responded to the motion by stating that the government "had taken measures" to investigate the contents of the book, and "I have considered the issue and found that it is not necessary to debate it."[8]

Conclusion

In August 2010, a principal of a national secondary school in Bukit Selambau, Kedah, reportedly accused the Chinese pupils of being insensitive toward their Muslim peers by eating in the school compound during the last Friday of the fasting month of Ramadan, and ordered them to return to China if they could not respect the culture of other races. In the same month, on the occasion of Merdeka (Independence) Day celebrations, a principal in a school in Johor was quoted in a police report as saying that "Chinese students are not needed here and can return to China or Foon Yew schools. For the Indian students, the prayer string tied around their neck and wrist makes them look like dogs because only dogs are tied like that."[9] Anecdotal evidence suggests that these are by no means isolated incidences, and are in fact symptomatic of the malaise identified and discussed in this chapter, which have cast a long shadow over education in multicultural Malaysia.

The government of Malaysia has established lofty goals for multiculturalism in Malaysia, toward which schools have been exhorted to labor. Yet in many ways, the evolution of the Malaysian education system—both form and substance—parallels the evolution of Malaysian's multi-ethnic society. To the extent that multiculturalism is a principle objective of the education system in Malaysia, it has led not only to the celebration of assumed differences and inequalities, but, paradoxically, also to the reification of the narratives that underpin them. From the above discussion, because of the intense politicization of education, it is clear that despite abstract allusions of inequality and harmony, the education system regards identities as "fixed" social realities that cannot be disputed or questioned, let alone challenged. The effect of this is that education in Malaysia cannot account for the systematic marginalization of certain communities.

The education system in Malaysia is defined by racialized discourses and the imposition of hegemonic narratives that tend to widen rather than bridge religious and ethical divides. Nowhere is this more evidenced than on the issue of *Ketuanan Melayu*, and the reactions to it in the discourses and narratives percolating beneath the lofty ideals of ministerial statements, that are "educating" the people of Malaysia. In 1957, the founding fathers and architects of the Malayan Constitution labored over the issue of special rights and privileges for the Malay community, and came to the conclusion that:

> We are of the opinion that in present circumstances (in 1957) it is necessary to continue these preferences. The Malays would be at a serious and unfair disadvantage compared with other communities if they were suddenly withdrawn. But, with the integration of the various communities into a common nationality which we trust will gradually come about, the need for these preferences will gradually disappear. Our recommendations are made on the footing that the Malays should be assured that the present position will continue for a substantial period, but that in due course the present preferences should be reduced and should ultimately cease so that there should then be no discrimination between races or communities. (Report of the Federation of Malaya Constitutional Commission 1957, para. 165)"

It appears that Malaysia is no closer to the founding fathers' vision of "the integration of the various communities into a common nationality" today than it was when these aspirations were articulated.

NOTES

1. Their argument was that the policy went against Article 152 of the Malaysian Constitution that proclaims the Malay language to be the national language in the country.
2. These groups included the politically influential Malay Writers Association (Gapena), the Abolish PPSMI Coalition (GMP), the Malay Consultative Council (MPM), and Perkasa.
3. This was exemplified most profoundly in the widespread opposition to the Malayan Union proposal, which sought to grant equal citizenship status to the ethnic Chinese and Indian minorities that were residing in British Malaya.
4. Conversation with Academic Head, Foon Yiew, 2 Secondary School, February 11, 2011, Johor, Malaysia.
5. Article 153 (1) reads: "It shall be the responsibility of the Yang di-Pertuan Agong to safeguard the special position of the Malays and natives of any of the States of Sabah and Sarawak and the legitimate interests of other communities in accordance with the provisions of this Article."
6. Interview with a Penang State Assemblyman, Kuala Lumpur, March 14, 2011.
7. http://satusekolahuntuksemua.wordpress.com/about-sss/, accessed April 13, 2011.
8. "Malaysian Parliament Shuns Debate on Novel Opposed by Indians." http://www.thaindian.com/newsportal/politics/malaysian-parliament-shuns-debate-on-novel-opposed-by-indians_100515197.html, accessed October 17, 2011.
9. "Racist Kedah Principal Apologises to Parents." *Malaysian Insider*, August 25, 2010. Available online, http://www.themalaysianinsider.com/malaysia/article/racist-kedah-principal-apologises-to-parents/, accessed April 12, 2011.

BIBLIOGRAPHY

Ahmad Fauzi bin Mohd, Mid Basri, Fo'ad bin Sakdan, and Asami bin Man. *Sejarah Tingkatan 1: Buku Teks*. Kuala Lumpur, Malaysia: Dewan Bahasa dan Pustaka, 2003.

Anwar Ibrahim. Keynote address at the CLAS Corporate Access Forum, held in Singapore, May 20, 2008.

Barone, Thomas N. "Civic Education and Citizenship in Malaysian Education." Paper presented at the Annual Meeting of the American Educational Research Association, held in New Orleans, April 1–5, 2002.

Barr, Michael D., and Anantha Raman Govindasamy. "The Islamisation of Malaysia: Religious Nationalism in the Service of Ethnonationalism." *Australian Journal of International Affairs* 64.3 (2010): 301.

Collins, Alan. "Chinese Educationlists in Malaysia: Defenders of Chinese Identity." *Asian Survey* 46.2 (March–April 2006): 298–318.

Hashim, Che Noraini, and Hasan Langgulung. "Islamic Religious Curriculum in Muslim Countries: The Experiences of Indonesia and Malaysia." *Bulletin of Education and Research* 30.1 (2008): 1–15.

Horowitz, Donald. *Ethnic Groups in Conflict*. Berkeley, CA: University of California Press, 1985.

Hussain, Abdullah. *Interlok*. Kuala Lumpur: Dewan Bahasa dan Pustaka, 1971.

Ibrahim, Rozita. "Multiculturalism and Education in Malaysia." *Culture and Religion* 8.2 (2007): 158–160.

Jamil, Hazri, and Nordin Abd. Razak. "Ethnicity and Education Policy in Malaysia: Managing and Mediating the Ethnic Diversity." *Journal of US-China Public Administration* 7.1 (2010): 81.

Kraince, Richard G. "Reforming Islamic Education in Malaysia: Doctrine or Dialogue?" In *Making Modern Muslims: The Politics of Islamic Education in Southeast Asia*. Edited by Robert W. Hefner, 106–140. Honolulu: University of Hawai'i Press, 2009.

Lee, Hock Guan. "The Limits of Malay Educational and Language Hegemony." In *Southeast Asian Affairs*. Edited by Daljit Singh, 180–197. Singapore: Institute of Southeast Asian Studies, 2010.

Lee, Molly N. N. "Education Reforms during Mahathir Era: Global Trends and U-Turns." In *Reflections: The Mahathir Years*. Edited by Bridget Welsh, 437–449. Washington, DC: John Hopkins University, 2004.

Liow, Joseph Chinyong. *Piety and Politics: Islamism in Contemporary Malaysia*. New York: Oxford University Press, 2009.

Liow, Joseph Chinyong. "Islamist Ambitions, Political Change, and the Price of Power: Recent Success and Challenges for the Pan-Malaysian Islamic Party, PAS." *Journal of Islamic Studies* 22.3 (2011): 374–403.

Malakolunthu, Suseela, Saedah Siraj, and Nagappan C. Rengasamy. "Educational Reform and Policy Dynamics: A Case of the Malaysian 'Vision School' for Racial R. Integration." *Education Research, Policy and Practice* 8 (2009): 127–129.

———. "Multicultural Education as a Reform Initiative: Reconstructing Teacher Preparation for Malaysian 'Vision Schools.'" *Asia-Pacific Education Researcher* 19.3 (2010): 453–464.

Manickam, Sandra Khor. "Textbooks and Nation Construction in Malaysia." Singapore: National University of Singapore, 2004. Available online, www.rchss.sinica.edu.tw/capas/publication/newsletter/N28/28_01_04.pdf. Accessed April 9, 2011.

Ministry of Education Malaysia. *Education in Malaysia: A Journey to Excellence*. Putrajaya, Malaysia: Ministry of Education, 2008.

Report of the Education Committee. Kuala Lumpur, Malaya: Ministry of Education, 1956.

Report of the Federation of Malaya Constitutional Commission, 1957. Available online, http://www.krisispraxis.com/Constitutional%20Commission%201957.pdf. Accessed October 18, 2011.

Santhiram, R. *Education of Minorities: The Case of Indians in Malaysia*. Kuala Lumpur, Malaysia: Child Information, Learning and Development Centre, 1999.

Santhiram, R., and Tan Yao Sua. "Ethnic Segregation in Malaysia's Education Choices: Preferential Policies and Desegregation." *Pedagogica Historica: International Journal of History Education* 46.1–2 (February 2010): 117–131.

Ting, Helen. "Malaysian History Textbooks and the Discourse of *Ketuanan Melayu*." In *Race and Multiculturalism in Singapore*. Edited by Daniel P. S. Goh, Matilda Gabrielpillai, Philip Holden, and Gaik Cheng Khoo, 3, 36–52. New York: Routledge, 2009.

8

Educating Citizens in America

THE PARADOXES OF DIFFERENCE AND DEMOCRACY

Ashley Rogers Berner and James Davison Hunter

> *The people of the United States need to know that individuals in our society who do not possess the levels of skill, literacy, and training essential to this new era will be effectively disenfranchised, not simply from the material rewards that accompany competent performance, but also from the chance to participate fully in our national life. A high level of shared education is essential to a free, democratic society and to the fostering of a common culture, especially in a country that prides itself on pluralism and individual freedom. (A Nation at Risk, 1983)*
>
> *What role should schools play in cultivating the civic virtues of a democratic society? A citizenry without the skills and virtues that support proceduralism, constitutionalism, and deliberation does not bode well for a democratic society. There is a great deal of concern these days that families, schools, and other social institutions are not cultivating such skills and virtues. There is also a great deal of cynicism about whether anybody or any institution has the will or knows the way to make a moral difference.*
> (Gutmann 2000, 79–80)

The Evolving Idea of Citizenship Education

Although Americans have spoken about the cultivation of citizenship for over two hundred years, the nature of the citizen ideal has been fluid and imprecise. Citizenship certainly presupposes attachment and moral habituation, but what exactly should the citizen be attached to? Democracy? The state? The local community? Their own personal interests? And what are the means of forming citizens? Rigorous academics? Community service? All of these ideals and methods have evolved over time.

The revolutionary and early Republican leadership viewed "citizenship" in political terms (e.g., white males who could vote), but their educational project aimed to encourage the democratic sensibilities of the entire non-slave population. Thomas Jefferson's "Bill for the More General Diffusion of Knowledge" (Virginia Legislature 1779) captured the prevailing rationale: to promote the kind of virtue and judgment that could preserve hard-won freedoms and guard against the encroachments of the state; and to create the conditions under which virtue, intelligence, and industry could supersede birth (Pangle and Pangle, 2000, 28; and found *in totem* at http://www.monticello.org/site/research-and-collections/bill-more-general-diffusion-knowledge).

The curricula of the founding period had roots in the aristocratic education that the founders themselves had enjoyed, but was deployed to democratize knowledge and nurture attachment to democratic freedoms. The educational writings of Thomas Jefferson, George Washington, John and John Quincy Adams, or Benjamin Franklin all reveal an uncompromising commitment to knowledge in service of moral and civic judgment. They conceived every subject as fostering democratic sensibility: literature and writing was to advance political participation and to prevent manipulation by the press; history was to show the dangers of tyranny and the power of individuals to change the world; science was to foster creativity and initiative; and political philosophy was to demonstrate the superiority of democratic liberties and to safeguard against their demise. As Thomas and Lorraine Pangle summarized, "the constant refrain of the Founders' concern with education in political history [was] the need to bring the young step by step to a steadily clearer and more sophisticated grasp of the truth and the intrinsic superiority of the most basic principles of political philosophy that underlie the American Constitution," such as natural rights, the social compact, indirect democracy, the reasons for a separation of powers, civil rights, property rights, free enterprise, and religious liberty (Pangle and Pangle 2000, 33).

As for religion, while not established by the state, it was considered the underpinning of virtue upon which the body politic relied, as was the family and local civic societies. As Benjamin Rush argued for his own plan for education in Pennsylvania in 1786, "religion is the foundation of virtue; virtue is the foundation of liberty; liberty is the object of all republican governments; therefore, a republican education should promote religion as well as virtue and liberty" (Butts 1978, 29). Statutes within various state constitutions reinforced this ideal. For example, Massachusetts's Constitution, ratified in 1789, called for the "support and maintenance of public Protestant teachers of piety, religion, and morality"; this was reaffirmed by the state legislature in 1827. The New Hampshire Constitution, framed in 1784, provided state support for "public protestant teachers of piety, religion, and morality" on the ground that "morality and piety, rightly grounded on evangelical principles, will give the best and greatest security to government" (Christenson 1986, 2). The Northwest Ordinance of 1787 likewise declared that "religion, morality, and knowledge, being necessary to good government and the happiness of mankind, schools and the means of education shall forever be encouraged" (Baker 1988, 539). In all schools everywhere, piety and good character remained the requirements for teachers. And religious orthodoxy defined the terms of piety and good character, even if religious ideals were expressed in a decidedly less sectarian fashion. Put simply, the child was located within overlapping communities that urged moral virtue and commitment to democratic ideals.

Formal education itself in the early decades of the new republic took shape in the framework of the "common school": schools that were locally organized and funded. In the increasingly dense, complicated, and diverse populations of the northeast, the common school was thought as serving to Americanize and homogenize the population divided by class, ethnicity, and faith. In the less populated regions, especially in the westward frontier, the common school was largely born out of the necessity of interdenominational cooperation. The number of Baptists, Methodists, Presbyterians, or Episcopalians in new small towns and cities was inadequate for any denomination to form its own school. Without "common schools" built upon a Protestant consensus, the children would have no schools at all (Tyack 1966; Smith 1967).

The main disagreements over education tended to revolve around the provision and control of this framework, rather than its purpose and content. For example, Jefferson's Virginia bill to provide state education failed, not because the legislators disagreed with him about the content or purpose of education, but because they felt that parents and local communities were better fit to administer it (Pangle and Pangle 2000, 22–41). Even through the mid-19th century, the major conflicts that occurred were more about the control of education than about its content.

Over the course of the 20th century, what was meant by "citizenship education" in schools became considerably more ambiguous. In the early 20th century, progressive educational reformers had begun to advance a vision of citizenship construed in broader public, rather than narrow, political terms. Yet, this reformist impulse also promoted greater attachment to the state and its administrative organs, rather than the suspicion of state power that the founders had favored. The consequences for curricula were significant: the new civics de-emphasized literature, constitutional history, political philosophy, and rhetoric in favor of "hands on" learning, such as visiting the offices of local officials, maintaining personal hygiene, and participating in a wide variety of social activities (Reuben 1997, 404, 414–416). As Charles Merriam wrote in *The Making of Citizens* (Chicago: University of Chicago Press, 1931), good behavior and psychological health were more important than political "indoctrination" of any kind—whether democratic, monarchical, or communist (Reuben 1997, 412).

Citizenship training in schools became even more complicated by the final third part of the 20th century. The Vietnam War brought in its wake a new disenchantment with American institutions, which made patriotism unseemly. In turn, history textbooks placed less emphasis on America's mythic ideal and heritage (Bruner 1977, xii; Kazin 2011, 141–149). In keeping with the times, some educational leaders even framed "citizenship" as a commitment to a society without capitalism, directing all pedagogy under this task (McLaren 2007, xvii, 39). In recent years, educational theorists have gone further still to propound the ideals of "global citizenship" that sets out a transnational ideal of civic responsibility (Dill 2010). Textbooks have followed suit. In short, the institutional framework for citizenship seems to have become somewhat unclear within the nation's schools.

In the realm of political philosophy and public policy, on the other hand, "citizenship" has, in recent years, become clearer and more precise. A new ideal has emerged that, according to William Galston, affirms many of the goals of the founders while also specifying the demands of a more plural society, such as respect for "the other" (Galston 2001, 218). Scholars analyzing the school effect in citizenship behavior commonly recognize four elements, which give form to this consensus:

- Participation in public-spirited collective action (community service);
- The capacity to be involved in the political process (civic skills);

- An understanding of the nation's political system (political knowledge);
- Respect for the civil liberties of others (political tolerance) (Campbell 2008, 489–490).

This emerging consensus recognizes the necessity of strong intellectual comprehension of, and emotional and practical commitment to, specific corporate ideals that are larger than the individual. At least among theorists, this represents a noticeable shift away from the moral skepticism and individualism of mid-20th century.

Civic Attachment and Citizenship Behavior

How do American citizens measure up to this general ideal? Are Americans knowledgeable of their political institutions and the history that shaped them? Can they articulate a clear vision of democracy, one that is capacious enough to honor deep difference and to articulate reasonable limits? Do Americans participate intelligently in the push and pull of political and public life, and do they know why they do so? Finally, are American public institutions capable of urging commitment to principles larger than the self?

By every metric, American citizens fall short and, it would seem, they fall more and more short as the years go by. Less than one-third of eligible voters cast Presidential ballots, less than one-fifth Congressional ones. When it comes to college freshmen, over the last thirty years "every single indicator of political engagement has fallen by at least half"—whether that means voting in Presidential elections, discussing political issues, or even reading newspapers (Galston 2001, 219). Not only political behavior but also civic knowledge is remarkably superficial, with 35 percent of high school seniors testing below the basic level, and another 37 percent testing at the basic level (Galston 2001, 221). Citing a recent study, Galston wrote that, "for many (though not all) categories of political knowledge, today's high school graduates are roughly equivalent to the high school dropouts of the late 1940s, and today's college graduates are roughly equivalent to the high school graduates of that earlier epoch" (Galston 2001, 222).

These problems come into focus when one looks at Americans' understanding of particularly important historical movements and events, such as the civil rights movement. Since public education aims to equalize opportunity, it is especially troubling to find that "in 2001, only 34 percent of eighth graders recognized that the phrase 'Jim Crow' referred to laws that 'enforced racial segregation' as opposed to laws that made liquor illegal, restricted immigration, or protected the environment"; or that in 2006, "only 38 percent of twelfth graders could identify the social policy reflected by a sign declaring 'COLORED ENTRANCE' above the door of a theater" (Paige 2011, 70). As a former secretary of education summed up, American students may have heard about Martin Luther King, Jr.'s "I Have a Dream" speech, but they do not understand why it was important or how the movement's longstanding arguments formed over time and shaped American history itself (Paige 2011, 69).

Furthermore, Conover and Searing's ethnographic work within the school populations of four American communities suggests that, even when one construes "citizen identity" in broad and colloquial terms such as "being an American," the picture is "sobering":

> Although most students have strong citizen identities, these identities are experienced as free-floating abstractions...most students have thin understandings of what it means to be a citizen, understandings dominated by a focus on rights and deficient in a sense of obligation. For most, being a good citizen requires only that one obey the law, vote, and act patriotically...particularly troubling is the finding that few students have a clear sense of their "future selves" as adult citizens (Conover and Searing 2000, 118).

Whatever else is happening in formal citizenship education, it is not the forging of thick, coherent civic identities that are understood coherently and enacted consistently. Why, then, do Americans demonstrate such under-achievement when it comes to the virtues, sensibilities, and practices of democratic citizenship? The short answer is that American culture makes it difficult to nurture *any* kind of commitment beyond the self.

American Culture and Commitment

The evidence suggests that the dominant institutions of American public life, intentionally or unintentionally, champion individual liberty with little constraint, authenticity with little clarity, and "values" without transcendence. Coercive "rules" exist, to be sure, but ones that "[instill] with intensifying moralism that specific moral outlook that requires the liberation of the individual from all ties of solidarity, responsibility, tradition and obligation that are not autonomously chosen" (Pangle and Pangle 2000, 23).

There are many reasons why this has come to be and the arguments are familiar. In short, American individualism has been severed from creedal communities that located individuals within larger moral obligations; furthermore, the institutions that might countervail the logic of "individual expressivism" or "moralistic therapeutic deism," have instead largely adopted it (Smith and Denton 2005, 162–170). In so many ways, American culture reinforces the ideal of the autonomous individual and the individual's own self-creation. This is, of course, a form of commitment—but a distinctly subjectivist one.

Religious Communities, Youth Organizations, and the Protocols of Psychology

The research focusing on students tends to show not only an unqualified belief in their own "personal development" and "happiness," but also a general inability to intellectually defend this position, or indeed any other position. This holds true even of children raised in worldview-intentional homes. The data from *Soul Searching: The Religious Lives of American Teenagers* is persuasive: outside of the Church of the Latter Day Saints and a few religiously orthodox enclaves, even American children raised in religiously observant homes tend not to be able to articulate their own doctrines coherently, nor explain the moral and social consequences of it (Smith and Denton 2005, 171, 262).

Religious communities themselves are partly to blame for this—and for different reasons. At one end, Jewish and Christian liberals tend to evacuate the transcendent sources of ethical thinking, and thus the compelling force from religious life, and at the other end, Christian evangelicals tend to privilege experience above knowledge and therefore devalue religious content (Prothero 2007, 105–121). The unintended consequence is that many religious communities are increasingly indistinct from the larger culture and less and less capable of articulating compelling reasons from their own tradition for living well and doing good.

There is evidence that some types of voluntary youth organizations have a modest positive impact upon adult political participation. "Service organizations, student council, drama clubs, musical groups, and religious organizations" are especially politically salient. Sports teams are not politically salient and, interestingly, neither are political and environmental campaigns. The reasons why some voluntary activities inspire a significant increase in the likelihood to vote as an adult seems to be a result of the intense time commitments and range of specific practices required, such as public speaking and other communal rituals that carry over into adult identity and behavior (McFarland and Thomas 2006, 412–420).

One of the reasons for the limited influence of faith-based and youth organizations concerns the dominance of the assumptions and conceptual frameworks of developmental psychology in educational theory and practice. For example, early versions of the Girl Scouts' Guidebook emphasized duty to community, family, friends, church, and school, and as well as loyalty to the "highest ideals" that she thinks are "right and good." By the 1970s, this had become "doing one's best" to "respect myself and others" (Hunter 2000, 57–59, 70–73).

It is certainly true that developmental psychology offers both tools for understanding cognitive growth and the development of morality, and it has expanded our resources for making sense of human behavior. However, despite its attempt to extricate itself from theological and secular metaphysics, it is also a carrier of particular, if varying, assumptions about human life (Rylance 2000, 24). The history of modern psychology and the therapeutic impulse in American culture have been explored elsewhere. Its relevance here is the extent to which its assumptions have been adopted by religious communities and youth organizations that are unaware of the resulting shift in moral focus—from adherence to goods and truths to the internal development of the individual.

These cultural dynamics are irreducibly ambivalent. Clearly psychology has not had a wholly or mostly harmful influence, and adherence to historic creeds by religious communities is far from sufficient for sustaining moral and civic responsibility. The factors are complicated, but the main civic institutions have become increasingly incapable of urging commitment to anything larger than the self—a prerequisite of a coherent and compelling citizen ideal.

Public Schools and the Education of Citizens

The founders of the Republic viewed the family and local communities as the makers of citizens, along side of formal education variously construed. For many historical reasons, public education now carries this weight almost exclusively. Indeed, one of the primary justifications for both the structure and legitimacy of American public education has been its claim to engender among the young a loyalty to the nation and its principles. Even those who bemoan the state of civic and religious knowledge maintain that only the public schools possess the capacity and the responsibility to create citizens who are civically literate (Prothero 2007, 127; Damon 2011, 43).

The modern character education movement is one illustration of the commitment that public schools have made to cultivate the high ethical standards that underwrite citizenship. In 1987, for example, the Washington, DC, Board of Education acknowledged the inadequacy of the moral relativism that had characterized many school systems in the 1960s and 1970s, and affirmed the following traits or values for its students: self-esteem; self-discipline; family, kinship, and belonging; moral and intellectual maturity; and responsibility to self and others (Hunter 2000, 90). The values selected are fairly typical of the dozens of character education programs, which most states require in their schools. The hope has been that talking about respect, kindness, and tolerance, and giving examples of their heroic outworking, would help children manifest goodness in their lives and communities.

The good intentions that animated the movement have produced little evidence of success (Hunter 2000, 151–152). On the contrary, the models often rest upon the same psychological sanctions that operate within the larger culture. They intentionally avoid addressing the enduring "why" questions of human experience (e.g., "Why should we be good?" or "Why should we eschew evil?") (Hunter 2000, 212). They operate with strong ideas but segregate them from the daily experiences of moral communities or the rich intellectual (and often religious) sources that make sense of them. Instead, these programs rest their advocacy of particular virtues upon self-interest and emotional well-being (Hunter 2000, 86–91). The imperatives of the autonomous, desiring self are built into the models.

In recent years, the character education regime seems to have shifted its emphasis from virtues to "competencies" and "pro-social skills." Stanford psychologist William Damon regrets that, "the most common topic in contemporary character education programs is 'social-emotional content' such as 'personal improvement/self-management and awareness,' 'relaxation techniques,' and 'emotional awareness'" (Damon 2011, 53–54, 56–57). In short, this important domain has become even more divorced from notions of moral commitment.

This, then, is the social conundrum: commitment in general, and loyalty to democratic principles in particular, requires intellectual, emotional, and practical commitment to something greater than the self, yet it is precisely this disposition that the schools can neither generate nor support.

There are two factors contributing to the problem that warrant further examination: the educational philosophy that dominates public education and its institutional structure.

Educational Theory

Educational theories grow out of implicit beliefs about the human person and the purpose of education itself. In brief, educational theories are both ontological and teleological. Over the past century, educational theory as taught in colleges of education, championed by superintendents, and accepted by teachers, has witnessed profound shifts in the dominant understanding of the child and the *telos* of education. The child is no longer seen as existing within larger relationships that inspire, demand, and constrain, but rather as an autonomous entity who bears the burden of self-creation. Education's purpose, then, is less about gaining the knowledge and the judgment to participate constructively in the larger human drama, as it is primarily about the development of the individual's personality and well-being (de Girolami 2008, 19).

This narrative has been well chronicled by Diane Ravitch and E. D. Hirsch. Both make the point that, taken together, the innovations of Progressive education—including the Project Method, the anti-reading movement, the calls for social efficiency, the protocols of "social adjustment," and the more recent focus on "skills and competencies"—place the individual child's interests at the center of the classroom. Resistance to an academically demanding, chronological progression of studies is often the by-product.

A striking example may be found in the contrasting strategies of Jerome S. Bruner, an educational psychologist at Harvard, and Neil Postman, a professor of education at New York University. In 1960, Bruner published the proceedings of an academic conference at which scientists and humanistic scholars discussed primary and secondary education. Their widely publicized conclusion was that university professors, knowing the full depth of each subject ("where it is *going*"), should help craft a K–12 curriculum that "spiraled" around the main themes and concepts according to the child's developmental ability. The conference participants assumed a coherent body of knowledge, mastery of which was desirable, and an authoritative role for scholars and teachers (Bruner 1977).

In 1969, Postman and Weingartner published their best-selling *Teaching as a Subversive Activity*. In their view, "relevance" and "interest" were paramount in schooling; a curriculum itself was oppressive. His sixteen recommendations for "making students into open systems" included "declar[ing] a five-year moratorium on the use of all textbooks (Postman and Weingartner 1969, 137)"; "have 'English' teachers 'teach' Math, Math teachers English, Social Studies teachers Science"; "dissolve all 'subjects,' 'courses,' and especially 'course requirements'"; "require all teachers to undergo some form of psychotherapy"; and "make every class an elective" (ibid., 139).

These publications came to represent opposing sides of what had become a fundamental divide among educators about the academic curriculum itself. Bruner's position was overwhelmed, as he acknowledged in the preface of the 1977 edition of his book (Bruner 1977, xii). The irony is that the goals of Postman and Weingartner's pedagogic strategy tends to be at cross-purposes with the creation of an informed and committed citizenry on the rich terms described by Galston and Campbell.

First, the ascendant strategy reinforced the self-referential trends within the dominant culture. As Hirsch explains in *The Making of Americans: Democracy and Our Schools* (2009), "The early [traditional] curriculum can be viewed as a set of concentric circles. At the core are the knowledge and skills all citizens should have. Beyond that is the knowledge, such as state history, that the individual state wants children to possess. Beyond that may be the knowledge and values agreed upon by the locality. And finally, beyond that, are the activities and studies that fulfill the needs, talents, and interests of the individual student" (Hirsch 2009, 24). Progressive education, by contrast, reverses this order (ibid.). In theory, the leading strategy of pedagogy claims to represent the child's interests but, as a matter of course, still represents a distinctive, ontological position held by adults about the child. It assumes the Romantic notion that children's cognition and personalities develop organically, and that that adult requirements quickly become oppressive.

On the ground, the prevailing view means that lesson plans follow what children might find interesting, instead of a more classical understanding of what the well-educated person—someone, by the way, capable of vetting candidates, critiquing public policy, and locating herself within global history—*needs* to know and understand. Recent variations, in the age of intense and high-stakes testing, present learning in terms of skill building, such as "critical thinking, problem solving, collaboration, global awareness, and even media literacy," at the expense of subject mastery, "which [such advocates] consider fungible." Certainly these skills are not new (one critic wrote, "[o]ne assumes that Aristotle tutored Alexander the Great in critical thinking long ago"). But their exercise within the public life still relies upon knowledge of "the proud, sometimes painful, complicated, and contentious history of the United States" and the "classic and ironic works that distill and define the essence of [a variety of] cultures and societies" (Rotherham 2011, 94–95). Despite heightened pressure for academic outputs, lesson plans still resist a coherent and factual narrative (Hirsch 2006, 22–50).

These trends have had a significant effect upon the subject matter most likely to advance civic attachment and engagement. Educational surveys of teacher knowledge bear this out: in 1996, "more than 50 percent of students in history and world civilization classes had teachers who neither majored nor minored in history." As a consequence, a 1999 study found that "more than 50 percent of high school government teachers could not adequately explain key subjects such as popular sovereignty, habeas corpus, judicial review, federalism, and checks and balances" (O'Connor 2011, 6).

Second, the loss of shared knowledge harms underprivileged children disproportionally. As Hirsch observed, "reading and writing require unspoken background knowledge, silently assumed"—not random assignments that promote "skills" (Hirsch 2009, 12). Children who arrive educationally under-prepared rarely have a chance to catch up. Low-income and minority parents have always known this and have fought, often in vain, for their children to receive the same advantages as the privileged.[1]

This disparity in privilege becomes even more troubling when one considers that it is not only civics class itself, but also the entire academic curriculum and the *ethos* of the school itself, which inspire strong citizenship. As Galston put it, "all education is civic education in the sense that individuals' level of general attainment significantly affects their level of political knowledge as well as the quantity and character of their political participation" (Galston 2001, 219).

Third, recent attempts to raise academic standards have yielded limited results, for they fail to consider the effect of the intellectual arguments cited above upon the longstanding culture of schooling. For instance, intermittent testing of student knowledge is a reasonable idea, but superimposed upon an educational culture accustomed to looking askance at precise subject matter, it has resulted, predictably, in conflict. Neither is rigorous evaluation part of teachers' own professional expectations, and for good reason: high marks are the cultural norm. Teacher dismissal rates are below .05 percent. Teachers rank themselves highly, and even those teachers who are on probation rank themselves as an 8 or 9 out of 10 (Weisberg et al. 2009, 23).

The troubling news about academic attainment is serious, and it is not new. The 1983 report, *A Nation at Risk*, noted the "rising tide of mediocrity" in American schools: "Many 17-year-olds do not possess the 'higher order' intellectual skills we should expect of them. Nearly 40 percent cannot draw inferences from written material; only one-fifth can write a persuasive essay; and only one-third can solve a mathematics problem requiring several steps" (*A Nation at Risk* 1983). Thirty years on, most districts and states *do* have curricular goals, and the federal government is currently prodding states to adopt the new national "core." Even having a core curriculum is something of an accomplishment, but many critics feel it is still too thin and does not provide the precise knowledge and chronological depth that a strong education demands (Wurman 2011; Stergios 2011; Wood 2011). In the global perspective, the dial has not moved: Harvard's recent study shows that United States' public and private students rank seventeenth in reading and thirty-second in math proficiency among the nations participating in international evaluations (Peterson et al. 2011).

Of course, the issue is not testing per se, or even its use in evaluating teacher performance. Neither is the issue the particular chronology of a history curriculum, or which literature should be required in an English class, or whether students memorize the periodic table. Rather, the problem is the well-established notion that education is *about something entirely different* besides the careful cultivation of academic abilities, civic sensibilities, and strong character. There are hopeful pockets of accomplishment to be found in both charter and traditional public schools, but they have succeeded only through opposition to the prevailing educational culture (Chenoweth 2007).

Finally, there is the absence of a framework for addressing the larger integrating questions that make us human. Not only do many children not read, but the big picture of the world in all of its varying history, geography, and *nomos* is absent, as is the habit of engaging in reasoned debate about the things that really matter ("What is the meaning of life?" "What is the just society?" "How do we live together with our deepest differences?"). Instead, as Robert Kunzman writes from his own experience, teachers shrink from substantive debates that might offend the peace of the classroom or trespass upon the Establishment clause of the Constitution (Kunzman 2006). Although discussions about religious and ethical systems are constitutional, both scholars note their rarity, attributable to a lack of such knowledge on the part of teachers and their (often unfounded) concerns about Establishment violations. Under these circumstances, it is hard to envision the steady cultivation of citizenship skills along the lines that Gutmann and Galston advocate.

In sum, the dominant educational philosophy strains to support an adequate concept of citizenship. It simply does not provide the conceptual framework or intellectual and moral resources to counteract the self-referential nature of the larger culture, nor does it particularly see this solipsism as a problem.

The Structure of American Public Education

Since the 1840s, America's states have adopted a "state control" model in which the government provides a common educational experience free of sectarian influence. Many other Western countries, in contrast, adopted a "civil society" model, in which the government supports a variety of school types that reflect the beliefs and commitments of the parents (Glenn 2002; Glenn 2011). Although these distinctive models are so embedded that we scarcely know they are there, they affect even our most basic definitions: in the United States, "public schooling" denotes educational uniformity; in Singapore, Sweden, and The Netherlands (for instance), "public schooling" indicates educational pluralism.

Both models developed in the mid-19th century as strategies for coping with plural populations. In the Netherlands, Protestants and Catholics worked in tandem to support their separate schools along side of the nonsectarian, state schools. In the United States, anti-Catholic prejudice prevented the American Protestant majority from endorsing state funding for *any* kind of confessional school. The "common school," it was hoped, could assimilate the foreign-born into a common culture. This gradually became the dominant view in the country at large and is now embedded in the national imagination. As Justice Stevens feared in his dissent to *Zelman v Simmons-Harris* (2002), the case that ruled state-funded vouchers constitutional, the resulting diversity will "weaken the foundations of our democracy" (536 U.S. 639, 644: 2002).

But is this true? The data suggests otherwise—that private schools actually support stronger citizenship behaviors. Although it is notoriously difficult to disaggregate the school effect from other cultural factors, three recent projects point in this direction. Their conclusions suggest that private and/or religious schools do a better job than public schools of forming citizens.

One study conducted by William Jeynes focused on three factors and their effect on the school performance of children from low socioeconomic backgrounds: religious adherence, religious schooling, and having an intact family. Our concern here is religious schooling. Jeynes used data from the National Education Longitudinal Study, or NELS88, of nearly 25,000 students from 1,050 schools, and analyzed "sixty studies that examined the relationship between religious schooling and academic outcomes" (Jeynes 2007, 6). He found that "in religious, mostly Christian, schools the achievement gap between white and minority students, as well as between children of high-and low-socioeconomic status, is considerably smaller than in public schools" (Jeynes 2007, abstract). Put differently: attending religious schools helps all students, but it particularly helps those at the lower end of the economic spectrum. Why?

First, the school culture is more amenable to academic accomplishment. Jeynes found that religious schools tend to be better than nonreligious schools in the following respects: school atmosphere, racial harmony, school discipline, school violence, and amount of homework done (Jeynes 2007, 110). This last quality may be further understood as fostering "learning habits that are most strongly related to academic achievement," i.e., "taking harder courses, diligence, and overall work habits" (Jeynes 2007, 13). In other words, religious schools generally do a better job of setting the conditions for the acquisition of deep knowledge—one of the prerequisites of strong citizenship.

Second, as James Coleman pointed out years ago, religious schools emphasize parental involvement and increase the social capital of parents themselves (Jeynes 2007, 14). These findings accord with other research demonstrating that when children move from public to Catholic schools, their parents become more civically engaged. Religious schools, in other words, encourage habits of participation.

Third, religious belief embodied in a religious school atmosphere can help children to "have an internal locus of control," which leads to better academic outcomes (Jeynes 2007, 15). The internal control mechanism helps students to "avoid behaviors that are typically regarded as undisciplined and harmful to educational achievement," such as pregnancy, drug use, or theft (Jeynes 2007, 15).

Other research by David Campbell further explores the relationship between citizenship education and different educational settings. His focus was on the four measures of citizenship set out above, that is, the habit of community service, skills adequate to political participation, historical and political knowledge, and tolerance of difference. He compared these qualities in the students of public versus private schools, importantly distinguishing between Catholic, religious non-Catholic, and secular, private school results. Campbell also compared assigned public schools to selective, magnet public schools. Beyond this, Campbell specifically isolated those factors that pertained to the school atmosphere. He discounted family factors (such as parental community service, education and income levels, and religiosity) and school-level structural factors such as "the school's size, whether the school arranges community service for students, has a student government, or encourages discussion of current events in classes" (Campbell 2008, 502).

What Campbell found is that Catholic schools did significantly better than public schools in fostering all four types of behaviors. Private secular and religious non-Catholic schools scored higher than public in all domains, but with one important exception: religious non-Catholic schools produced graduates who were less tolerant of others. Magnet schools showed a slight but not statistically significant uptick in the four behaviors.

The lack of tolerance evidenced by graduates of religious non-Catholic schools is indeed troubling. At the very least, the belief that private schooling can lead to intolerance is not without some empirical justification. What is warranted is further differentiation within this category, especially Jewish, Quaker, and Protestant fundamentalist schools, to delineate what exactly are the beliefs and practices that sponsor a mistrust of the other.

The Cardus Education Survey (2011) offers the largest scale study to date of *graduates* (ages 24–39) of Catholic, Protestant, home, secular, private, and public schooling. Their operative question was whether the outcomes of the religious schools matched their stated intentions, and as such, there is limited overlap with the questions we are pursuing here. Cardus (a think-tank in Canada) was interested in discovering the school effect upon such things as private religious observance, congregational leadership, or the prevalence of divorce. What Cardus's research does show in sum is that the private school effect results in graduates who are more stable members of their local communities, more capable of sustained commitment, and more intellectually capable. There is, of course, variation. Catholic and private non-religious schools do a superior job of academics and of encouraging higher education than either Protestant or public schools; Protestant school graduates are less involved in politics than Catholic and public peers. As the report concludes, "these findings should... provide relief for those in larger society who are concerned about the polarization of society along the lines of religious conservatives versus secular liberals, as it is clear that Christian schools are a public good in many ways. These findings should ferry us past this debate" (Pennings 2011, 14).

While not conclusive, these studies are highly suggestive and, on the face of it, counter-intuitive. For these reasons, Galston is right in arguing that it is time "...to rethink some long-held beliefs about sources of civic unity in the United States, and to reflect anew on the relationship between the *ethos* of individual schools and the civic purposes of education" (Galston 2001, 231).

Public Schooling and the Democratic Ideal

At the level of political theory, there is a widespread concern about the mechanisms that underwrite private schooling. The dynamics of private schooling, it is argued, lead to pure, parental control without the influence of other citizen-stakeholders. Public schools are, by contrast, "an essential welfare good for children" (Gutmann 1999, 70). The state-control model not only provides "the primary means by which citizens can morally educate future citizens," but also the best means for balancing—through democratic deliberation—the varying intentions and aspirations of the state, parents, and professional educators (Gutmann 2000, 84). In this sense, advocates of the present system contend that the state-control model of public education is inherently amenable to democratic processes in ways that private schools are not.

In theory, perhaps; but in practice, this contention is highly debatable in at least two respects.

First, the power of teachers unions and other professional teachers associations generate nearly insurmountable imbalance in local and state educational politics. This imbalance affects every aspect of the school's structure: from the length of school day, to limits on parent-teacher conferences, to the frequency of faculty meetings, to the strict salary "lanes" that raise salaries mechanically and irrespective of performance, to the detailed bureaucratic processes for dismissal. In principle, democratically elected officials represent all the various interests within their constituency. Teachers through their unions, by contrast, constitute the biggest spending bloc in local and state elections. Few if any other constituencies can mobilize this kind of political power (Brill 2011; Moe 2011).

Second, the politicization of the curriculum through textbook contracts diminishes democratic dialogue within school districts and between them. Large states and districts have such vast purchasing power that they can virtually determine which textbooks will be produced for the rest of the country. Even within one constituency, competing political ideologies vie for control of the academic agenda, often changing the academic curriculum whenever an election takes place (Hickok 2011, 54; Paige 2011, 72–73).

In this real-world setting, it is difficult to assert that public education is inherently disposed to "democratic deliberation." The state-control model we now have privileges the employment priorities of professional educators as well as the political ideologies of whichever party happens to be in power.

Conclusions

The paradox of citizenship-education is that the mainstream of educational theory, policy, and practice aspires to form the young into an ideal of citizenship, but it cannot deliver in large measure because it is rooted in conceptual strategies and organizational structures that, by their very nature, render its ends unattainable. Good intentions abound, but there are "design flaws," if you will, that make the best of intentions unrealizable.

Recent initiatives from outside the dominant institutions are attempting to address the problems discussed, and with some success. For example, Supreme Court Justice Sandra Day O'Connor started iCivics, which offers opportunities for civic learning to teachers and students (O'Connor 2011, 10). Likewise, the Close-Up Foundation "brings students to Washington D.C. for interactive lessons about government" and "exposes teachers to ideas from peers and Close-Up staff about how to teach civics in engaging, substantive ways" (Rotherham 2011, 95). However promising, these initiatives are not embedded in the basic routines or training activities of schools (Rotherham 2011, 95). And then there are government-sponsored programs, such as the USA Freedom Corps and the National Endowment for the Humanities' "We the People" program—which are designed to help teachers impart the basics of American history. Here, the problem is that these programs are subject to competing political interests and thus face defunding or shifts of emphasis (Bridgeland 2011, 42–43; Cole 2011, 85–86). One illustration of a promising initiative inside the schools is found in the Democracy Prep Charter Schools that marry strong academic content to civic engagement (Andrew 2011, 99–109). These have shown good results, not least for minority children. Initiatives such as these could very well make a small difference in the civic knowledge imparted to the next generation.

Yet the problems with America's dominant "education for citizenship" are formidable: a culture that reinforces the ideal of an autonomous and unencumbered self; a pedagogy that has for a century devalued academic content in favor of the possibilities of psychological well-being; and a structure that neither reflects a democratic process nor honors democratic pluralism. Challenging these settled realities is no easy or quick task.

Challenging these realities, though, require one to acknowledge the limitations of "democratic citizenship" in the first place, however richly it is conceptualized. While "democratic citizenship" should certainly play a role in youth organizations and in the range of educational institutions, it cannot constitute their rationale because human beings are not reducible to their role vis-à-vis the political community. "Children," as one scholar has observed, "are not merely immature citizens in a republic. They are not mere creatures of the state." They are simultaneously children in homes, students, playmates, members of churches, synagogues, and mosques, and eventually employees and employers (Skillen 2004, 102). Democratic citizenship, in other words, is bound by laws and orientations that point beyond itself. This is perhaps the strongest argument to consider not only educational pluralism, but also a more capacious public square that affirms the variety of human commitment.

NOTE

1. In the 1910s, they demanded Latin (against the condescension of the establishment); in the 1950s, they resisted the "new math"; in the 2010s, they ask for more homework assignments—only to be turned away (Ravitch 2000, 263, 272, 400). The result is that children attending Exeter, Stuyvesant High, or the Convent of the Sacred Heart can translate *The Aeneid* or deconstruct Acts of Congress; children from inner-city Camden cannot. This cannot be blamed upon poor neighborhoods or uneducated parents. France, which insists upon high educational standards in its curriculum, closes the achievement gap by the sixth grade (Hirsch 2009, 148).

BIBLIOGRAPHY

Andrew, Seth. "Fighting Civic Malpractice: How a Harlem Charter School Closes the Civic Achievement Gap." In *Teaching America: The Case for Civic Education*. Edited by David Feith, 99–110. Plymouth, UK: Rowman & Littlefield Education, 2011.

Baker, John S. "Parent-centered Education," *Notre Dame Journal of Law, Ethics, and Public Policy* (Summer 1988).

Bridgeland, John M. "My White House Mission after September 11." In *Teaching America: The Case for Civic Education*. Edited by David Feith, 41–50. Plymouth: Rowman & Littlefield Education, 2011.

Brill, Steven. *Class Warfare: Inside the Fight to Fix America's Schools*. New York: Simon & Schuster, 2001.

Bruner, Jerome. *The Process of Education: A Landmark in Educational Theory*. Cambridge, MA: Harvard University Press, 1977 [1960].

Butts, R. Freeman. Public Education in the United States: From Revolution to Reform. New York: Holt, Rinehart and Winston, 1978.

Campbell, David E. "The Civic Side of School Choice: An Empirical Analysis of Civic Education in Public and Private Schools." *Brigham Young Law Review* 4 (2008): 487–524.

Chenoweth, Karin. "*It's Being Done*": *Academic Success in Unexpected Schools*. Boston: Harvard Education Press, 2007.

Christenson, Bryce. "Against the Wall," *Persuasion at Work* 9, 2 (February 1986): 2.

Chronicle of Higher Education Innovations Blog; "The Core Between the States," blog entry by Peter Wood, May 5, 2011. Available online, http://chronicle.com/blogs/innovations/the-core-between-the-states/29511.

Cole, Bruce. "Revolutionary Ignorance: What Do Americans Know of the Original Tea Party?" In *Teaching America: The Case for Civic Education*. Edited by David Feith, 81–88. Plymouth, UK: Rowman & Littlefield Education, 2011.

Conover, Pamela Johnston, and Donald D. Searing. "A Political Socialization Perspective." In *Rediscovering the Democratic Purposes of Education*. Edited by Lorraine M. McDonnell, P. Michael Timpane, and Roger Benjamin, 91–126. Lawrence: University of Kansas Press, 2000.

Cooling, Trevor. *Doing God in Education*. London: Theos, 2010.

Damon, William. *Failing Liberty 101*. Palo Alto, CA: Stanford University Press, 2011.

de Girolami, Marc O. "The Constitutional Paradox of Religious Learning." Public Law & Legal Theory Working Papers, Columbia Law School, 2008. Available online, http://lsr.nellco.org/columbiapllt/08146.

Dill, Jeffery. "The Making of Global Citizens: The Moral Vision of Schooling for a Global Imaginary." PhD diss., University of Virginia, 2010.

Galston, William A. "Political Knowledge, Political Engagement and Civic Knowledge." *Annual Review of Political Science* 4 (2001): 217–224.

Glenn, Charles L. *The Myth of the Common School.* Amherst: University of Massachusetts Press, 2002 [1988].

Glenn, Charles L. "What the United States Can Learn from Other Countries." In *What Americans Can Learn from School Choice in Other Countries.* Edited by David Salisbury and James Tooley, 79–88. Washington, DC: Cato Institute, 2005.

Glenn, Charles L. *Contrasting Models of State and School: A Comparative Historical Study of Parental Choice and State Control.* New York: Continuum, 2011.

Gutmann, Amy. "Challenges of Multiculturalism in Democratic Education." In *Public Education in a Multicultural Society: Policy, Theory, Critique.* Edited by Robert K. Fullinwider, 156–182. Cambridge, UK: Cambridge University Press, 1966.

Gutmann, Amy. *Democratic Education.* Princeton, NJ: Princeton University Press, 1999 [1987].

Gutmann, Amy. 2000. "Why Should Schools Care about Civic Education?" in *Rediscovering the Democratic Purposes of Education.* Edited by Lorraine M. McDonnell, P. Michael Timpane, and Roger Benjamin, 73–90. Lawrence, KS: University Press of Kansas.

Hickok, Eugene. "Civic Literacy and No Child Left Behind: A Lesson in the Limits of Government Power." In *Teaching America: The Case for Civic Education.* Edited by David Feith, 51–60. Plymouth, UK: Rowman & Littlefield Education, 2011.

Hirsch, E. D., Jr. *The Knowledge Deficit: Closing the Shocking Education Gap for American Children.* New York: Houghton Mifflin, 2006.

———. *The Making of Americans: Democracy and Our Schools.* New Haven, CT: Yale University Press, 2009.

Hunter, James Davison. *The Death of Character: Moral Education in an Age without Good or Evil.* New York: Basic Books, 2000.

Jeynes, William H. "Religion, Intact Families, and the Achievement Gap." *Interdisciplinary Journal of Research on Religion* 3.3 (2007): 1–22.

Kazin, Michael. "Good History and Good Citizens: Howard Zinn, Woodrow Wilson, and the Historian's Perspective." In *Teaching America: The Case for Civic Education.* Edited by David Feith, 141–150. Plymouth, UK: Rowman & Littlefield Education, 2011.

Kunzman, Robert. *Grappling with the Good: Talking about Religion and Morality in Public Schools.* Albany: State University of New York Press, 2006.

McFarland, Daniel A., and Rueben J. Thomas. "Bowling Young: How Youth Voluntary Associations Influence Adult Political Participation." *American Sociological Review* 71.6 (2006): 401–425.

McLaren, Peter. *Life in Schools: An Introduction to Critical Pedagogy in the Foundations of Education.* Boston: Pearson, 2007 [1998].

Miller, Helen. "Meeting the Challenge: The Jewish Schooling Problem in the UK." *Oxford Review of Education* 27.4 (2001): 501–513.

Moe, Terry M. *Special Interest: Teachers Unions and America's Public Schools.* Washington, DC: Brookings, 2011.

MonolithIC3D; "Education to Raise Technology Consumers Instead of Technology Creators," posted by Ze-ev Wurman, April 8, 2011. Available online, http://www.monolithic3d.com/2/post/2011/08/education-to-raise-technology-consumers-instead-of-technology-creators.html.

National Commission on Excellence in Education. *A Nation at Risk: The Imperative for Educational Reform.* Washington, DC: United States Department of Education, 1983.

O'Connor, Sandra Day. "The Democratic Purpose of Education: From the Founders to Horace Mann to Today." In *Teaching America: The Case for Civic Education.* Edited by David Feith, 3–14. Plymouth, UK: Rowman & Littlefield Education, 2011.

Paige, Rod. "Forgetting Martin Luther King's Dream: How Politics Threatens America's Civil Rights Memory." In *Teaching America: The Case for Civic Education.* Edited by David Feith, 69–80. Plymouth, UK: Rowman & Littlefield Education, 2011.

Pangle, Lorraine Smith, and Thomas L. Pangle. "What the American Founders Have to Teach Us about Schooling for Democratic Citizenship." In *Rediscovering the Democratic Purposes of Education.* Edited by Lorraine M. McDonnell, P. Michael Timpane, and Roger Benjamin, 21–46. Lawrence: University of Kansas Press, 2000.

Pennings, Ray. *Cardus Education Survey: Do the Motivations for Private Religious Catholic and Protestant Schooling in North America Align with Graduate Outcomes?* Hamilton, Canada: Cardus, 2011.

Peterson, Paul E., Ludger Woessmann, Eric A. Hanushek, and Carlos X. Lastra-Anadon. *Globally Challenged: Are U.S. Students Ready to Compete?* Boston: Harvard's Program on Education Policy and Governance and Education Next, 2011.

Postman, Neil, and Charles Weingartner. *Teaching as a Subversive Activity.* New York: Dell Publishing Co., 1969.

Prothero, Stephen. *Religious Literacy: What Every American Ought to Know—and Doesn't.* New York: Harper Collins, 2007.

Ratcliff, Admiral Mike. "Donor Intent: Strategic Philanthropy in Higher Education." In *Teaching America: The Case for Civic Education.* Edited by David Feith, 171–183. Plymouth, UK: Rowman & Littlefield Education, 2011.

Ravitch, Diane. *Left Back: A Century of Battles over School Reform.* New York: Simon & Schuster, 2000.

Reuben, Julie. "Beyond Politics: Community Civics and the Redefinition of Citizenship in the Progressive Era." *History of Education Quarterly* 37.4 (1997): 399–420.

Rieff, Philip. *The Triumph of the Therapeutic: Uses of Faith after Freud.* Chicago: University of Chicago Press, 1987 [1966].

Rotherham, Andrew J. "Core Curriculum: How to Tackle General Illiteracy and Civic Illiteracy at the Same Time." In *Teaching America: The Case for Civic Education.* Edited by David Feith, 89–98. Plymouth, UK: Rowman & Littlefield Education, 2011.

Rylance, Rick. *Victorian Psychology and British Culture 1850–1880*. Oxford: Oxford University Press, 2000.

Sandstroem, F. Mikael. "School Choice in Sweden: Is There Danger of a Counterrevolution?" In *What Americans Can Learn from School Choice in Other Countries*. Edited by David Salisbury and James Tooley, 23–40. Washington, DC: Cato Institute, 2005.

Skillen, James W. *In Pursuit of Justice: Christian-Democratic Explorations*. New York: Rowman & Littlefield, 2004.

Smith, Christian, with Melinda Lundquist Denton. *Soul Searching: The Religious and Spiritual Lives of American Teenagers*. Oxford: Oxford University Press, 2005.

Smith, Timothy. "Protestant Schooling and American Nationality, 1800–1850," *Journal of American History* 53.4 (1967): 679–695.

Stergios, Jim. "Testimony to the Texas Committee on State Sovereignty." Boston: Pioneer Institute, 2011. Available online, http://www.pioneerinstitute.org/pdf/110414_TX_Stergios.pdf.

Thomson, Mathew. *Psychological Subjects: Identity, Culture, and Health in Twentieth-Century Britain*. Oxford: Oxford University Press, 2006.

Tyack, David. "The Kingdom of God and the Common School: Protestant Ministers and the Educational Awakening in the West." *Harvard Educational Review* 36 (Fall 1966).

Waldron, Jeremy. "Multiculturalism and Mélange." In *Public Education in a Multicultural Society: Policy, Theory, Critique*. Edited by Robert K. Fullinwider, 90–120. Cambridge, UK: Cambridge University Press, 1966.

Weisberg, Daniel, Susan Sexton, Jennifer Mulhern, and David Keeling. *The Widget Effect: Our National Failure to Acknowledge and Act on Differences in Teacher Effectiveness*. Brooklyn, NY: New Teacher Project, 2009.

Witte, John, Jr., and Joel A. Nichols. *Religion and the American Constitutional Experiment*. 3rd ed. Boulder, CO: Westview Press, 2011.

Afterword

Adam Seligman

WELL OVER HALF a century ago, when I was in third grade and Armistice Day was still observed in the United States, I was a student in a religious Jewish day school in Brooklyn, New York. I well remember coming home one day in early November, proud as can be and reciting to my parents, by heart, the poem we had just learned in school:

In Flanders Fields the poppies blow
Between the markers [sic] row on row,
That mark our place; and in the sky
The larks, still bravely singing, fly
Scarce heard amid the guns below....

I was rather taken aback that my father well knew that poem by John McCrae, and though he congratulated me on my good memory, said I had made only one mistake. That it was not "Between the markers row on row," but "Between the crosses row on row."

The next day in school, I checked the mimeographed sheet we had received in class and, sure enough, saw that it had "markers" and not "crosses" printed on it. When I showed this to my father, he became very upset and, to my great embarrassment and shame, demanded a meeting with the Principal and made a huge fuss on how dare they fiddle with the text of poems, what nonsense was this, not wanting little Jewish children to even say the word "crosses" and so on.

While the type of religious close-mindedness evinced by the school authorities may recall the case of the Jewish schools in Paris studied by Kimberly Arkin, this would be a mistake. We all felt very American, following baseball avidly, poured over historical comics of the American Civil

War, many of our parents had fought in World War II, and we never experienced any tension between following the arcane rules of stoop ball on the one hand and that of the Babylonian Talmud on the other.

I tell the story here, because it epitomizes many of the conflicts and trade-offs that are raised in the chapters of this volume. Moreover, and though it was a private and parochial school (and certainly in the milieu I grew up in—liberal, democratic, Jewish) no one—among either observant or less-observant Jews—ever questioned the strict separation of Church and State and the responsibility of a religious community to pay for its own schools if that was what they desired, to guarantee their collective continuity. The story highlights however, just how subtle are the type of issues raised in the Silvio Ferrari's survey of different EU state policies on religious education; e.g. the conundrum of denominational or non-denominational teaching of religious traditions—which, as we have seen, is a serious issue in quite a number of the cases reviewed in this volume. Can the terms of an inclusive citizenship be generated, or even augmented, from a particularistic tradition with clearly delineated boundaries, terms of membership, and commitments, that are by definition exclusive if not exclusionary? Can the Israeli polity generate such terms of membership for all its citizenry out of the unique language of the Jewish tradition? Can Malaysia or Turkey from an Islamic vocabulary, or Bulgaria from an Orthodox one? What of Cyprus—split as it is along national and religious lines? What sort of citizens will be produced from local, parochial, and under-supervised religious schools in France (and elsewhere) we may ask?

Denominational schooling in religion is clearly focused on preserving itself and asserting its own boundaries and truths. Non-denominational schooling, often accused of being "relativistic," is however, I would claim, problematic in very different terms. For it can provide no sense of belonging. Yet, without a shared sense of community (and communities always have boundaries, however labile and penetrable they may be), mutual commitment and trust the religious perspectives provided in such schooling will be incapable of providing the sense of meaning, values, and goal-orientations; that is the reason people turn to religious traditions in the first place. There is no easy answer to this conundrum. As we have seen, different countries—with different religious and national heritages, facing very different challenges to the terms of citizenship—are devolving different types of answers.

Yet, a problem remains. For even when reaching out and sharing in the broader culture of citizenship, as my school authorities clearly were interested in doing—by teaching (by heart no less) a poem written by a Canadian physician at the battle of the Ypres salient in 1915—these same authorities attempted to obfuscate one of the most core aspects of that broader culture (i.e., that it was Christian). The challenge of bringing particularistic and universalistic assumptions and commitments together is not an easy one. The 20th century has taught us the horrors of both particularism and universalism, when taken to extremes; and more recent decades have illuminated just how impossible it is to construct a polity, or a life, by attempting to eschew the very choice. The current crises in humanistic education in North American universities and beyond are not unrelated to this state of affairs.

The challenge, I would suggest, is not to be met by some particular set of curricula desiderata or syllabus content; rather, I will argue, by adopting a particular approach, one that I will attempt to outline below.

And so, to close this volume, I would like reflect a bit on what I think would be involved in moving beyond the often state-centered models so admirably analyzed in the chapters above, and to privilege a type of practical paidea over the forms of legally mandated and state generated practice, characteristic of so many of the cases analyzed above. To explore, what type of pedagogy would be necessary to develop new forms of living with difference in the context of the increasingly pluralistic societies that make up the world we are living in.

I would like to claim that one way to approach this problem was suggested by the dictum attributed to the Scottish philosopher, David Hume, that: "Explanation is where the mind rests." Now minds are very busy things, constantly moving, restless, questioning and querying—people spend a lifetime of yoga and meditation to get the mind to rest. If so, then, indeed, when does the mind rest? One place it rests is, most often, when the particular purpose of its questioning has been fulfilled. In slightly different terms, the mind rests when the purpose for which an explanation has been pursued has been met. Unpacking this idea may just allow us another way to think of radical difference in a more malleable manner, and so perhaps develop new approaches to the challenge of deep pluralism in the civic realm.

What I would like to suggest is that in these contexts of deep pluralism, we change the place where our minds "rest." We need to transform the purposes of knowledge (especially knowledge of the other, of he or she who is different and yet, shares the city streets, buses, voting booths, and health offices with me). We need to transform the fundamental purposes of our knowing (and thus of our explanations), from providing a knowledge of, to providing a knowledge for. Not an idea *of* the other, rather ideas *for* certain joint purposes—for a set of to-does is the goal toward which our explanations should be oriented. For explanation is not in fact, the end of experience, but rather, very much at its beginning. It is the place where already-before-the-event, I know where I will locate it. In essence then, what we must strive to do is reject any final explanation—agree to set apart broad, inclusive and generalized explanations. And while none of us questions our own belonging to meaning-giving communities (which could be Jewish, Moslem, Christian, or secular-humanist) we must, in our shared civil life, eschew the types of explanations and ideas such communities of belonging provide to our understanding of the other, and seek an experience relatively free from such pre-existing interpretive grids predicated on sameness and difference.

The idea is relatively simply, I believe. For rather than think that we need to know the other in order to trust her, or share civil space with him, we should begin with the assumption that we can never fully know the other—if truth be told, we rarely, fully, know even ourselves. If trust is to be based on knowledge (and so on a "full" explanation), we can never be trustful. There will never be sufficient knowledge, especially of another who refrains from eating and drinking that which we eat and drink (pork and wine, say), or who prays and fasts on different days, who reveres other prophets and other prophetic books and is, in his and her most intimate relations, a total cipher to us and what we take for granted. Only by becoming this other could we possibly know her; and then, of course, we have simply switched moral communities, rather than extending the boundaries of our own (for now I would no longer partake in the Easter ham with my family). We must therefore hold in suspension any claims to knowledge of the other and not make such knowledge a precondition for shared civil life.

What is demanded is, in fact, a new form of thinking through experience, suspending judgment even as one forms new conjectures leading us to new forms of action, and I would hazard, new forms of civic belonging as well. One would, in this scenario not ignore, or try to hide, the fact that the world outside certain sections of Brooklyn, is, in fact, Christian. Rather, and in an age-appropriate way, discuss the challenges of, say, maintaining particular identities in the context of a majoritarian culture; one experienced oftentimes as less than accommodating and how difficult this could be in a combat situation—where trust across peoples of different religious and ethnic communities is crucial for a military unit to function properly.[1]

So, rather than have our minds rest, that is, reach a place of comfort and security on the basis of our knowledge (or, in the case of my story, total and willful ignorance) of the other, I suggest that we reorient the objects of our knowledge. Explanation should be oriented toward a particular task. Our knowledge of the other should be oriented not to some secret place inside the soul, but rather to a well defined practical task. If, for example, I need to organize a community action together with Muslims and Jews—say to demand benches in the park, or a larger education budget for local schools—well then, what must I know of Muslims and Jews (in general, but only in so far as it pertains to these particular Muslims and Jews with whom I will be working) to be able to work together with them on these projects? Well, I must know what they eat and what they don't eat (to pack the proper sandwiches). I must know when they pray (not to schedule meetings at prayer time)—this sort of thing.[2] Once we have this sorted, we may go on to more complicated joint projects, at which time I will be required to know more of them (and they will, as well, need to learn quite a bit about me) in order to scale up, from our first community organizing event, to—let us say—running a joint campaign for an elected official. And so on, and so on. There is no need in these joint actions to plumb the depths of Jewish halachic reasoning and Talmudic views of Jesus, or Muslim attitudes toward divorce or the greater *Jihad*. There are very specific things I need to know to do, very specific projects, together with my neighbors who are different from me. As we (if we) do more together, I will learn more of them, and they of me; and as we learn, we will be building a shared context, a shared experience—in fact, a set of shared experiences—of embodied knowledge that is learned in the doing and that will serve as the grid through which my more abstract knowledge of being Jewish or Moslem or Sikh or for that matter, disabled or poor, will begin to be refracted. Together, through a joint "doing," we will be constructing precisely those interpretive frames and meaning-giving contexts through which my understanding of the other will take place. We will thus begin to teach our children about the other, in a similar way that we teach them to tie their shoes. And just perhaps they will wear their citizenship with as much pride as their sneakers. This in fact, is the logic behind the type of "practical tasks" required by students in current civic education classes in the religious sectors of Israeli society, as discussed in Shlomo Fischer's paper above.

All of this brings us to what I like to call the idea of embodied knowledge, that is, knowledge focused on particularities and hence what is, in essence, experience. Experience, as Dewey (2004, 134) has taught us, is the central component in thinking. "To learn from experience," he tells us, "is to make a backward and forward connection between what we do to things, and what we enjoy, and suffer from things in consequence. Under such conditions, doing becomes a trying; an experiment with the world to find out what it is like." In this process, the intellect cannot be separated from experience and the attempt to do so leaves us with disembodied, abstract knowledge that all too often emphasizes "things" rather than the "relations or connections" between them (ibid, 137). In so doing, it is of precious little help in our attempt to connect the multitude of disconnected data that the world presents into a framework of meaning.

Meaning, as is clear to all, rests not on the knowledge of "things," but on the relations between them. These relations, in turn, as Dewey so brilliantly argues, can only be assessed through experience—because only through experience do we bring the relevant relations between things into any sensible sort of juxtaposition. (Hence, the relevant relations between fabric, wood, staples, hammer, stain-pot, brush, etc. are only made relevant in the construction of the chair. Without the experience of chair-making, the relations between the components, even the definition of the component elements, is open to endless interpretation. Moreover, if I were building a light glider the relevant relations—of tensile strength, thickness, suitability of material, etc.—would be different). Thus meaning, emergent from experience, can only be supplied by the goals toward which we aspire—as indeed, experience, as opposed to our simple passive subjugation to an event, is always in pursuit of a practical aim. This, I would submit, is the real way forward in our quest for civic enculturation: shared practical goals and the establishment of those social frameworks needed to achieve them, not only within, but most especially across different religious, ethnic, racial, and communal boundaries. Religious education needs be reframed not in terms of a generalized knowledge of others, or of one's own community. Rather, religious education must be conceptualized as a mode of living together differently. It must become a particular type of knowledge "for"— and the "for" involved is that of civil engagement and the building of a city where all belong. In this sense, the model of religious education developed in Birmingham, England, and noted in the introduction is very relevant.

Each and every one of us brings infinite possibilities to our encounters with other human beings. These cannot be circumscribed by the idols of the tribe, or the marketplace, or for that matter, by our grandmothers' stories. It is not by expanding or universalizing the boundaries of trust (which is a utopic dream), but by radically recalibrating them, that we can learn to live together differently. The constant search for infinitely calculable degrees of moral sameness—or absolute otherness—is dangerous. Such an exercise will always leave us with a not-too-negligible human remainder whose position outside the boundaries will be a constant threat to all. The challenge of really living with difference demands great moral courage. It demands us to act and to take stands in situations of moral ambiguity and in circumstances of less-than-full knowledge. Yet, if the great religious traditions of the world have anything to offer us, it is precisely this courage in these circumstances. At the end of the day, this may indeed be the most important contribution of religious traditions to the process of civic enculturation.

NOTES

1. Elementary school children can be pretty sophisticated about such matters, as I learned when I spoke to my own daughter's fifth grade class, more than a dozen years ago, on different Jewish and Christian understandings of love.
2. Lest this seem too obvious, let me point out that a few years ago I was asked to speak at an inter-faith event at the US Naval Academy on September 30, 2008. I pointed out that this was one of the holiest days in the Jewish liturgical calendar, Rosh Hashanah (the New Year) and I would be at synagogue all day. After thanking me for my quick response, my interlocutor asked if I could suggest anyone else. I observed that given the sanctity of the day, I doubted if he would find anyone knowledgeable who would be available. I did not hear back. It seemed that even after my second message, my interlocutor was still ignorant of the problem.

BIBLIOGRAPHY

Dewey, John. *Democracy and Education*. New York: Dover Books, 2004.

Index

Abdul Razak Hussein, 176–77
accreditation issues, 85–86, 88
achievement gaps, 211
Act on Churches, n8
Adams, John, 194
Adams, John Quincy, 194
Administration of Religious Education, 143
admission standards, 115
African religions, 57
agnosticism, 78
AK Party, 61, 157–59, 160–62, 164
Alawites, 61, 62
Alevis, 4, 18, 20, 157–58, 163
Alexander the Great, 204
Algeria, 102, 103, 105
Alsace-Moselle, France, 32, n1
American Joint Distribution Committee, 102
Angkatan Belia Islam Malaysia (ABIM), 173
Anglicanism, 18, 20
animism, 170
Annan, Kofi, 46
Annan Plan, 52, 53
anti-Semitism, 96, 102, 104
anti-Zionism, 121
Arabs
  Arabic language, 58, 76, 122, 126, 129, 154, 173, 184
  and French day schooling, 103–5
  and Israeli citizenship, 12, 122–25, 143
  and Israeli education, 125–29
  and Israeli political environment, 133, 136, 143, 145n11
Aristotle, 204
Arkin, Kimberly, viii, 5, 8, 216–17
Armenian Orthodoxy, 54
Armenians, 54, 58, 74
Armistice Day, 216
Ashkenazi Jews, 102–3, 105, 112–13, 116n8, 126–27
assertive secularism, 154–56, 156–59, 163–64, 165n5
Association for Civil Rights in Israel (ACRI), 128
Association of Universal Love and Brotherhood, 62
Ataka (Attack) Party, 84, 91n5
Atatürk, Mustafa Kemal, 54, 59–60, 63–64, 154, 156–57. *See also* Kemalist policies and reforms
atheism, 74, 78, 85, 89
Austria, 37nn16 –17, 38n18
Autocephalous Greek Orthodox Church of Cyprus, 54
Aviner, Elisha, 136
avodah zarah, 112

Baden-Wuttemberg, Germany, 2
Balakov's Commission, 80–82
Balkans, 4, 10, 75

Bangsa term, 179
Bank of Israel, 128
Baptists, 195
Bar-Ilan University, 138, 142
Barisan Nasional (BN), 187
Başgil, Ali Fuat, 153
"Basis for a Comprehensive Settlement of the Cyprus Problem," 46
Belgium, 37n16, 38n22, 38n24
Benayoun, Mme, 109–10
Berner, Ashley Rogers, 10, 15
"Bill for the More General Diffusion of Knowledge," 194, 195
Birmingham, England, 21, 221
bishul akum, 111, 112
Bourdieu, Pierre, 103
British Empire and colonialism, 45, 46–47, 48, 169, 171–72, 178–79
Bruner, Jerome S., 202, 203
B'Tzelem, 128
Buddhism, 57, 60, 170
Bulgaria
 and the Balkan War, 4
 and citizenship challenges, viii
 and citizenship definitions, 12
 and civic enculturation, 3
 and collective identity, 11–12
 context of religious education, 70–71, 71–77
 and the European Union, 5, 21, 38n19, 38n24, 80, 89
 and nation-state formation, 18–19
 post-communist attitudes on religious education, 77–85
 and secularism, 6, 10–11
 and social "otherness," 18
 and state-sponsored religious education, 20
 and teacher training, 85–91
 and World War II, 21, 22n1
Bulgarian Constitution, 70, 76–77
Bulgarian Exarchate, 71–73, 91n3

Bulgarian Ministry of Education, 73–74, 76, 78–79, 79–80, 84, 86, 88
Bulgarian National Television, 88
Bulgarian Orthodox Church, 10, 21, 73–74, 78–85, 88–89, 91n2
Bulgarian Parliament, 77, 84
Bulgarian Principality, 73
Bulgarian Socialist Party, 78, 91n5
Bulgarian University Ranking System, 91n8
Bumiputera, 170, 176

Campbell, David, 203, 207–8
Cardus Education Survey, 208
Catholicism
 and American education, 206, 208–9
 and Bulgarian education, 77, 87, 89
 and civic enculturation, 6, 10
 constitutional protection in Cyprus, 54
 and French education, 99
 Italian Concordat of 1984, 2
 and Parisian day schools, 97–98
 and religious education in the European Union, 30–31, 32, 37n9, 37n15, 38n19
 and Turkish education, 151
cemevis, 163
Central Bureau of Statistics (CBS), 122
character education movement, 201
Chief Mufti's Office, 70–71, 80, 84, 88
Chief Rabbinate (Israel), 125
Chinese minority communities
 and Malaysian multiculturalism, 168–69, 170–74, 178, 180–81, 183–88, 190n3
 and social "otherness," 18
 and state-sponsored religious education, 20
Chinese religions, 57
Chitrit, Mme, 111, 113–14
Christianity

and American culture, 199
and Bulgarian teacher training, 87, 89
and Cypriot education, 60
and Malaysian multiculturalism, 170
and religious education in the European Union, 26
See also specific Christian denominations
Christ is the Truth: Orthodox Christian Education, 56
Christ's Path: Orthodox Christian Education, 56
Chrysostomos II, 51, 63
Church of the Latter Day Saints, 199
Church Slavonic, 91n1
church/state separation, 9–10, 18, 217
citizenship education
  and American education, 193–97
  challenges of, viii, 217–20
  and civic attachment, 197–98
  and context of Israeli education, 119–21
  and French Republicanism, 97–101
  and fundamental challenges of society, 1–2
  and Israeli civic culture, 126–27
  and Israeli liberal citizenship discourse, 127–28, 142–44, 144–45
  and Malaysian multiculturalism, 175, 178–79, 190n3
  and nation-state formation, 19
  and pluralistic societies, 14–18
  and religious education in the European Union, 26, 33
  and religious requirements, 10
  terms of, 14
  and Zionism, 136, 142–44
civic culture and identity, 16, 126–27, 182, 197
civic skills, 196
civil rights and liberties, 128, 145, 197

civil society
  and civic enculturation, 6, 8
  and Malaysian society, 168, 186
  models of education, 206
  and religious education in the European Union, 35
class tensions and conflict, 103–4, 116n3, 116n9, 204
Clermont-Tonnerre, Stanislas, 12, 146n15
Close-Up Foundation, 210
Cohen, Adar, 141–42
Cohen, Asher, 141, 143
Coleman, James, 207
collective action, 196. *See also* civic culture and identity
collective identity, 11–12, 140, 141
Commission on Religion, 78
Commission on the Affairs of Religious Teaching in School, 80–82
Committee of Ministers (Council of Europe), 36n6
common schools, 195, 206
communism, 9, 70, 76, 89, 90
Communities Engaging with Difference and Religion (CEDAR), vii
communities of belonging, 219
community service, 196
compulsory religious education, 29–30
confidence, 17–18
Confucianism, 170
Congress of Berlin, 72
Conover, Pamela Johnston, 198
conservatism, 157–58, 209
Constitutional Court (Bulgaria), 70
Constitutional Court (Turkey), 150, 161, 162, 165n5
Constitution of the Republic of Cyprus, 53–54, 60
contrat d'association, 98–99
Convention for the Protection of Human Rights and Fundamental Freedoms, 25

conversion, religious, 75
core curricula, 205
corporatist-state economy, 126–27
cosmopolitanism, 136
Council of Europe, 25, 34, 36nn5–6, 39n32, 52–53
Council of Higher Education (YÖK), 162
Council of State, 159
Council on State Religious System, 126
Counter-Reformation, 10
cultural assimilation, 79, 206, 211
Curriculum Committee, 143–44
Cyprus
  and citizenship challenges, viii
  and citizenship definitions, 12
  and civic enculturation, 3–5
  and collective identity, 11–12
  competing narratives on divided Cyprus, 49–53
  context of religious education, 45–46, 46–49
  and goals of education, 63–64
  informal religious education in, 57–58
  and interreligious dialogue, 62–63
  and nation-state formation, 18–19
  religious and ethical education in, 53–57
  and religious education in the European Union, 38n17, 38n20, 38n24
  religious institutions and associations in, 61–62
  and religious minorities, 58–60
  and secularism, 10
  and state-sponsored religious education, 20
  and tensions over religious education, 60–61
Cyprus Turkish Islam Association, 62
Czech Republic, 27–28, 37n16, 38nn22–23

Damon, William, 201
DAP party, 187, 188
Debray, Régis, 26
Debré laws, 98–101, 106, 151
Declaration of Independence (Israel), 119, 122, 139
decolonization, 171–72
Demetriou, Andreas, 51
democracy
  and American citizenship education, 211
  and challenges of pluralism, 9
  and civic attachment, 197–98
  and civic enculturation, 6
  and expressivist religious Zionism, 136
  ideals in American public education, 209–10
  and Israeli civics curricula, 130–38, 139
  and Israeli political theology, 134
  and religious education in the European Union, 33
  role of education in, 193
  and Turkish education, 158
  and Zionist theology, 121
Democracy Prep Charter Schools, 211
Democratic Left Party, 159
"A Democratic Regime vs. the Culture of Democracy" (Bin-Nun), 136
demonstrations, 100
Denmark, 36n9, 37n13
denominational religious education, 26, 28, 30–32, 35, 35n11, 38n24, 217
Denominations Act, 79
Department of Education (France), 101
Department of Statistics (Malaysia), 170
Deuteronomy, 135
Dewan Bahasa dan Pustaka (Institute for Language and Literature), 175
Dewey, John, 221

dietary restrictions, 101–2, 113, 125
dinnim, 109–10
Directorate of Religious Affairs (Cyprus), 58, 61–62
Directorate of Religious Affairs (Turkey), 155–56
Diskin, Avraham, 141
"dispositions" of religious education, 22, 23n2
"divine state" concept, 132, 133
Diyanet, 155–56, 158
Dong Jiao Zong (DJZ), 185, 186
Dong Zong, 185
Douglas, Mary, 110–11
Durkheim, Émile, 18, 97

Eastern Malaysia, 170
Eastern Orthodoxy, viii, 8, 11, 70, 78–79, 91n3
Eastern Rumelia, 73
Ecclesiastical Academy, 89
Edirne, 73
Education Ordinance Act, 171
elections, 145n1, 160, 161
Elkana, West Bank, 138
Elkin, M. K. Zeev, 141
embodied knowledge, 221
English language, 180–81
Enlightenment, 2, 90–91
EOKA B, 49
Episcopalians, 195
Erbakan, Necmettin, 157
Erdoğan, Tayyip, 151, 157, 163
Ergenekon, 161
eschatological theology, 110, 134
Establishment clause, 205–6
Estonia, 36n9, 37n10
ethics education, 54–58, 201. *See also* morality and moralism in education
ethnic identity and conflict
and civic enculturation, 2–3, 6
and context of Israeli education, 123
and Cyprus, 45, 49–50
ethno-religious hostilities, viii
and expressivist religious Zionism, 136–38
and French education, 103–6, 115
and identity politics, 12–13
and Malaysian multiculturalism, 169, 186
and national identity, 2–3, 63–64, 136–38
European Court of Human Rights, 29, 37n12, 165n8
European Union (EU)
and Bulgaria, 21, 38n19, 38n24, 80, 89
context of religious education, 25–27
countries with denominational religious education, 26, 30–31
countries with non-denominational religious education, 26, 28–30
countries without religious education, 26, 27–28
and Cyprus, 46, 50–51, 57
evolution and limits of denominational education, 31–32
and models of religious education, 32–35
evangelicals, 199
exemptions from religious education, 34, 37n12, 55
expressivist religious Zionism, 130–31, 133–36, 136–38
extremism, 90, 91n5

faith-based organizations, 200
fascism, 9
Federation of Malaya Constitutional Commission, 189
Ferguson, Adam, 12
Ferrari, Silvio, vii, 2, 5, 16, 21–22, 217
Ferry laws, 98

Finland, 37n16, 38nn21–23
First Additional Protocol, 25
Fischer, Shlomo, 8, 21, 220
Fonds Social Juif Unifié (FSJU), 102
Foon Yew Schools, 188
forced conversion, 75
Foucault, Michel, 106–7
France
  and church/state separation, 18–19
  and civic enculturation, 3, 6
  and context of religious education, 96–97, 97–101
  and Debré laws, 98–101, 106, 151
  and declining pluralism, 101–7, 107–15
  and denominational religious education, 32
  and educational achievement gaps, 211
  and nation-state formation, 18–19
  and pluralism dialogue, viii
  and religious education in the European Union, 26, 28
  secularism in, 152
Franklin, Benjamin, 194
French Department of Education, 96
French Republicanism, 97–101
French Revolution, 146n7
Freud, Sigmund, 17
Frey, Frederick, 154
fundamentalism, 84, 208
funding for religious education, 38n23, 99, 102–3, 115
The Future Vision of the Palestinian Arabs in Israel, 129

Galston, William, 196, 203, 204, 209
Gavison, Ruth, 120
Gaza, 120, 124, 128, 145
Geiger, Yitzchak, 139–40
gender issues, 12–13, 165n5
Germany, 31, 38n23
Ghannem, Assad, 129
Girl Scouts, 200

Glicksberg, Bilha, 141, 144
globalization, 127–28
Gökalp, Ziya, 154
Goldstone Report, 120
Great Britain, 37n14. *See also* British Empire and colonialism
Greater Land of Israel, 133
"Great Turkish Nation" curricula, 51
Greece, 2, 38n20, 38n24, 48
"Greece-Cyprus Unified Education" policy, 51
Greek Cypriots
  and bicommunal religious education, 53–54
  and competing narratives on divided Cyprus, 49–53
  and context of Cypriot education, 45–46, 46–49
  and interreligious dialogue, 62
  and minority religious education, 58
  and national identity, 63–64
  and religious/ethical education, 54–57
Greek Ministry of Education, 50
Greek minority populations, 4
Greek Orthodoxy
  and Cypriot education, 46–47, 54–58
  and Greek national identity, 3–4
  interreligious dialogue in Cyprus, 62–63
  and religious education in the European Union, 38n20
  and Turkish education, 163
group identity, 11–12
group rights, 144
Grunspan, Mme, 109
Gül, Adbullah, 161, 162
Gül, Ozdemir, 62
Gülen movement, 151, 159, 164
Gush Emunim, 124

Habib-Deloncle law, 99
Hacı Bektaşşi Veli Derneği, 62

Hagar, 114
Haifa, Israel, 122
halakhic tradition, 100–1, 112, 113, 116n8, 136
Halki Seminary, 163
Hanafi Islam, 59
Haredi Judaism, 100, 104–10, 116n5, 123–24, 126, 134, 145n11
Hartman Institute, 21
Hasan and Eylem Zengin v. Turkey, 30
headscarf bans, 13, 150–51, 159, 161, 163, 165n7
Hebrew University, 141
Hegel, Georg Wilhelm Friedrich, 12, 132
Hellenism, 50, 51
Henry Luce Foundation, vii
High Council of Judges and Prosecutors, 162
Higher Evangelical Theological School, 85
Higher Islamic Institute, 85, 86, 87–88
Hinduism, 57, 60, 170
Hirsch, E. D., 202, 203–4
historical revisionism, 50, 52–53, 54
Holocaust, 116n4
Holy Synod of the Bulgarian Orthodox Church, 73, 76, 83–84, 86
homogenization, cultural, 105–6, 108
homophobia, 96
humanism, 218
human rights, 13, 119, 120, 127–28, 138
Hume, David, 218
Hungary, 28
Hunter, James Davison, 10, 15
Hussain, Abdullah, 169

Ibrahim, Anwar, 187
iCivics program, 210
Id, 7
Idadi school, 47
identity politics, 12–13
Ignatieff, Michael, 13

"I'm a Malaysian" movement, 185
Imam-Hatip schools, 20, 151, 154, 155–56, 159–60, 162
inclusive citizenship, 217
India, 10
Indian minority communities
    and Malaysian multiculturalism, 169, 170, 178–79, 180, 188, 190n3
    and social "otherness," 18
    and state-sponsored religious education, 20
indigenous cultures, 170
individualism, 199
individual rights, 14. *See also* civil rights and liberties
"In Flanders Fields" (McCrae), 216–17
informal religious education, 57–58
Institute for Culture and World Affairs (CURA), vii
Institute for Language and Literature (*Dewan Bahasa dan Pustaka*), 175
intercultural dialogue, 87
Interlok (Hussain), 169, 188
intermarriage, 116n2
Internal Revolutionary Macedonian Organization (VMRO), 84
International Covenant on Economic, Social and Cultural Rights, 36n4
international law, 25
Internationmal Islamic University Malaysia (IIUM), 184
interreligious dialogue, 62–63
Ishmael, 114
Islam and Muslims
    and Bulgarian education, 74–77, 78, 83–85
    and citizenship challenges, viii
    and civic enculturation, 7, 8
    and Cypriot education, 46–48, 54, 57–59, 62–64
    and education in the European Union, 26, 30, 38n24

Islam and Muslims (*Cont.*)
  Islamic law, 47
  and Malaysian education, 170–74, 176–77, 181–84, 187–88
  and pluralism dialogue, viii
  Shia Islam, 158
  and state-sponsored religious education, 20
  Sufism, 164
  Sunni Islam, 59, 62, 157–58
  and Turkish education, 150–52, 152–54, 154–56, 156–59, 159–60, 163, 164, 165n5
Islamist Felicity Party (SP), 157
Israel
  and citizenship discourse, viii, 12, 142–44
  and civic culture, 3, 11–12, 126–27, 127–28
  and civics curricula, 127, 128–30, 138–42
  education system in, 20, 119–21, 125–26
  and expressivist religious Zionism, 136–38
  and nation-state formation, 18–19
  and religious national identity, 4, 11, 133–36
  and secularism, 10
  and social "otherness," 18
  social structure of, 122–25
  theology and politics in, 130–33, 133–36
Israel Democracy Institute (IDI), 123, 125
Israeli-Arab conflict, 140
Israeli-Palestinian conflict, 20
Italy, 31, 32, 37n16, 38n22

Jackson, Robert, vii
Jaffa, Israel, 122
Japanese religions, 57

Jawa script, 183
Jefferson, Thomas, 194, 195
Jehovah's Witnesses, 18, 82, 84
Jesus, 90
Jewish National Fund, 128
Jeynes, William, 207
Jiao Zong, 185
Judaism and Jewish populations
  and American culture, 199
  and American education, 208
  and anti-Semitism, 96, 102, 104
  Ashkenazi Jews, 102–3, 105, 112–13, 116n8, 126–27
  and Bulgarian education, 74, 77, 87
  and civic enculturation, 7, 8
  and Cypriot education, 57, 60
  and French education, 101–7, 107–15
  halakhic tradition, 100–101, 112, 113, 116n8, 136
  Haredi Judaism, 100, 104–10, 116n5, 123–24, 126, 134, 145n11
  and Israeli demographics, 122
  Jewish minority populations, 4, 5
  non-Observant Jews, 123
  rabbinic Judaism, 110, 125
  and religious education in the European Union, 26
  Sephardic Jews, 102–3, 113
  and state-sponsored religious education, 20
  and World War II Bulgaria, 21, 22n11
Justice and Development (AK) Party, 150–51

Kalkandjieva, Daniela, 5, 11, 21, 91n4
Kamus Dewan, 175
Kant, Emmanuel, 138
kashrut (*kashruth*), 101–2, 125
Kemalist policies and reforms
  and assertive secularism, 152
  and Bulgarian Pomaks, 75–76
  philosophic influences, 154

Index

and Turkish Cypriots, 49, 54, 63
and Turkish education, 156–57
kesrette vahdet (unity within diversity), 164
Ketuanan Agama, 176
Ketuanan Melayu, 175–79, 179–81, 181–82, 184–86, 188–89
ketubah, 116n2
kibbutzim, 128
King, Martin Luther, Jr., 198
Knesset, 121, 122, 125, 139, 145n1
Kook, R., 131–33, 133–37
kosher laws, 111–12
Kremnitzer, Mordechai, 143–44, 146n15
Kremnitzer Committee, 129, 138, 139, 143–44, 146n15
Krishna, 82
Kunzman, Robert, 205
Kurds, 4, 18, 165n3
Kuru, Ahmet, 4, 8, 14

labor unions, 209–21
Labor Zionist movement, 126–27, 140
"late modernizer" countries, 3
Latif, Dilek, 3–4, 5, 8
Latins (Roman Catholics), 54
Latvia, 37nn16 –17, 38n21, 38nn23–24
Law for the Development of the Academic Staff of the Republic of Bulgaria, 86
Law of Education (1909), 73
Law of Political Parties, 156
Laws and Principles of *awqaf* (Ahkamül Evkaf), 53–54, 58
Leo XIII, 151
Leyla Şahin vs. Turkey, 165n8
liberal citizenship, 8, 12, 120, 127–28, 142–44, 144–45
The Life with Christ: Orthodox Christian Education, 56
Likud Party, 139, 141
local cultures, 1

loi Debré, 98–101, 151
Lomasny, Martin, 15
Lutheranism, 36n9
Luxembourg, 37n16, 38n22

Macedonia, 73
Madison, James, 10
madrasah schools, 183–84
magnet schools, 208
Mahathir bin Mohammad, 168, 179, 180–81
Maimonides, Moses, 116n8
majoritarian culture, 219
Makarios III, 48, 54
The Making of Americans (Hirsch), 203
The Making of Citizens (Merriam), 196
Malaysia
    and citizenship challenges, viii
    and citizenship definitions, 12
    and civic enculturation, 3–4
    and collective identity, 11–12
    Constitution of, 175, 189, 190n1
    context of Malaysian education, 168–70, 170–74
    and cultural pluralism, 188–89
    and Islamic education, 8, 181–84
    and *Ketuanan Melayu*, 175–79, 179–81, 184–86
    Malayan Union proposal, 190n3
    and Malay language, 190n1
    Malaysian Indian Congress, 169
    and nation-state formation, 18–19
    and racial politics, 187–88
    and the religion/secular divide, 6
    and secularism, 10
    and social "otherness," 18
    and state-sponsored religious education, 20
Mandatory Palestine, 126, 140
mandatory religious education, 70–71, 79–80
Mandel, Maud, 116n4

Manickam, Sandra, 178
Maronites, 54, 58
Marxism-Leninism, 82
Massachusetts Constitution, 195
math, 205
Maxim of Bulgaria, 84, 91n6
McCrae, John, 216–17
medreses, 47, 77
Melaka Sultanate, 179
Merdeka Day celebrations, 188
Merriam, Charles, 196
Merton, Robert, 15
Methodists, 195
Middle East, 10
millett system, 47, 54, 71–72
Ministry of Education (Cyprus), 49, 56, 139
Ministry of Education (Greece), 56
Ministry of Education (Israel), 121, 126, 129, 145n1
Ministry of Education (Malaysia), 172, 174
Ministry of Education and Science (Bulgaria), 86
minority populations, 58, 73. See also specific nationalities and ethnicities
Mitterrand, François, 99
monarchy, 134
Moral Education syllabus, 178
morality and moralism in education
    and American education, 193–95, 198–99, 199–200, 201, 206, 209
    and Bulgaria, 74, 81, 85
    and the civil sphere, 14–18
    and Cyprus, 59
    and the European Union, 22, 36n4, 38n21, 39n28
    and France, 97–98
    and Israel, 131–32, 140
    and Malaysia, 177–78, 182
    moral autonomy, 14
    and secularism, 10, 14–16

Mormonism, 82
Morocco, 102, 103, 104, 105, 116n5
Morris, Benny, 128
moshavim, 128
mosques, 60–61, 163
Motherland Party, 161
Movement for Rights and Freedoms, 78, 91n5
Muhammad (prophet), 59
multiculturalism
    and arenas of social interaction, 17
    and Bulgaria, 82
    and Cyprus, 51, 53
    and Israel, 120, 123, 128, 139–40
    and Malaysia, 8, 19, 168–74, 175–79, 179–84, 184–86, 187–88, 188–89
    and the Turkish Republic, 152
    See also pluralism

Najib Tun Razak, 170, 181
National Action Party, 161
National Agency for Assessment and Accreditation, 88
National Cultural Policy (Malaysia), 177
National Education Longitudinal Study (NELS88), 207
National Endowment for the Humanities, 210
National Front (Malaysia), 169, 170, 187
nationalism and national identity
    and Bulgaria, 74, 84, 90
    and civic enculturation, 2–3
    and Cyprus, 52, 54
    and France, 106, 108, 146n7
    and Israel, 123, 124–25, 127, 130–33, 137–38, 138–42, 144–45
    religion's role in, 11
national languages, 176, 190n1
National Parliament (Bulgaria), 84
National Unity Party (UBP), 53
A Nation at Risk (National Commission on Excellence in Education), 193, 205

Index

nation-state system, 8, 13
Neophytos of Morphou, 63
Netanyahu, Benyamin, 121, 139
Netherlands, 34, 37–38, 206
Neuberger, Benny, 129
New Agreed Syllabus Conference, 22
New Bulgarian University, 85
New Hampshire Constitution, 195
New Testament, 56
Nikolay of Plovdiv, 81, 86
non-denominational religious education, 26, 27–30, 32, 34–35, 35n1, 40n33, 217
non-governmental organizations (NGOs), 120
non-Observant Jews, 123
Northern Europe, 29
North Nicosia, 20
Northwest Ordinance, 195
Norway, 29
Nuvvab school, 77

O'Connor, Sandra Day, 210
Old Testament, 56
1Malaysia, 170
"One School For All" movement, 186
Open University, 129
"Operation Cast Lead," 120
optional religious education
  and Bulgaria, 79–80, 87–89
  and Cyprus, 59, 61, 64
  and the European Union, 31, 35n1, 37n10
  and France, 99
  and Turkey, 162
Orthodox Christianity
  in Bulgaria, 73–74, 81, 83, 86, 89
  in Cyprus, 46–49, 57–58
  in the European Union, 30, 32
  in Israel, 134
Orthodox Ecclesiastical Academy, 85
Orthodox Judaism, 100, 123–25, 134

Oslo peace accords, 124, 128
"otherness"
  and Bulgarian teacher training, 87
  and challenges of inclusive citizenship, 219–20
  and the Cyprus conflict, 50, 51
  and Muslims in Bulgaria, 76
  and religious education in the European Union, 33–34
  and terms of citizenship, 17
  See also ethnic identity and conflict
Ottoman Empire
  and character of the Turkish Republic, 152–54, 164
  and Cyprus, 46–47
  millet system, 47, 54, 71–72
  and modern attitudes toward Islam, 83
  and religious pluralism, 4–5
  and Turkish education, 164, 165n3
Özal, Turgut, 161

Pakatan Rakyat, 187
Palestinians, 18, 120–23, 126
Pandakir Amin Mulia, 188
Pangle, Lorraine, 194
Pangle, Thomas, 194
Pappe, Ilan, 128
Parisian day schools, 97
Parliamentary Assembly (Council of Europe), 34, 36n5, 39n32
parochial education, viii
Parti Islam Se-Malaysia (PAS), 173–74, 187, 188
Parti Keadilan Rakyat (PKR) party, 187
passive secularism, 156–57, 160–63, 164
Patriarchate of Constantinople, 71, 91nn2–3
patriotism, 139, 196. See also nationalism and national identity
Peace of Westphalia, 8
pedagogical skills and training, 85–91, 99, 108–10, 114–15, 143

Pengajaran dan Pembelajaran Sain dan Matematik dalam Bahasa Inggri (PPSMI), 168, 180
Penilaian Menengah Rendah (PMR) public examinations, 171
Peoples' Alliance, 187
People's Justice Party, 187
Peron, Shai, 145n1
physical education, 183
Plovdiv, Bulgaria, 85
pluralism
  and American education, 206
  and Bulgarian teacher training, 85–91
  and Cypriot education, 46–49
  e pluribus unum concept, 164n2
  and French education, 96
  impact of Jewish day schooling, 101–7
  interreligious dialogue in Cyprus, 62–63
  Israeli liberal citizenship discourse, 145
  kesrette vahdet (unity within diversity), 164
  and the Ottoman Empire, 4–5
  and post-communist Bulgaria, 82
  problems of, 9–14
  and religious education in the European Union, 26, 32–33
  See also multiculturalism
Poland, 32, 37n16, 38n19, 38nn22–23
political parties, 122–24, 187–88, 210
political polarization, 150, 209
political theology, 133–36
polytheism, 114
Pomaks, 4, 75–77, 78–79, 84
Portugal, 31, 37nn16–19, 38n23
Post-Communist societies, viii, and citizenship challenges 77–85
Postman, Neil, 202–3
post-Zionism, 121
prayer in schools, 13
Presbyterians, 195

Principality of Bulgaria, 72
private schools, 77, 97–99, 151, 158–59, 174
privatization of religion, 14
professional teachers associations, 209–10
Progressive education, 202, 203
Project Method, 202
property rights, 156, 162
Protestantism
  and American education, 195, 206, 208–9
  and Bulgarian education, 77, 89
Protestant Reformation, 7, 10
  and religious education in the European Union, 28–29
"Provisional Regulations for Religious Governance of the Christians, the Muslims and the Jews," 72
"Provisional Regulations for Religious Governance of the Muslims in Bulgaria," 75

Quakers, 208
al-Qubrusi, Nazim, 62
Qur'an
  and Bulgarian Pomak community, 76, 77
  and Cypriot education, 59–60, 61
  and Malaysian education, 183
  and Turkish education, 154–56, 159–60, 162

rabbinic Judaism, 110, 125
Rabin, Yitzhak, 129
racism
  and Jewish day schooling, 113
  and Malaysian multiculturalism, 177, 185–86, 187–88, 189
  See also ethnic identity and conflict
Rahman Talib Educational Review Committee Report, 176–77

Rakyat term, 179
Ramadan, 7, 188
Ravitch, Diane, 202
Razak Report, 171–72, 176–77
Reconciliation Commission, 53
Regulations for Unified State Standards, 86
religion
   and citizenship requirements, 10
   and identity politics, 12–13
   religion/secular divide, 5–9, 9–10
   religious rights, 54
   religious syncretism, 11
   religious Zionism, 130
   and terms of citizenship, 14
   See also specific religions
"Religion, Culture and Ethics," 61
Religion and Democracy, 34
religious communities, 199
Religious Culture and Morality (ethics course), 59
religious holidays
   and the Bulgarian Constitution, 70
   and challenges multiculturalism, 222n2
   and ethnic conflict in Malaysia, 188
   and identity politics, 12
   and Jewish day schooling in France, 101–2, 105
   Jewish holidays in Bulgaria, 22
   and post-communist Bulgaria, 78, 81
Renaissance Process, 79
Report of the Education Committee of 1956, 176
republicanism, 12, 136–38, 144–45
Republican Party (US), 10, 194
Republican People's Party (CHP), 156, 159, 161
Republican Turkish Party (CTP), 53, 59
Republic of Cyprus, 45–46, 48–49, 50–53, 55
right-wing politics, 123

Rokkan, Stein, 18–19
Roma, 78
Roman Catholic Church, 57. *See also* Catholicism
Romania, 38nn18 –19, 38n22, 74
Rosh Hashanah, 222n2
Rousseua, Jean-Jacques, 131
Rubenstein, Amnon, 120
Rukunegara, 177–78
Rum, 71
Rumi, Mawlana Jalal al-Din, 62
Rumi Institute, 62
Rush, Benjamin, 194–95
Russian Orthodox Church, 91n3

Saar, Gideon, 139, 141
San Stefano Bulgaria, 72, 74
Santhiriam, R., 179
Satu Bahasa (One Language), 186
Satu Sekolah Untuk Semua (SSS) movement, 186
Saya Anak Bangsa Malaysia (SABM), 185
Schnitter, Maria, 5, 11, 21
Searing, Donald D., 198
secondary schools, 98–99
secularism
   and civic enculturation, 7–8
   and Cypriot education, 49, 51–52, 54, 58, 60, 61, 63–64
   and the European Union, 26
   and French education, 97–98
   and Jewish day schooling in France, 110, 115
   non-Observant Jews, 123
   religion/secular divide, 5–9, 9–10
   and Turkish education, 14, 150–52, 152–54, 154–56, 156–59, 160–63, 163–64, 165n5
segregation, 105–6, 110–12, 169
Sekolah Agama Kebangsaan (national Islamic schools), 172

Sekolah Agama Negeri (state Islamic schools), 172
Sekolah Agama Rakyat (people's religious schools), 172, 173
Sekolah Agama Swasta (private Islamic schools), 172
Sekolah Jenis Kebangsaan (national-type schools), 172
Sekolah Kebangsaan (national schools), 172, 174
Semi-Higher Islamic Institute, 85
Sephardic Jews, 102–3, 113
September 11 terrorist attacks, 83
Sermon on the Mount, 90
service organizations, 199
Sezer, Necdet, 159, 160
Shabbat observance, 101–2, 109–10
Shas system, 126
Shia Islam, 158
Shlaim, Avi, 128
Shumen, Bulgaria, 85, 87
Sijil Rendah Pelajaran (SPR) examination, 171
Singapore, 206
Six Day War, 133
Slovenia, 28, 37nn9–10
Sofia, Bulgaria, 72, 86
Sofia Synod, 73
Sofia University, 76, 78, 85, 86–87, 89
Sofiianski, Stefan, 78
Soul Searching (Smith and Denton), 199
Southern Dobrudzha, 74
South Nicosia, 20
Spain, 31–32, 37nn16–19, 38nn22–23
spirit cults, 7
sports, 199
state-control model of education, 206, 209–10, 218
State Education Law (1951), 126
State General Educational System, 125
State Religious system (Israel), 126
"Statutes for the Religious Organization and Government of the Muslims in Bulgaria," 75
Steffens, Lincoln, 15
Stern, Yedidyah, 141
Sufism, 164
Suicmez, Yusuf, 61
Sunday schools, 81, 89
Sunni Islam, 59, 62, 157–58
Supreme Court (Israel), 127, 128
Supreme Court (US), 151
Svimer, Valt, 52
Sweden, 10, 29, 36n9, 206
symbols, religious, 13
Synodal Concept of 2008, 81
Synod of the Bulgarian Orthodox Church, 70–71, 91n4

Tamils, 4, 20, 168, 171–74, 177, 181, 186, 190n3
Tamir, Yulie, 130
Tanzimat Edict, 153–54
Taraf (newspaper), 158
Tarnovo Constitution, 72, 73
Taylor, Charles, 130–31
teacher performance, 205
teachers unions, 209–10
teacher training, 85–91, 99, 108–10, 114–15, 143
Teaching as a Subversive Activity (Postman and Weingartner), 202–3
tekkes, 47
Tel Aviv University, 141
Ten Commandments, 13
terrorism, 83
testing of students, 204–5
Tevhid-i Tedrisat (Unification of Education) Law, 154
textbooks
    and American education, 196, 203, 210
    and Bulgarian education, 75, 82, 91n1

and Cypriot education, 49–50, 52–53, 56–57, 59–60
and European Union education standards, 29, 31, 38nn17–18
and Israeli education, 120–21, 129–30, 139–41
and Malaysian education, 175, 178–79, 182
theocracies, 9
Third Republic, 6, 151
Thrace, 73
To be Citizens in Israel (Ministry of Education), 129, 139
Torah, 133
tosafit, 112
totalitarian systems, 9
traditionalism, 100, 102
Treaty of Berlin (1978), 72
Treaty of San Stefano, 72
TRT (Turkish television), 165n3
trust, 1, 16, 17–18, 222
tuition rates, 102
Tunisia, 102, 103, 104, 105
Turkey
  and assertive secularism, 152–54, 154–56, 156–59, 163–64
  and citizenship challenges, viii
  and citizenship definitions, 12
  and civic enculturation, 3
  and collective identity, 11–12
  context of religious education, 150–52
  and Cyprus, 47, 48
  and ethnic identity, 12
  and national identity, 4
  and nation-state formation, 10, 18–19
  and Ottoman legacy, 152–54
  and passive secularism, 152, 156–57, 160–63, 163–64
  Republic of Turkey (1923), 152, 153–54
  and social "otherness," 18
  and state-sponsored religious education, 20

Turkish Cypriots
  and bicommunal religious education, 54
  and competing narratives on divided Cyprus, 49–53
  and context of Cypriot education, 45–46, 46–49
  and interreligious dialogue, 62–63
  and minority religious education, 58–59, 61
  and national identity, 63–64
  religious institutions and associations in the North, 61–62
Turkish Federated State of Cyprus, 46
Turkish Ministry of Education, 59
Turkish Republic of North Cyprus (TRNC), 4, 46, 58, 60–61
Tutu, Desmond, 63

ultra-Orthodox Judaism. *See* Haredi Judaism
UMNO party, 181, 187
UNESCO Convention against Discrimination in Education, 36n3
United Chinese School Committees' Association (UCSCA), 185
United Chinese School Teachers' Association (UCSTA), 185
United Kingdom (UK), 18, 20, 21, 36n9, 37n14. *See also* British Empire and colonialism
United Nations (UN), 45–46
United States
  and American culture, 198–99
  and church/state separation, 9–10, 18–19, 157
  citizenship education in public schools, 200–2
  and civic attachment, 197–98
  and civic education, 10
  and civic enculturation, 3, 6
  Constitution, 194, 205–6

United States (*Cont.*)
  and democratic ideals in public education, 209–10
  and educational theory, 202–6
  and evolution of citizenship education, 193–97
  and paradox of citizenship education, 210–11
  and pluralism dialogue, viii
  and religious communities, 199–200
  secularism in, 10, 152
  and structure of public education, 206–9
universalism, 217
University of Plovdiv, 86, 87
University of Veliko Tarnovo, 84–87, 89, 91n8
USA Freedom Corps, 210
US Naval Academy, 222n2

Veliko Tarnovo, Bulgaria, 84–87, 89, 91n8
vernacular schools, 168, 171–72, 174, 176–77, 179–81, 184, 186
Vichy France, 98, 116n4
Vietnam War, 196
Vision School Project, 179–80
voluntary teaching, 35n1
voting, 197

waqfs, 47, 53
Washington, DC, Board of Education, 201
Washington, George, 194
Weingartner, Charles, 202–3
West Bank, 120, 124, 128, 138
"We the People" program, 210

With the Grace of Christ: Orthodox Christian Education (Ministry of Education and Culture of Cyprus), 56
With the Love of Christ: Orthodox Christian Education (Ministry of Education and Culture of Cyprus), 56
Women's rights, 165n7
World War I, 74
World War II, 21, 73–74, 91n4, 103, 116n4, 216–17

xenophobia, 83–84, 123. *See also* ethnic identity and conflict; racism

Yakobson, Alexander, 120
Yang di-Pertuan Agong, 190n5
Yehuda, Tzvi, 133
Yesh Atid Party, 145n1
Yesodot—Center for Torah and Democracy, 21, 138, 143
Yonlour, Ahmet, 63
Young Turks, 154
youth organizations, 199–200, 211

Zameret, Zvi, 139–40, 140–41, 144
Zelman v Simmons-Harris, 206
Zionism
  and Israeli citizenship, 119, 124–25, 142–44
  and Israeli civic culture, 126
  and Israeli civics curricula, 130–38, 138–42
  and Israeli education policy, 121
  and Israeli political theology, 133